# Developing
## A *Heart* for
# Mission
### Five Missionary Heroes

# Developing A Heart for Mission

## Five Missionary Heroes

# Roy Robertson

**NavMedia**

Jesus Christ commanded us to go into all the world

and preach the Gospel to every person

*(Mark 16:15).*

The Navigators is an international, interdenominational
Christian organization. Our mission is to advance the
Gospel of Jesus and His Kingdom into the nations through
spiritual generations of laborers living and discipling
among the lost. We envision multitudes of diverse people
in every nation who have a passionate love for Christ,
live a lifestyle of sharing Christ's love, and multiply
spiritual laborers among those without Christ.

Nav Media is the publishing ministry of The Navigators,
Singapore. Nav Media publications help believers learn
biblical truth and apply what they learn to their lives and
ministries. Our mission is to stimulate spiritual formation
and disciplemaking fervour and skills among our readers.

ISBN 981-04-7425-3

Unless otherwise identified, all Scripture quotations in this
publication are taken from the original King James Version
of The Holy Bible.

# edication

To the memory of

Dawson E. Trotman,

whose ministry, vision and example

made a life-changing impact

on my life and ministry,

to the glory of God

# Contents

# PART IV

# PART V

# Foreword

The story Roy Robertson tells in this book needs to be told far and wide. It is about an exciting, and little known, era of Christian missions in Asia that followed World War II. He focuses on five missionary leaders he calls "The Powerhouse Five." These were ordinary men with heroic commitment to fulfilling the Great Commission. What they did was extraordinary.

Roy Robertson is a missionary hero. Sent to China in 1948 as The Navigators first missionary, Roy launched Navigator ministries in several countries of Asia and went on to form an organization devoted to training national evangelists.

He is still going strong today—54 years later. I call him intrepid, characterized by resolute fearlessness, fortitude and endurance. Having been deeply involved with The Powerhouse Five, Roy tells in this book his firsthand story. It smells not of library dust, but of smoke of the battle.

Living now in Hong Kong with his wife, Phyllis, Roy continues recruiting and training Asian evangelists.

**Lorne C. Sanny**
*The Navigators*

reface

Sometimes I hear a person say, "The day of the traditional missionary is past." I react very strongly against such a statement. What, has God's Word changed? Is the Great Commission out of date? Have Chinese or Indian or Islamic strongholds been evangelized?

Someone else will say, "But missionaries are no longer welcomed in most countries of the world." The answer to this is simple. When were missionaries ever welcomed by people rebelling against the one true God of the universe? In fact, all through history missionaries and prophets of God are hardly ever invited; they are sent! Even today they are sent out by God to do a "Mission Impossible"—that is, impossible except for the fact that the Lord Himself promises to go with those who obediently forsake their own plans and culture in order to carry the Gospel to all the world.

Missionaries indeed have had a glorious history and accomplished amazingly great things for God under extreme difficulties. The "Golden Age of Missions" is generally recognized as the period between 1790-1940. This era begins with William Carey, rightly called the father of modern missions. Carey went to India in 1792 and spearheaded a great missionary advance for those who followed his pattern.

By 1861 major Protestant denominations had successfully planted Christian churches along coastal regions of China, but the interior remained unreached. Then God laid a burden on the heart of Hudson Taylor to reach the twelve unevangelized provinces of inland China which even then comprised a population of more than 300 million. Hudson Taylor established the China Inland Mission, and many other missionary agencies have followed in this pattern to target unreached people groups. The advances following in the wake of these two great missionary pioneers continued to expand until the withdrawal of most missionaries because of World War II. England provided the missionary base for the first two missionary advances.

However, for sheer magnitude of countries penetrated and multitudes reached with the Gospel, the greatest surge of missions took place from 1945-1955 spearheaded by veterans of American military service. With the defeat of Japan at the close of World War II, General Douglas MacArthur issued an emotional challenge to the American churches to send out 10,000 missionaries to Asia. The Americans responded in unprecedented numbers and more than 10,000 new missionaries did enter into Asia over the next ten years. In Japan alone 4,000 missionaries representing 145 missionary organizations began a new missionary enterprise in Japan.

Missions today continues to advance building upon all three of these foundations. The denominational missionary follows in the traditions of William Carey, and God is blessing this movement. Following in the footsteps of Hudson Taylor, missions have spotted and targeted many unreached tribal and ethnic groups. Dozens of missionary agencies today are focused on the reached people groups. Emulating the patterns of Youth For Christ, The Navigators and Campus Crusade, tremendous opportunities exist today to further develop the ministries of public evangelism and personal discipleship. This book concentrates on spotlighting the adventures and struggles of five missionary heroes during the dramatic missionary advance of 1945-1955.

Still, in my opinion the greatest challenge for expanded missionary enterprise lies before us now. The September 11, 2001 attack by terrorists on the New York Trade Center has rudely awakened many complacent Americans to the worldwide conflict that rages everywhere. We are not immune from attacks or smugly secure to pursue our own personal lifestyle, isolated from the world around us. The worldwide conflict between the forces of evil and the forces of the Gospel will continue to get more fierce until Jesus comes again. Because America represents Christianity and stands beside Israel, we have become the enemy; the whole world opposes the advance of the Gospel of Jesus Christ.

God raises up a nation in order to glorify His holy name and to witness of His eternal message which offers grace to deliver whosoever will believe out of judgment. Every Christian should do his part in witnessing for Christ, but the Lord Jesus Christ Himself calls for some to become foreign missionaries. They will spearhead the Gospel advance into enemy territory. Perhaps they could be compared to the green berets of modern warfare. The requirements are tough—the missionary is required to leave behind his own home, brothers, kindred, personal plans and comfortable culture for the sake of the Gospel (Mark 10:29-30). His assignment is to enter into a foreign, resistant culture to become salt to the people of that country and then to shine forth the light of the Gospel message (Matt. 5:13-16).

A personal word in closing—I am at the end of my life having reached into my eighth decade by the grace of God. My generation including some of the leaders whom I have been privileged to know intimately were anointed by God to carry the message of the Gospel in unprecedented numbers into different countries and cultures. The principles and patterns under which they worked are still effective today. My prayer is that God will raise up a new generation of committed, full time foreign missionaries who will carry the glorious Gospel into other strongholds still controlled by Satanic influences. The Lord has asked us to pray for more missionaries that will be available to labor in His harvest. As never before, the harvest is truly great, but the laborers are few.

# Introduction

After I was released from my squadron as a Navy fighter pilot following World War II, I had the privilege of living for several years in the home of Dawson and Lila Trotman, founders of The Navigators. Their home, commonly called "509" after its street address (509 Monterey Road, South Pasadena, California), was a large, three-story colonial style house. Fuller Evangelistic Foundation, administered by Dr. Charles E. Fuller of the Old Fashioned Revival Hour, rented it at a token rate to The Navigators, a Christian organization ministering mainly among U. S. Navy, Army and Air Force personnel.

Nearly the entire headquarters staff of The Navigators, then consisted of the six men and 12 women who were housed in this home. One of the women, Phyllis Hapke, would later become my wife, following the death of my first wife, Lois, in 1959. To avoid complications, the young men and women living in the home at that time were not allowed to date. However, true love can find a way; and Daws did announce engagements from time to time to the delight and sometimes, surprise of many in the household.

In those days many Christian leaders from around the world visited the Trotmans, who were known for their hospitality and concern for works other than just their own organization. The family and guests, sometimes as many as 30 people, would gather around the huge dining room table with Daws and Lila at each end. After a leisurely meal interspersed with lively discussion, testimonies and a planned practical joke or two, the guests would be invited to share their vision and dreams with the Trotman family and staff. A time of prayer generally followed.

To Daws, prayer formed an integral part of one's life. He had a heart for the whole world, and a special commitment to assist "other works." Every Tuesday morning Daws met regularly for prayer with a small group of dedicated, like-minded leaders. These men are the focus of this book. They became my lifelong friends through my association with Daws.

Indeed, those were thrilling days following World War II when American influence reached its height. After years of fierce struggle the war had been won and now these Christian missionary leaders believed the Gospel could reach into the whole world in their generation. These men dreamed great things. Their faith stirred and challenged my own heart.

Daws would often tell his staff, "We have a great God! Don't just pray for peanuts; pray for continents!" I will never forget the prayer Daws uttered on my behalf just before I left his home to go to China, *"Lord, open the eyes of this young man and lay on his heart what is on Your heart—the world!"*

This book is an effort to show how a few men of faith—ordinary men with an extraordinary grasp of what was on God's heart—could, and did, change a world for Christ. The principal characters of this book—David Morken, Hubert Mitchell, Dick Hillis, Dawson Trotman and Bob Pierce—set in motion great movements that continue to the present day even though three of the five have been called to Glory. Scores of other mission groups have followed in their footsteps to accomplish mighty deeds for the King of kings.

God continues to repeat this process today through any small group of dedicated, prayerful and committed people. God's power is still available to us—the power of prayer, the power of faith and the power of a clear pattern for others to follow.

In the first part of II Chronicles 16:9 we read, "For the eyes of the LORD run to and fro throughout the whole earth, to shew himself strong in the behalf of them whose heart is perfect toward him."

Even today God is searching for ordinary people who through faith and commitment can become missionary heroes in the sight of God.

# Part 1

## Modern Missionaries in Action

# THE POWERHOUSE FIVE

*1935 - 1946*

Basic Missionary Patterns

# INTRODUCING THE POWERHOUSE FIVE

Dawson Trotman, a man of great faith, claimed promises from the Word of God and engaged in disciplined prayer sessions with a few selected prayer partners. During the mid-1940s, he met regularly on Tuesday at 5:00 A.M. with these Christian leaders. Their prayers reflected a united concern for the spiritual life of the servicemen who passed through the Los Angeles area.

Daws, Hube Mitchell and David Morken, as close friends, already gave much of their time toward reaching American servicemen. At the close of World War II their prayers focused on reaching the youth of Los Angeles, then expanded to the youth of California, and eventually to the youth of the whole world. They were later joined by Dick Hillis and Bob Pierce, who with Hubert Mitchell and David Morken were linked in a new movement called Youth for Christ (YFC).

The men gathered for prayer on the roof of the Willard Hotel, adjacent to the Bible Institute of Los Angeles (BIOLA) or sometimes in a bomb shelter in Mitchell's back yard. The headquarters of The Navigators occupied the first floor of this hotel. On the roof, a small building housed the elevator shaft and electric generator. Daws called it "The Powerhouse," which carried a double meaning—the power of electricity and the power of prayer. These five men who met there for prayer became leaders in the YFC movement and then prominent in world missions. I have dubbed them appropriately "The Powerhouse Five".

I met all these men during my training in the Trotman home. When the Youth for Christ leaders requested a Trotman-trained man to join them to handle the follow-up program in Asia, Daws sent me out to work under these men. They became my mentors and missionary heroes; I came to know them well.

In this section I have tried to relate some incident or vignette in the early experience of each man to show how God led them through struggles and testings that helped mold their character. They were very human, like us, yet God chooses such earthly vessels to carry the unsearchable riches of the Gospel to a darkened world without hope.

# Chapter 1

## A STRANGE DREAM

*T**his steamy, tiger-infested jungle is indeed the end of the earth,* thought David Morken, overwhelmed and discouraged.

In America he had responded with joyous obedience to God's call to carry the Good News of the Gospel to the uttermost parts of the earth. After reaching Sumatra, the largest island of modern Indonesia, David left the base city of Palembang and traveled into the roadless jungle by dugout canoe with his wife and two small daughters until he found the remote Kubu tribe. They were the most primitive of the five major tribes of the Batak people who inhabited the mountains, lakes and jungle portions of Sumatra.

"These people are hopeless," complained David to the Lord after struggling for many weeks to introduce them to the Savior.

The Kubus live in primitive conditions. Enslaved by ignorance and superstition, they struggle to survive in the dense, hostile jungle amid wild elephants, tigers, pythons and poisonous snakes. They offer sacrifices to their gods and on their arms they wear fetishes empowered by Satan.

While David pondered his failure, a young man lay dying of a high fever while the villagers prepared for a night of devil worship. The men adorned their practically naked bodies with white chalk paint; the women placed food sacrifices for the spirits in miniature baskets that hung on strings attached to the ceilings of their huts. Covered with itching sores, the villagers danced and wailed to the demons—their bodies diseased and their souls enslaved by Satan.

The chanting and dancing continued through the night, getting wilder and wilder. The witch doctor pricked the body of the dying man with sharp, pointed spears that had been dipped in cobra blood. The victim grimaced and wailed, then fell into a trance. The drums beat louder, the dancers jumped faster, the women shrilled to a higher pitch; but the life of the young man slipped away into the blackness of a Christless hell as Satan claimed another victim.

David felt helpless and miserable as he sat on his bed in the missionary hut at the end of the village and listened to the dreadful sounds emitted by a people possessed by the power of the devil. Their cries came from hearts filled with dread, fear, submission and hope-lessness.

## A Call to Royal Service

After graduating from Bible School, David had ministered about four years in the Midwest. Then in 1935 he married Helen Mitchell (sister of Hubert Mitchell who had become a missionary in Indonesia). Helen had been working in Wooster, Ohio for about five years. David proposed to her on the Wooster College campus.

In 1936 David and his wife Helen with their baby daughter moved to Lodi, California, where David became pastor of a strong and growing church.

One day, while doing research in the city library, he stumbled onto some articles telling about a tribe of people in Dutch New Guinea who had just been discovered by explorers from the outside. They lived deep in the interior of an area labeled on the maps of that time as Wissel Lakes; the inhabitants of this densely populated valley were cannibals living as if in the Stone Age. Although the data intensely interested David, he read all the accounts in a somewhat detached way since they were so far removed from his world in California.

But that night as he tried to go to sleep, it seemed as though David heard the heart cry of God saying, "Let My people go that they might serve Me!" He recalls his encounter with the Lord that night in vivid detail: "I was still awake, so I asked myself, 'Do these cannibals belong to God? Are they His people?' Then I asked God, 'Lord, do they belong to You?'"

"And, of course, the answer was, 'Yes, they do by every known law of proprietorship, by creation, by love and by redemption.' Scripture flooded my mind and heart. I saw afresh how 'God so loved the world' and how by our Lord's death and resurrection He saves and sets men free—free from the deadly power of sin and from the tyrannical rule of Satan. God sets them free indeed, free to worship Him and satisfy His broken heart."

"That was a life-changing hour for me because the Lord said, 'David, you have the only message that can set these people free to serve Me. I want you to GO—go for My sake, because for them there is no alternative for salvation.' In the morning I told my wife, Helen, and she was ready to go!"

First-term missionaries were not sent alone to the interior jungle tribes, so David and Helen, with their small children, joined forces with the Mitchells in Sumatra under the umbrella of Christian and Missionary Alliance (C&MA). Their first task, as in any mission-ary work, was to learn the language of the people to whom they were being sent. The tribal people had their own dialect, but the main trade language throughout Sumatra was then known as "High Malay," which the missionaries had studied diligently and which was known by the Kubu people.

The type of Malay spoken in Sumatra would later become the basis for the modern Indonesian language, now spoken by more than 150 million people in that nation. Providentially, being familiar with the national Indonesian language would later prove useful to David when he returned to Indonesia in the 1950s to conduct citywide crusades in that country.

### "Kami Bodok"

David worked with two national co-workers from Borneo, Suelan and Oedjang, who had been converted through the ministry of C&MA missionaries. They had finished courses at the Bible school in Makassar, capital of the southern part of Celebes (Today Sulawesi). They had been sent to Sumatra to help David among the Kubus, and were present with him that night when the young man with a high fever lay dying.

The missionaries had come with medicine to relieve the itching and pain of Dyak scurvy, a skin disease that covered the bodies of many. This medicine is just a temporary help, David thought. We must communicate the Gospel of eternal salvation from the sin and bondage that has enslaved them.

As the villagers prepared that night to offer sacrifices to the demons as part of the burial ceremony, David tried to tell them the story of Jesus and the redemption He came to bring to men. However, his efforts to explain the Gospel fell on dull ears. In response the village chief admitted, "*Kami bodok* [we are stupid and cannot understand]."

Others who listened to the Gospel story passed it off with a shrug. "*Itu kabar kosong* [your message is empty wind]." No one in that village believed. Such negative responses were disheartening.

The next morning at daybreak, David slipped out from under a mosquito net and climbed onto a fallen tree. Pacing back and forth on the large log, he felt too discouraged even to pray. Finally he was able to say, "Jesus!"

After some time, he told the Lord what a big failure he was. Maybe the Lord will feel sorry for me, he finally decided. Instead he felt the voice of the Lord speaking to him clearly.

"David, do you remember when I called you to come out into the jungles?"

"Yes, I remember."

"Remember how I said, 'Therefore go'?"

"Yes, I remember."

"And I said, 'Lo, I am with you always.' Remember, David?"

"Yes."

"Do you think I have broken My promise?"

And David answered, "No, You are still with me."

Finally David felt the Lord speaking clearly to his heart. "The reason I made this promise is because we are co-laborers. I created heaven and earth with my spoken Word, but the work I am doing now is far greater than creating this planet, the earth, and all the creatures in it. I have determined not to do it alone but to do it together with men like you."

The Lord continued to speak to his heart, "I have many people in these jungles whom I must bring to Myself. I have a work in these jungles that will bring Me glory forever. David, you can quit and go home if you want to and I will get someone else. Or, you can stay and we will work together in My greatest work, which is calling a people out of bondage to worship Me for all eternity."

The thought of being a co-worker with God was overwhelming. David broke down and wept like a baby. Sobbing, he told the Lord, "I'll do whatever You want me to do."

Two days after his deep experience with the Lord, David and his companions from Borneo made their way back into the jungle; suddenly they came to a clearing that led to another Kubu village. The people of this tribe build their houses in the trees, with a ladder that can be pulled up for safety. David could see their dwellings up in the trees, but no people. Then he observed two small women huddled together, chatting while preparing food.

In the custom of this people a man may not speak directly to a woman. However, since David and the men with him could see no one else in the village, they finally inquired of the women if any men were around. The women did not answer with words but pointed by protruding their lips toward a little hut in a tree on the other side of the clearing.

David and his companions walked to the area beneath the tree hut and called out the Kubu greeting, *"Apa kabar, tuan* [What's the news, sir?]." A man came to the opening. Seeing the white-skinned David, he began trembling all over. With a shaking voice he replied, *"Tidak ada kabar* [I don't have any news]."

David immediately assured the man in the tree hut that he and his friends had some marvelous news and had come a long way to tell him about it. He asked permission to climb up the ladder to enter the little house.

"*Silakan masuk* [Please come in]."

David and his companions climbed the ladder and seated themselves on the bamboo slat floor with the villager.

The missionary began by telling him something about his family and his work. "We are not hunting tigers or elephants, nor do we represent the government. We have come to tell you the greatest story ever told." After hearing David's account of God's redemptive plan, the slender Kubu tribesman agreed that it was indeed the most wonderful news he had ever heard.

"*Tuan* [Mr.], I believe that. Will you tell this story to the other men in our village?" he asked.

"Where are they?" inquired David.

"Most of them are out hunting, but I will gather them together so they can hear you tell this amazing story."

The man, who turned out to be the village witch doctor, gathered 17 men, women and children. David was eager to communicate with them, but noted that the women and children were fearful; so he gradually won their confidence by telling them about his own two little girls. David's native companions, Suelan and Oedjang, also gave words of greeting and encouragement.

Then David told, as simply and as clearly as he could, the story of God's great love for people in sending His Son Jesus to die for the sins of the world and to rise again from the dead.

After he finished telling of the resurrection, the chief's brother spoke up, "*Tuan*, may I say something?"

**The Dream**

The man began to tell about a dream he had the previous night. He related that in his dream three men had come to visit his village. He did not know their names, but he learned the title of one of the men who spoke to him. It was Maharajah—the King of all kings—Lord of all lords.

"Where did you hear that?" David asked.

"In my dream," was the reply.

"Have you ever heard that name before?"

"No."

And none of the other villagers had ever heard that name either.

"What did he say to you?" asked David.

"This great man spoke to me about receiving that which would satisfy all the desires of my heart. In my dream this man told me that I had deep desires, but having children cannot satisfy these deepest desires. Even if I were wealthy like the *Orang Belanda* [Dutch people], I would not be satisfied. The man in my dream then told me the only way these heart desires can be satisfied is to seek God and follow Him.

"Then I woke up wondering how I could seek God and tried to go back to sleep and dream some more, but I couldn't sleep. The reason I did not go out hunting today was to find out how I could seek this God. First, I thought maybe I should kill a chicken as a sacrifice, but a voice seemed to say to me, *'Jangan* [don't do that].' Then I thought of going to inquire at a Muslim village, but again my heart was troubled. Other ideas came to my mind, but each time I felt that they were not the way. Now you have come and have told us about *Isa Anak Allah* [the Son of the one true God]."

As David and his companions listened in awe, the chief's brother began to tell the other villagers how this Jesus must be the man who came to him in his dream. It was a supernatural comprehension.

Turning to his fellow villagers, he said, "Something in my heart tells me that this is the way."

To David he affirmed, "*Saya percaya dan saya terima* [I believe and I also receive]." His wife, who recently gave birth to a baby boy, was lying nearby, chewing betel nut and cheroot. She opened her stained, blackened teeth and spoke simply, "I also believe." (Chewing

*David Morken preaching the Gospel in Japan.*

betel nut, a type of pepper plant bean, together with its leaf, produces a thick, red paste, which has a narcotic effect on the person and is highly addictive. The older people of these primitive tribes, especially the women, chewed these nuts constantly even though it affected their gums and teeth.) They named their first-born baby boy Daud [the Kubu equivalent of David] in honor of the missionary who has just brought them the good news of salvation.

The hearts of the people of this remote Kubu village had been divinely prepared. God sent His discouraged messenger into a ripe harvest. Many Kubu people from this village came to Christ and soon a church was formed. They turned from the worship of demon spirits to worshipping the true God who satisfied all the desires of their hearts.

At the beginning of World War II David was driven out of the Dutch East Indies by the Japanese armies. He spent the rest of that war ministering to American servicemen. Then with Youth for Christ, one of the new movements that was an outgrowth of the war, David entered China to preach to thousands of people in a great spiritual harvest that preceded the fall of China to communism. As we will read in the following chapters, God began to put together a team to preach to the multitudes in Asia.

# hapter 2

## A NAIL AND A PHANTOM SHIP

The news is incredible! The Japanese have bombed Pearl Harbor! America has declared war; Japanese invasion troops are already moving toward Singapore and Sumatra.

This startled Eva Mitchell, the paternal aunt of Hubert Mitchell whose wife had recently passed away, leaving behind four motherless children. Yet Hube and his small band of missionary co-workers continued to do missionary work among the primitive Kubu people deep in the jungles of Sumatra. *They may not even know of the great dangers they face*, she thought.

The news reports give an increasingly alarming assessment of the situation. Some British troops are stationed in Singapore, but Sumatra, the largest island of the Dutch East Indies, later to be called Indonesia, has practically no protection. The meager Dutch garrison is no match for the military might of Imperial Japan. The next Japanese military objective will be to capture the vitally important oil production port city of Palembang, through which the missionaries will need to travel in order to evacuate Sumatra.

In Los Angeles, California, as Aunt Eva listened to the news reports of successful Japanese conquests, her heart ached for the missionaries of her family who lived so remotely in the jungles of Sumatra half a world away.

Earlier, Aunt Eva had learned of an "Amazing Radio" that had been manufactured for the explorations and travels of the famous Frank Buck, who had made a movie called "Bring 'Em Back Alive" about animals in the jungle. After the European war started, Buck's plans had changed and so he put up his jungle radio for sale. Aunt

Eva heard of this sale and persuaded some prayer supporters of the Mitchell family to buy it and send it out to Sumatra.

*I must tell Hube about this immediately,* she decided. So she sent a message to the Frank Buck radio receiver to warn the missionaries of plans for a Japanese invasion.

At that time in December 1941 Hubert Mitchell led a missionary task force under the Open Bible Mission; they worked under the umbrella of Christian and Missionary Alliance, assigned to a church planting mission targeting the Kubu tribal people in Sumatra. The Kubus lived within a roadless and bridgeless virgin jungle area where the white man had never penetrated until the arrival of Hube and his missionary team. Hube, his four children, and the family of his brother-in-law, David Morken (see Chapter 1) lived at a pioneer missionary outpost near the Kubus.

## One Chance in Four Billion

As Hube became more proficient in the High Malay language, he began to communicate the glorious truth of the Gospel to these tribal people—that Jesus Christ had died on the cross for our sins and had risen again from the dead (see 1 Corinthians 15:3-4). But he soon met with intriguing difficulties.

When Hube had first explained the Gospel to the primitive Kubus, they asked him, "What is a *salib* [cross]?"

He had demonstrated his answer by cutting down two saplings and laying one across the other in the form of a cross. "How can a man die lying upon two trunks of trees?" the Kubus asked him.

"Wicked men drove nails into the hands and feet of Jesus, and the blood left His body," Hube had explained carefully.

"What is a *paku* [nail]?" inquired the tribesmen who had never before seen a nail, even though the word existed in the trade language.

Hube and his companions searched in vain in their packs for a nail. "Please, Lord," he prayed, "give me some way to explain a nail to these people, so they can believe in Jesus."

After a typical native lunch of rice and dried fish, the Kubus watched Hube take a can of mandarin oranges from his knapsack. He usually carried two or three of these fruit cans with him on his trips to the villages because they were light in weight and the fruit refreshed him in the jungle heat. The cans had been packed in Japan and purchased at a Chinese store 100 miles from his base.

Hube had poured the oranges from the can into his tin dish. As he started to throw the can away, he heard a rattling sound; to his amazement he saw a shiny three-inch nail inside the can.

"Look," he shouted, "This is a nail! This is like the long ones they used to nail Jesus to the cross!" (Later, a mathematics professor calculated there was one chance in four billion that a nail would be in that particular can.)

After hearing the story again, the people wept and said, "How great is the love of God!" Many responded to this Good News and a community of Christians came into being. The new believers then led Hube and his companions on a two-week trek through the trackless jungle because they wanted all their neighboring tribes to hear the Good News as well.

Kubu tribesman, however, were set free to worship God out of this stronghold of Satan only at the cost of great hardship and suffering by the messengers of the Gospel. Hubert and his co-workers had begun to build a mission station among the Kubu people. They cleared trees, chased tigers and snakes out of the area, and hired a Chinese carpenter to cut wood. Everyone joined in the work as they labored together in constructing some buildings on a small hill by a river. The missionary ladies helped lay the tile roof. The team then named their forward missionary base Bukit Berkat [Mount of Blessing].

Under these strenuous living conditions, Hubert's wife, Helen, died of childbirth complications and was buried in that far-off country away from her homeland. Hube, however, stayed on in the jungle with his four small children to guide the rapidly growing Kubu church.

Hubert's sister (also named Helen) was married to David Morken (Chapter 1), who joined forces with Hube to lead many more Kubu people to Christ. After Hubert's wife died, his sister, Helen

Morken, had taken care of the four Mitchell children—David (10), Paul (8), Daniel (6), and Jean Marie (18 months). The Morkens also already had two children of their own at this time—Andrea (5) and Arlita (3).

## The Flight Across the Islands

Having heard the news from Aunt Eva on their jungle radio, the small missionary group huddled to discuss plans in view of an impending invasion by the Japanese armies. One set of parents volunteered to stay on to live among the Kubu Christians in the jungle because they could speak the language fluently. But everyone overruled that plan. If the parents were to be shot by the Japanese, the children would be orphans. Besides, their staying might attract the Japanese to the area and endanger the young Kubu Christians.

Fresh news on the radio reported a force of Japanese ships heading for Sumatra. All Americans were ordered to flee the country. So the missionary community, comprised of Hubert with his four children, David and Helen Morken with their two children, and several others from the Open Bible Mission reluctantly prepared to leave; but nearly all of their belongings had to be left behind.

Among the few possessions that Hube carried with him was his precious accordion. In the face of all the trying circumstances of those times, he remained steadfast in his faith. When the Lord took his wife to be home with Himself, he quoted the immortal words from the Scriptures, "O death, where is thy sting?" (1 Corinthians 15:55). While he fled from the Japanese with his small children, he frequently sang and played a song he had composed that was based on Annie Johnson Flint's grand poem, "He Giveth More Grace."

> *He giveth more grace when the burdens grow greater,*
> *He sendeth more strength when the labors increase,*
> *To added affliction He addeth His mercy,*
> *To multiplied trials, His multiplied peace.*
> *When we have exhausted our store of endurance,*
> *When our strength has failed e'er the day is half done,*
> *When we reach the end of our hoarded resources,*
> *Our Father's full giving has only begun.*

*Chorus:*
*His love has no limit, His grace has no measure,*
*His power has no boundary known unto men,*
*For out of His infinite riches in Jesus,*
*He giveth, and giveth, and giveth again!*

After reaching the provincial city of Jambi, the group proceeded by bus, then by truck, to the coastal city of Lubeng Lingaw [Bandar Lampung today] on the southern tip of Sumatra. The missionary party hurried along to keep ahead of the rapidly advancing Japanese forces. As they traveled southeastward toward the coast, they saw many Japanese planes, most of which were filled with paratroopers, flying overhead toward their objectives. The Japanese army quickly overran the weak defenses of the Dutch army and captured the important city of Palembang, which was the hub of the rich oil and rubber fields of Sumatra, the major objective of the Japanese.

Crossing by ferry to the island of Java the missionary party hurried on to Batavia [now called Jakarta], the capital of the Dutch East Indies. By now Singapore had fallen and the relatively weak Dutch and native forces would not hold out much longer.

Officials told them of the possibility of an American ship reaching Surabaya, 450 miles to the east. So the Mitchells, the Morkens, and two other missionary families rushed onward by road to Surabaya, hoping to catch some friendly ship. The group of missionaries arrived just in time to board the S.S. *President Madison* of the American President Lines, the last American ship to reach Java before it fell to the Japanese. They did not have enough money for tickets, but the U.S. government took responsibility for evacuating the Americans.

## "The Phantom Ship"

By now the Japanese navy controlled the sea routes in all directions. Its submarines and warships sank every allied ship they encountered. So the skipper of the *President Madison* took a long evasive route and headed toward India instead of trying to cross the Pacific. A perilous, uncomfortable journey ensued, because the overloaded ship contained a great variety of frightened passengers of many occupations and social strata, all desperately trying to survive. Overwhelmed by the pressures of war, one passenger tried to commit suicide. The overworked crew held frequent emergency drills in which they assigned passengers to lifeboats. Rumors flew about constantly that other American passenger ships had been torpedoed and sunk.

After playing hide-and-seek in the Bay of Bengal to avoid enemy subs, the *President Madison* stopped briefly in Madras, India. Some missionary friends, mainly from the British Commonwealth countries, met Hube and his party and urged them to stay in India and help with their missionary work. However, the Americans were not part of the Commonwealth and had no visas to remain in the country, so they were required to return to the ship.

When the *President Madison* arrived in Colombo on the island of Ceylon [Sri Lanka today], they learned that three other American ships had been sunk in that area by patrolling Japanese submarines. From Colombo they began a 92-day circuitous sea voyage around South Africa, stopping only at Durban, then across the Atlantic to South America. To avoid detection, now by German submarines, the captain maintained radio silence throughout the voyage. Meanwhile rumors circulated in the United States that the *President Madison* had also been sunk by Japanese or German submarines.

When they arrived unannounced in New York harbor in April 1942, newspaper headlines reported the story of "the phantom ship" that glided through enemy waters eluding the Japanese and Germans on a miraculous 92-day voyage.

When the weary missionary party stepped ashore in America, they did not seek worldly entertainment, seclusion or rest. Their greatest hunger was for spiritual food. The Morkens and Mitchells attended Calvary Baptist Church in New York City to hear well-known evangelist Gypsy Smith. What wonderful preaching of the Word! How thrilling to see their fellow Americans, especially the youth, responding to the public invitation to receive the Lord Jesus Christ as Savior. How heavenly to hear a great choir sing the sevenfold "Amen." It seemed that heaven had come down, and joy flooded their parched souls.

But what about the Kubu people left behind in the jungles of

Sumatra? Hubert and David had been laying down their lives to take the Gospel to them, and they had witnessed God's blessing upon their work in a wonderful way. Why did God close the doors to such a promising start in helping the Kubu people build a church? Why did God allow the missionary efforts in Southeast Asia to be overrun by opposing forces? At this time only God Himself knew the full answer.

The angels of God surely had been watching over the *President Madison* with its precious cargo of some of God's chosen missionary servants. In spite of the fact that large parts of Asia had fallen to a military power that opposed Christianity, Hube and David had not finished their work in Asia.

God had far bigger plans for His faithful servants. And God would use those long war years to prepare His servants in many ways to preach the Gospel in some of the largest cities of Asia with dimensions of receptivity that would be far beyond their wildest dreams.

## An Open Door

When Hube returned from Sumatra, he didn't know precisely what to do. Taking care of four motherless children, he was unable to travel to do the public preaching that he dearly loved. Church friends arranged for day-help to assist in the chores of fixing meals and doing the laundry.

One day the chairman of the board of Union Rescue Mission located in downtown Los Angeles approached Hube. The chairman talked to Hube about establishing a new kind of rescue mission.

"We see a need for reaching the thousands of American servicemen who flood into downtown Los Angeles with idle time on their hands and plenty of opportunities to engage in the fleeting pleasures of sin," he explained. "We are challenged to provide the servicemen with a place of wholesome Christian atmosphere as an alternative to the enticement of sin. Our mission is located at 220 South Main, just a few blocks from the Greyhound bus terminal. We plan to rename it "Victory Service Club.""

In 1943 Hubert accepted the invitation to direct this new kind of mission. With endorsement by the United Service Organization (USO), more than 200 churches in the Los Angeles area participated with volunteer help. Ladies served coffee, doughnuts, cake, cookies, sandwiches and gallons of root beer from a giant barrel. Soldiers, sailors, marines and airmen, along with a roving shore patrol and military police, flocked to the service center for food and fellowship. The committee, however, cautioned Hube not to have "too much religion" because that might drive away some of the servicemen.

"Fellas, we're going to close the canteen for a few minutes," Hube would announce. "We'll sing some ol' hymns, and have a word of prayer for our buddies serving overseas."

With Hube's exuberant singing voice and talent for playing the accordion, accompanied by gifted pianists, quartets and soloists, a lively program would follow which was quite different from formal church services back home. The format and style of presenting the Gospel in this service center was later followed in the huge Saturday night youth rallies that began toward the end of World War II.

In those days the Center produced a popular radio program broadcast throughout that area on Saturday nights. Bob Bowman, founder of Far East Broadcasting Company (FEBC), handled the mike. John McCrosson wrote "On the Jericho Road" and other numbers for the quartet. At the end of each program they issued a public invitation for men to come forward to receive Christ. These men were led into a back room for counseling. God began to work in a marvelous way, and hundreds of servicemen found Christ.

Victory Service Club became a popular place for servicemen to enjoy fun, food and fellowship, and also to hear the Good News about Jesus Christ and His salvation. At least once a day they held a special Gospel service. On weekends, sometimes they had as many as five a day. The Victory Service Club was located near a large Catholic church. On one occasion, as Hubert counseled a serviceman to receive Christ, the church prayer bells began to ring.

"They're celebrating your coming to Christ," Hube announced.

Months later when he was standing at the coffee bar, a serviceman walked up to him and said, "Hube, remember me?" At first he couldn't.

When the serviceman said a few more words, Hube indeed remembered him. "You're the guy who prayed in the room when the bells rang." Some 15,000 other men received the Lord during those years.

## The Thriving Kubu Church

But what about the Kubus? What happened to the struggling infant church on Sumatra? Did it survive or did it perish?

While in Indonesia toward the end of the 1980s I had the privilege of attending a Christian conference at which Hube and his young son Paul gave a thrilling report on their recent trip back into

*Hubert Mitchell (right rear) with some of the Jambi Kubus he was visiting when this "small miracle" occurred.*

21

the jungles of Sumatra to visit the Kubu people. One of Hube's early converts met them at the airport in Palembang, then escorted them into the jungles to visit village after village that now had a thriving church with buildings constructed by the Christians themselves from indigenous materials.

Even then the area remained primitive. Travel was exceedingly tedious. Young Mitchell, who had obviously experienced severe culture shock, reported, "On this trip I learned how to hurry up and wait!" He continued, "We would rush to get ready, then wait for hours till the next means of transportation became available to take us farther into the jungle."

Yet it proved to be a wonderful experience for father and son. The Kubus welcomed back one of their original missionaries with a lavish display of appreciation and love. The days were filled with feasting, storytelling, native music, preaching and praising God. The Kubus possess a natural talent for singing; Hube had carried his beloved accordion again into the jungle. Father and son spent many happy hours singing and rejoicing with their Kubu brothers and sisters in Christ.

# Chapter 3

## RIGHT MESSAGE—WRONG METHOD

In the middle of the night, Dick Hillis tossed and turned upon the rough bedding in his mud-plastered room. His language teacher, Elder Kung, plus a donkey and some other animals, also occupied the same room. However, not just the cold, damp air in an unheated Chinese house kept him awake that night. The lack of response to his preaching troubled Dick. He felt discouraged and distressed,

He lived in north central China's densely populated wheat-growing area. Surrounded by farming people who clung to their own peculiar customs and spoke no English, this young 24-year-old American missionary, though tenacious in his work for the Lord, experienced loneliness.

One can feel ever so lonely and uncomfortable under the constant gaze of crowds of people who stare at your big nose, blue eyes, blond hair and pale skin. You long for a companion of your own language and culture with whom you can share your opinions, dreams, doubts, observations, inner struggles and feelings.

It was not the usual China Inland Mission practice to send a young missionary to work alone in a remote mission outpost. Originally Dick had come to assist a veteran missionary couple. The Tomkinsons ministered in the market town of Shen Kiu, a city of about 13,000 people in the province of Honan known as the breadbasket of China. The two Chinese characters forming the word Ho-nan mean "south of the river." The river, of course, is the great Yellow River. It originates  in the Gobi desert wasteland near Mongolia and flows on a winding 5,000-mile journey across the entire breadth of northern China before emptying into the Bohai Sea.

The Tomkinsons were able missionaries, well acquainted with the local language and customs. The people spoke basic Mandarin (the official language) adorned with their own regional accent and idiomatic expressions.

Dick's grasp of Honan's tough tonal language was adequate, but tedious at times. To help their young missionary recruit make good progress in language study, the Tomkinsons outlined an excellent program for him. They assigned Dick a full time language teacher, Elder Kung, a zealous Christian.

Every day, Monday through Friday, teacher and student pondered over lessons in a study room at the small mission headquarters. Dick's mentor, slightly better educated than the average person in Shen Kiu, dressed in the long-sleeved gown of a teacher. As the two sipped tea, they read the Bible together and discussed points of Chinese grammar by the hour. After a week of such concentrated language study, the restless young American felt eager to get out among the people and practice what he had learned.

The experienced Tomkinsons wisely scheduled practice sessions on alternate weeks for their young trainee. They sent Dick out in the company of Elder Kung to talk to people in the villages. He conversed with men at traditional Chinese teashops. He invaded boisterous market centers and bought hot noodles from vendor stalls along the roadside—mingling and chatting with friendly but skeptical people as best as he could. The missionary's early efforts to share the Gospel usually led to a partial communication breakdown, which kindled renewed dedication to study harder during the following week of scheduled class work.

After eight months, the Tomkinsons left unexpectedly for another station. The mission had no one available to join Dick in the work. He faced a choice of staying on alone or abandoning the station. Dick immediately accepted the challenge to remain in Shen Kiu. The church expected him to preach in the regular services. Bombarded by Chinese sounds and characters all hours of the day and forced to use the language on all occasions, he made great progress in language study. He now preached and prayed in Chinese with a degree of fluency. Others would say he was doing well.

But during the next three years only one family came to Christ. Mr. Ho, attended church but was demon-possessed, so Dick and several Chinese elders in the district joined in prayer for him. They called on the name of Jesus and pleaded the blood of the Lord Jesus Christ for victory in casting out the demon. Dick's poorly educated co-workers prayed with great zeal and faith. Dick admitted in his heart that he felt a little frightened; this sort of thing was new to him. Yet the demon was cast out, and Mr. Ho was saved along with some of his family members.

"But this was not my fruit," Dick humbly told the Lord, as he tossed wakefully on his rough Chinese cot. "This was the fruit of the faith and prayer of the elders. And why only one family in three years? What is wrong? Why is there not more fruit?"

## A Divine Summons

When Dick left America he had such high expectations of what God would do through him as a missionary. He had been converted at seventeen in an evangelistic service at the Church of the Open Door in Los Angeles, California. At that time he was already attending the Bible Institute of Los Angeles (BIOLA), located on Hope Street in downtown Los Angeles where his twin brother, Don, studied.

After the love of Jesus conquered his restless and rebellious spirit, Dick felt an immediate compulsion to dig into the Word of God and to share his faith. Within weeks after his conversion he attended a missionary conference and seriously began to consider a missionary career.

The affirmation came from the Scriptures, particularly Mark 16:15, "Go ye into all the world, and preach the Gospel to every creature." He applied each phrase to his own heart in a personalized manner.

Go . . . *That means to leave America*, thought Dick.

Ye . . . *Yes, me, Dick Hillis.*

Into all the world . . . *Some far off place like Africa or China.*

25

*Dick Hillis in Honan. The idea of the bridge illustration was developed from this picture.*

Preach the Gospel . . . *Yes, proclaim the Good News of salvation to darkened, heathen hearts.*

To every creature . . . *God means that every single person must have the opportunity to hear the wonderful message of salvation. No one has the right to hear the Gospel twice until everyone has had the chance to hear it once.*

## A New Method

So Dick applied to, and was accepted by, the China Inland Mission (CIM) to carry the Gospel into unreached areas of China. When he arrived in Shanghai in 1933, he was only 20 years old—the youngest missionary from America to begin the mission's formal program of language study and indoctrination. After six months of study in Mandarin at the CIM men's language school at Anking in central Anhwei Province, he proceeded immediately to Shen Kiu to assist the Tomkinsons. Now, three years of preaching had brought forth little fruit.

Dick recalls, "Guess what I was preaching. I was urging the Christians in our area to go into all the world and preach the Gospel to every creature. But they were not responding; they were not going.

"In spite of this lack of response, Elder Kung and I faithfully went out day after day seeking to get to every village in our county. We faced an enormous, discouraging task . . . just the two of us doing the work of the Gospel.

"I felt ready to throw in the towel. One night in a little Chinese room with Elder Kung and a couple of donkeys, I could not sleep because nothing was happening.

"Christ has said, we have not chosen Him, but He has chosen us that we might go out and bear fruit. "I had borne no fruit. Hence, I felt discouraged and ready to go home.

"While I was thinking and praying and lying in that dark, damp, cold Chinese room, the Spirit of God brought to my attention Matthew 4:19. This records that Jesus said to a group of poorly educated fishermen, 'Follow Me, and I will make you fishers of men.'

He simply said in effect, 'In order for you to become what I want you to become—true disciples—true evangelists—true witnesses—here is My plan. Follow Me as we go out together.'

"And the Spirit of God brought to my attention that though I had urged the Christians of our area to go, probably the reason they were not going out was that they didn't know what to do. I had been guilty of having the right message but the wrong method.

"A little later on when it got light, I turned to the book of Acts which I was reading. I came to that great verse, Acts 20:4, speaking of Paul's strategy in his travels: 'And there accompanied him into Asia Sopater of Berea; and of the Thessalonians, Aristarchus and Secundus; and Gaius of Derbe, and Timotheus; and of Asia, Tychicus and Trophimus.' I knew that Paul had trained some men at Ephesus, but I realized that on this particular trip a group of men both from Asia and Europe accompanied him to learn how to do the work of the Gospel.

"And as I thought about it, I realized that is exactly what Christ's method was. Paul discipled believers just as Jesus discipled His followers. Jesus became the model to lead men out into evangelism and passed on this pattern to Paul and to all subsequent generations.

"Then as I looked through other portions of the Scriptures, I found that again and again Paul wrote to the churches and said words such as these: 'Be ye followers of me, even as I also am of Christ' (1 Cor. 11:1); and to the church of Thessalonica he said, 'And ye became followers of us' (1 Thes. 1:6) and in the following verses he mentions that they also bore fruit, for others followed them. And I realized that I had been preaching the right message and urging them to do something, but they couldn't do it because they had never been shown how."

The next Sunday Dick excitedly preached the morning message. He used Acts 1:8 as his text. "But ye shall receive power, after that the Holy Ghost is come upon you: and ye shall be witnesses unto me both in Jerusalem, and in all Judaea, and in Samaria, and unto the uttermost part of the earth."

According to Chinese custom, the women and children sat

together on the left and the men on the right. Even husbands and wives did not sit together in the Chinese churches in old China. About 40 adults, 13 men and double that number of women, attended the service. Dick wanted to challenge the men alone, so after the service he dismissed the women and children and asked the men to stay behind. Then he shared with the 13 men what God had revealed to him.

"So I told them what I had discovered in the Word of God—that Paul taught and trained men just as Jesus did—by taking people with Him; therefore I had determined that I would never go out alone to these villages where there were no Christians. These were Buddhist villages where the people worshipped demons, idols and the ancestral tablets. I said that I would leave them in their darkness unless these Christians in my area would go with me. I informed the men that I believed that when Jesus commanded His believing disciples to go, He meant everyone should go, not just a few. Not everyone should go to the same place, not everyone the same distance, not everyone with the same gift, but everyone should go to wherever God would send them, starting as a witness in his own 'Jerusalem.'"[2]

These men were farmers. They immediately came up with a series of tough questions in their thinking.

"How can we preach with so little education?" Most had only three years of formal school—the minimum required to be able to read and write in limited fashion.

"The disciples of Jesus were also unlearned men," responded Dick.

"We are not accustomed to speaking in public."

"I will teach you how."

"We have no money."

"Take wheat flour and vegetables from your houses, and we will cook and eat together."

So they launched out together on this new method of preaching the Gospel to the village people. During the cold winter months when the farmers had nothing to do but feed their animals, the gospel team went out together to spend several days in other villages. In the winter season the farmers were bored, with little to occupy their time, so out of curiosity many came to listen.

Dick preached first. The people listened politely. Then Elder Kung preached. He had more education and training than the other team members. And the people listened to him more closely than to the missionary. He understood their ways and feelings, yet he believed in this new God. Then the other men spoke, at first with difficulty; but with practice they grew in confidence and ability.

The missionary had to instruct the new lay evangelists not just to attack the Chinese gods and superstitions, but rather to preach about God and His Son Jesus Christ in a positive way. The supreme God of all gods—*Shang Ti*—had a son *Yesu* [Jesus] who came into the world to die on the cross for our sins and to rise again from the dead.

The new method worked; as Elder Kung and the other Chinese farmers gave testimonies people began to respond to the Gospel, to believe in Jesus and to receive Christ as Savior. Later the Chinese farmers learned to proclaim the Gospel with increasing power and effectiveness. Soon new preaching centers and house churches were springing up in nearby villages. In turn, the farmers began teaching these new Christians how to witness and to share their faith.

During the following winter, the seasoned Shen Kiu gospel team ventured into other parts of Honan Province. Led by their missionary, they took enough vegetables and flour to last for several weeks as they shared the Gospel of Christ in places where the message had never been preached before. The team members often slept on the floor of shops or houses of Chinese farmers. The Gospel, especially when given through the lips of one of their own people who had been delivered from the clutches of sin, indeed demonstrated the power of God.

The Gospel spread rapidly from village to village, from town to town. The Christians of Shen Kiu formed new gospel teams from other areas. Elder Kung became an outstanding evangelist, and the Holy Spirit raised up other gifted leaders from among this rural people. Eventually they set up a women's team to reach the women and children of the area. The Scripture was fulfilled, for from their "Jerusalem" (Shen Kiu) the Gospel spread through the witness of the people in their district, into another district, and eventually through-out the whole province.

## God's Provision and Deliverance

Dick was attracted to Margaret Humphries while still in Bible School, but she was not ready at that time to go beyond a casual acquaintance. As Dick spent several lonely years in China, he thought often of Margaret. Then when he learned that God led her to work under the China Inland Mission he felt God's leading to declare his love to her by letter. She arrived in Shanghai in October 1936. After Margaret finished her formal language study in Shanghai the couple married on April 8, 1938. Following a brief honeymoon she joined Dick at his isolated station in Honan Province.

In the beginning of 1941, Dick became seriously ill. Dick and Margaret Hillis with their children traveled through communist lines in order to get to the CIM hospital in Shanghai. When they finally reached the hospital, he was rushed into the operating room to remove an appendix that was about to burst.

The operation left Dick very weak. Because he had lived under strenuous conditions in the interior of Honan for eight years without a real vacation, the CIM leaders sent him back to the United States for furlough in July 1941.

## A New Assignment

Then came Pearl Harbor. The war in the Pacific would last a long four years; the Japanese interned many missionaries from allied nationalities in China and those on furlough could not return to their fields.

By the fall of 1943 Dick Hillis, who had begun to teach missions at BIOLA, had joined the Tuesday morning prayer group led by Dawson Trotman. These men challenged and inspired each other—Dick with his stories of what God had done in China, Hube and David with the accounts of the wonderful deliverance out of Sumatra and the great harvest of service men receiving Christ through the servicemen's centers, and Dawson Trotman with the exciting stories of how God had raised up a powerful multiplying ministry among American servicemen.

## "The Jesus Nest"

Dick Hillis had thus learned a method that he would use later to lead Youth for Christ teams in Taiwan into some of the most fruitful gospel preaching in missionary history; that gospel message would turn the whole island upside down.

As for Honan, the Communists overran the province, but the missionaries continued work there during China's early civil war. The Nationalist army of Generalissimo Chiang Kai-Shek in the south and the Communists in the north fought fiercely to control this province, a major food supply for north China. So between 1935 and 1941 the Communists took the province on two occasions only to be routed by the Nationalists. In the midst of these battles the churches were in a state of constant fear and harassment.

In 1949 the Communists finally took the province. The new regime was particularly hard on the Christians because its leaders believed that they had sided with the Nationalists. Later, during the terrible days of the Cultural Revolution (1965-1975), when every church in China was closed, the Christians in Honan were again targeted for harsh treatment. The Communists had boasted that they would destroy Christianity, but here in Honan the Christians still persisted. The Communists were wrong because Jesus had promised, "I will build My church; and the gates of hell shall not prevail against it" (Matthew 16:18).

After the death of Mao Tse-Tung, the first church reopened in Shanghai on Palm Sunday in 1979. Some 12,000 people crowded into the five services at the former Moore Memorial Church (Mo En Tang) on that first Sunday celebrating the reopening of the Chinese church. In subsequent years hundreds of church buildings that had been turned into factories or banking houses during the Cultural Revolution were returned to the Christians and reopened to the preaching of the Gospel.

# Chapter 4

## THE POWERHOUSE

*I'm drowning!* thought Dawson Trotman, as his head bobbed in the water. Daws and his girlfriend had accompanied a group of young people on a picnic beside a southern California lake. Some of the party had started across the lake in rented canoes.

Suddenly Daws's canoe tipped over, throwing him and his girlfriend into the water. He soon realized she could not make it to the other side. At birth Daws had weighed only three pounds, and a partial blood blockage to his lower extremities left him with weak legs. As he pumped his thin legs vigorously in a gigantic effort to keep himself and the girl afloat, he realized his past sinful life and rebellion against God. His stepmother had tried to push her experience-oriented Christianity on him, but he felt unsure, for this view of religion, to him, lacked reality and love.

Now he felt desperate. *Lord,* he cried out in his heart, *If You save me, I will serve You!* His lungs sucked in water as he went down below the surface for a second time. *Lord, if You will save me, I promise to serve You for the rest of my life!*

He came up briefly, and just as he was going down for the third time to certain death, hands of rescuers grabbed hold of his thick, bushy hair and held on. They pulled him and the girl to shore and frantically pumped water from their lungs by artificial respiration. Daws's life and the life of the girl were spared.

"Yet, like most people, I soon forgot my promise to God," Daws related afterwards. So God reminded him. A few weeks later, the police picked him up in a drunken state. In desperate trouble again, he remembered his stepmother's pleading against his rebelliousness.

"Son, if I ever hear of your getting into trouble with the police, it will kill me."

As the policeman took him to jail, Daws once again pleaded with God. *O Lord, if You will get me out of this mess without my mother finding out, I promise to serve You the rest of my life!*

He felt desperate. Once again a gracious God heard his prayer. The police officer noticed something in the face of the troubled young man that softened his heart.

"Son, you don't like this kind of life, do you?"

"Oh, no sir," he confessed hopefully. "Please, sir . . ."

The officer let him go without pressing charges.

This time, true to his promise, Daws went the very next Sunday evening to a church youth group in his hometown of Lomita, California. To stimulate interest, the two women sponsoring the youth group, Miss Ethel Mills and Miss Laura Thomas, divided the young people into two groups so they might compete against each other. Daws noticed the prettiest girl and sat down beside her. Miss Thomas assigned each person ten Scripture verses and promised to give a point for each verse memorized by a team member during the following week. "At the end of the contest," she announced, "the losing side will provide a picnic lunch for the winning side."

Daws, though still unsaved, wanted to make a good impression, so during the following week he memorized all the verses perfectly. To his surprise, none of the others in the group had done the assignment.

"To get more points for your side," the sponsors explained, "you must quote all ten verses again next week plus ten new ones." This assignment forced Daws to review the first ten verses while tackling the second ten. Through this "review . . . review . . . review . . . " principle, Daws discovered the secret of effective Scripture memory.

Daws would walk to work with a lunch pail in one hand, while in the other he reviewed the verses which he had written out on a set of memory cards. He shuffled through the cards and quoted out loud John 5:24: "Verily, verily, I say unto you, He that heareth My word and believeth on him that sent me, hath everlasting life, and shall not come into condemnation; but is passed from death unto life." Suddenly the truth of that verse struck home to his heart. "Why, I can have eternal life right now!" He paused on the street and prayed to receive the Lord Jesus Christ into his heart.

## Scripture Memory and the First Witness

Thereafter Scripture memory became a meaningful and exciting project. He set himself the goal of memorizing a verse a day and then reviewing all he had learned in a systematic way. In the first three years of his Christian life he memorized more than 1,000 verses. In years to come the Lord would use Daws and The Navigators "Topical Memory System" that he created to introduce thousands of servicemen, college students, ministers and lay people to the blessing of hiding the Word of God in one's heart.

Memorizing Scripture became a tool for sharing the Gospel. Soon after his conversion, Daws began witnessing in his place of work at a lumber yard. But it was not easy. Daws quickly experienced the stigma attached to becoming a bold witness for Jesus Christ. One could not be a friend of the world and have close communion with the Lord at the same time. "Love not the world, neither the things that are in the world. If any man love the world, the love of the Father is not in him" (1 John 2:15).

A small Christian group met once a week at noon at the lumber yard where Daws worked. A local minister came each week to lead a Bible study for a small group of men; the other workers had labeled the regular attendees of this group "religious do-gooders." By identifying with this group Daws knew he would come under close scrutiny by all the men and lose his popularity among his former friends with whom he had been associated through gambling, drinking and swearing. Although tempted to compromise, he joined this group openly at its noon Bible study.

The leader, who was glad to see him, tested his commitment and loyalty for a few weeks, then invited Daws to lead the Bible study one week. Daws did not immediately accept the offer but made excuses, "I am not qualified . . . I have no formal training . . . Let someone else do it." Other young Christians use the same excuses time and again when faced with a similar opportunity.

Daws would later comment that this was probably one of the great tests of his early Christian experience. The week following his refusal to the minister proved to be a miserable one for him. He found it hard to review verses, hard to read the Bible and even hard to pray.

Daws rationalized with God, "Lord, I am willing to do anything You want, but surely You don't want me to lead the Bible class. Lord! Lord!" But still he experienced no peace in his heart.

Toward the end of the week, he finally prayed in submission, "Lord, I am willing to do anything You want and lead this Bible study. I don't understand why You want me to do this, but I will do it!" Almost immediately peace and joy flooded his heart. The following week Daws told the minister he would lead the class, then spent additional time in preparation and prayer.

When Daws arrived at the lumberyard on the day of his inaugural teaching session, he noticed a large handwritten sign on the bulletin board: "Porky will preach today at noon—All invited!" His friends called him "Porky" because his bushy crop of dark reddish hair on the top of his head stood up like porcupine quills. Word began to spread like wildfire that the former cussing, drinking and gambling convert would give his testimony that day.

As Daws prepared to speak at the place of the meeting he saw not just a handful of the faithful few, but more than 100 noisy, laughing, skeptical men before him. "What shall I say?" he asked the Lord.

Nervously, hesitatingly, he began to quote Scripture and wove in his personal experience in a simple straightforward manner. As he proceeded, the Spirit of God began to touch hearts and some of the smirks turned into tears. This began his ministry before his fellow peers. In due course, he led seven of his bosses to Christ, several of whom would enter the ministry or missions as full-time servants. One of these men, Eber Hazelton, spent his life in China under the China Inland Mission.

## Lessons Learned

Early in his ministry Daws learned a lesson. Any specific invitation from a spiritual leader needs to be carefully considered, for it could be the voice of God speaking to you through that person. Daws always believed that if he had refused that first ministry assignment from "the preacher," at the lumberyard, God would not have entrusted to him the development of the ministry which followed. The global ministry of The Navigators would never have materialized. The biblical principle is this: "He that is faithful in that which is least is faithful also in much: and he that is unjust in the least is unjust also in much" (Luke 16:10).

A second lesson Daws learned was to take an open stand for Jesus alongside the local Christian brethren; he identified with the on-site Christian group at the lumberyard, even though they were not considered to be dynamic or attractive. So on mission fields of the world today new believers are taught to be baptized and to join a local church, even in communist-dominated countries. In most Asian cultures a person is not considered a true believer unless he has been baptized and is openly identified with some local church. The distinguishing mark of a Navigator during World War II in the U. S. Navy was that he carried openly a big black Bible and notebook for all to see. While I served as a naval officer on an aircraft carrier, Navigators taught me to carry my Bible and notebook in my left hand and then salute the colors with my right hand whenever I left the ship to go ashore. Carrying the Bible openly certainly deterred one from all sorts of evil.

## Meeting God In the Morning

Not only had Daws made a habit of Scripture memory, but he determined to form the habit of meeting with the Lord every morning. Some of the Old Testament promises he memorized invite fulfillment. Among these are Jeremiah 33:3: "Call unto me, and I will answer thee, and shew thee great and mighty things, which thou knowest not."

Daws decided to claim these promises at face value, so he asked a friend to join him every morning at 5:00, before they went to work, because "That if two of you shall agree on earth as touching any thing that they shall ask, it shall be done for them of My Father which is in heaven" (Matthew 18:19).

They prayed that God would use them in their local area of greater Los Angeles, then extended their request to the State of California. Next they prayed that God would use them in every state of the United States of America. Later, they bought a map of the world and asked the Lord if He would make them a blessing in each of the 160 countries shown on the map as they put their fingers on each country. After 40 consecutive early morning vigils, Daws believed that the Lord had heard and would answer their prayers.

## Witnessing To Someone Every Day

Daws also began witnessing daily to individuals he met, often quoting Scriptures that make clear God's plan of salvation. After a year at the Bible Institute of Los Angeles (BIOLA), he became so involved in ministry that he left the Bible school to devote more time to God's work. He strictly disciplined his life to spend an hour a day in prayer and to memorize a new verse of Scripture every day. He also covenanted with God to witness to some individuals each day. "An hour a day, a verse a day, a life a day" became his motto and a desired standard for the men he would train.

As leader of the local Christian Endeavor group, Daws had the privilege of driving guys and girls to and from the meetings. This inter-denominational teenage Bible club movement spread throughout California and into other parts of the United States during the 1930s and 1940s. He formed the practice of selecting one girl to drop off last so he could witness to her to see if she really knew the Lord. After one embarrassing case in which he found himself kissing the girl instead of witnessing, he learned to let her out of the car first before he began his conversation.

One day Daws gave an attractive young girl a ride home from Sunday School.

"Why don't you come to Christian Endeavor?" he asked her.

"I have no way," she replied.

"I'll pick you up along with the rest," he promised.

Taking her home last after the C.E. meeting, he let her out of the car, then asked, "Are you a Christian?"

"I've gone to church all my life," she answered without hesitation.

"I didn't ask you if you are a churchian, but are you a Christian?" he asked again.

"Well, I was baptized," she said, a little less confident.

Opening his New Testament, Dawson explained verses describing the salvation Christ offers without conditions to those who receive Him. "Don't go to sleep tonight until you have settled it," was his parting word.

Settle it she did. At 2:00 in the morning Lila Clayton knelt beside her bed and became a new creature in Christ.[1]

Lila was only 13 years old when Daws led her to the Lord. As he joyously began to shepherd her in the faith he fell deeply in love with this young Christian. He had to wait until she graduated from high school before her parents assented to the marriage. They were wedded on July 3, 1932.

Immediately after their wedding, they opened their home to servicemen as Daws began to disciple U.S. Navy personnel who would become known as "The Navigators." This nautical term allegorically compares one's life to a ship at sea with Jesus as the Captain and the Word of God as a compass. By the time World War II began, hundreds of servicemen were memorizing Scripture systematically and "navigating" for Jesus Christ.

## Servant To Other Works

"One verse I rest on," Daws would often tell his Navigator gang, is 2 Corinthians 9:8, 'And God is able to make all grace abound toward you; that ye, always having all sufficiency in all things may abound to every good work'. Based on that promise I'm asking the Lord somehow to let us serve 'every good work' in America and in the world."

So claiming the promise from the passage in 2 Corinthians to serve every good work, he followed the instructions found in Philippians 2:3-4. Rather than being absorbed in just his own little world, Daws began to practice the principle of serving "Other Works."

One of the works that Daws would be serving effectively later became known as Youth for Christ (YFC). Simultaneously, yet independently of one another, God had begun raising up Saturday night youth rallies in some of the large cities of the United States; these great rallies blossomed and grew in Los Angeles, Chicago, New York and Philadelphia. Led by different committed and far-seeing men, these would later join together loosely and grow into a worldwide movement to be called Youth for Christ International. Years later Daws shared the burden of his heart in these words:

"I believe the need of the hour is an army of soldiers, dedicated to Jesus Christ, who believe not only that He is God, but that He can fulfill every promise He has ever made and that nothing is too hard for Him. It is the only way we can accomplish the thing that is on His heart—getting the Gospel to every creature."[2]

### "The Powerhouse"

Uprooted from the mission field by the ravages of war, David Morken, Hubert Mitchell and Dick Hillis all relocated in Los Angeles by the summer of 1942. Each one of these men became involved in ministering to the youth of a nation at war

God brought these three men in touch with a kindred spirit—a restless young man who had been converted through memorizing the Scriptures and had launched a fast-growing ministry among Navy personnel whose ships berthed at the Long Beach harbor just outside of Los Angeles.

Hube first met Dawson Trotman at Mount Hermon, a Christian conference center located among the great redwood trees about 350 road miles northwest of Los Angeles in the San Francisco Bay area. Their mutual interest in servicemen's work drew them together; Hube had just begun his work at the Victory Service Club when he met Daws at a Mount Hermon conference in the summer of 1943.

They agreed to meet together every Tuesday morning at 5:00 for prayer. Most of the time they met at "The Powerhouse" on the roof above The Navigators' office at the Willard Hotel, or occasionally in the cement igloo bomb shelter behind the Mitchell home. Though they both dearly loved the Lord and became giants in prayer, they had contrasting styles that must have amused the angels in heaven. Hube, in the style of the great prophet Elijah, would call unto the Lord in a thundering voice. Daws, in his own individualistic way, would sometimes almost whisper, as a reminder that the Lord is close at hand. But each greatly loved and respected his prayer companion.

A few months later they were joined by David Morken who also had become involved in directing a servicemen's center for thousands of Marines stationed in Santa Ana. Soon these three men were not only memorizing single key verses of Scripture, but eventually David and Hube committed whole books of the Bible to memory, from which they would often quote liberal portions in their preaching.

From that small beginning of a few men meeting together in prayer at "The Powerhouse" God began to do a mighty work in fulfillment of His promise, "Call unto me, and I will answer thee, and shew thee great and mighty things, which thou knowest not" (Jeremiah 33:3). As these men prayed together, joined later by Dick Hillis, Bob Pierce, and a few other prayer partners from time to time, God strengthened their faith to call on Him for greater and mightier things. They went to pray, not just to talk to one another. They poured out their hearts before God for the youth of Los Angeles, for people in California, for servicemen overseas, for the countries of Asia and the world—that God would use them to get the Gospel out to people in all parts of the earth. God mightily answered their prayers in His own time and in His own way.

ENDNOTES:
1.  Betty Lee Skinner, Daws, *A Man Who Trusted God*, Colorado Springs, Colorado: NavPress, 1994, pages 48-49.
2.  Dawson Trotman, *The Need of the Hour*, Colorado Springs, Colorado: NavPress, 1976, pages 6-7.

# Chapter 5

## TO CHINA WITHOUT FUNDS

The awaited day arrived—June 29, 1947—and lines formed outside the famous Hollywood Bowl of Los Angeles, California. That evening the long-planned and prayed-for special Youth for Christ (YFC) rally drew more than 20,000 young people who filled the bowl to overflowing. Billy Graham handed Bob Pierce a Bible to present to President Chiang Kai-Shek in Nanking, China with these inscribed words:

"To Chiang Kai-Shek, President of the Republic of China, from Youth for Christ and the young people of America, who are praying for you and for the great country of China that it may come to know Christ."

On Monday, July 1, the front page of a Los Angeles newspaper featured a large picture of Bob receiving the Bible to take to China.

However, imagine his shock upon learning that after paying all rally expenses, no money remained to send him to China!

"God wants me to go to China and preach. I am sure of this," he said to friends. "Then why doesn't He supply the money? What has gone wrong?"

Another thing bothered him. What will people say? He had promised many people he would go. After his picture had appeared in a front-page newspaper report on the rally, Bob was human enough to be troubled by a punctured self-image. So he laid the matter before God in prayer.

His request was partially answered when a friend gave him enough money to buy a ticket to Honolulu on the Pan American

Clipper. With this token of God's approval he started out by faith, trusting the Lord to supply the rest. So with only enough money to buy a one-way ticket, he boarded his plane at the Los Angeles International Airport.

When Bob reached Honolulu, he checked at Western Union as he had been instructed. Hallelujah! YFC Los Angeles friends wired him an additional $500—enough to buy a ticket to the Philippines. John Sycip, a wealthy businessman and YFC's business representative in that country, met him. He would sponsor Bob's ministry in the island archipelago.

Bob received a warm welcome in the Philippines and spoke in various cities on the northern island of Luzon. Then Sycip, who owned the second largest airline in the country, flew him to other islands for outdoor rallies where he preached from the tops of trucks provided by Christian servicemen from America.

On the island of Bohol at the first anniversary celebration of Philippine independence, July 4, Bob preached to some 5,000 people, including government and Catholic officials, who packed the auditorium. Afterwards, a Catholic priest told Bob in private that he had harbored doubts in his heart about the Bible being the Word of God and Jesus being the only way of salvation, but now he wanted to make the decision to trust the Lord Jesus Christ as his Savior.

During all the meetings with large crowds throughout the Philippines, John Sycip had taken no public offerings. In the last meeting, a rally in John's own Chinese church where 22 young people came forward to receive Jesus as their Savior, still no offering was taken. How could Bob get to Hong Kong without money for a ticket? God had the answer waiting. Sycip would fly Bob to Hong Kong on one of his own planes so that Bob could witness to his pilot about Christ.

In Hong Kong, Bob again spoke at various meetings. Sycip provided him a room in the luxurious Peninsula Hotel where very few missionaries would have had enough money to stay. However, in future years the missionary community would gather at this hotel every Friday afternoon for tea and prayer. Until a later change, these facilities were provided for only the cost of a cup of tea. Many times over three decades I have attended this Friday afternoon missionary meeting to be refreshed by God and encouraged by my missionary friends.

The main evangelistic services were held at the Central YMCA, ideally located just a few minutes walk from the busy Star Ferry Pier in Kowloon. From this pier ferries shuttled across the waters every few minutes, linking Kowloon on the mainland with the Island City of Hong Kong. Wherever Bob preached, many people responded to the gospel invitation.

After the Hong Kong meetings ended, Bob prayed in his hotel room, thanking God for the meetings and the many decisions people had made to receive Christ. However, he kept wondering how he could get to Shanghai, which was still about 850 miles away.

Then Bob remembered something. Before John Sycip's pilot left to return to the Philippines, he had handed him an envelope. In the rush of the meetings Bob had forgotten about it. Now he opened it and found three crisp one hundred dollar bills—enough to buy his ticket to Shanghai, China.

The Lord supplied his needs step by step. God kept testing Bob's faith, but never once did he lack funds for the next step. He was learning to trust God for the needs for the next trip, and the next, and the next.

## Reaching Servicemen on Skid Row

As a youth, Bob Pierce was graduated from the Nazarene College in Pasadena, California, and then joined a gospel quartet that traveled to many gospel meetings. At the age of 22 he married Lorraine Johnson and looked forward to a settled home and fixed income. Yet while attending special services with his father-in-law, Nazarene evangelist Floyd Johnson, Bob felt the call of God to surrender himself and all that he had to the cause of getting the Gospel out to the whole world. He and his wife would depend completely on the Lord to supply all their needs "according to His riches" (Phil. 4:19).

He soon became involved as an evangelist among the youth of his denomination, The Church of the Nazarene. But he struggled at this time, both in his ministry and in his own spiritual life. He needed help and guidance, but where would he get it? He heard about a young pastor named Torrey Johnson, who had a dynamic youth evangelism program in Chicago. This same Torrey Johnson later would spearhead the formation of the Youth for Christ organization and become its first president.

Even then Torrey Johnson as a pastor greatly impacted the youth of that large city with its many suburbs. The more Bob learned about this man the more he became convinced that Torrey could give him the counsel and direction he so desperately needed. So he told his young wife, "I must go to Chicago to meet this man."

Bob's encounter with Torrey was not just a casual meeting; rather it was a divine appointment, which made a lifetime impact on his life and ministry. Torrey, who Bob would later describe as "a man's man," asked many penetrating questions and gave some tough counsel; yet Bob's heart was bonded in a special relationship with this wise and dynamic leader. Torrey became his role model and mentor for the rest of his life.

Soon after returning home in 1943 Bob took charge of the youth ministry at the Los Angeles Evangelistic Center where he began to hold youth rallies, following the pattern of Torrey Johnson in Chicago. He also developed a close friendship with Hubert Mitchell and David Morken, stalwarts of the Powerhouse prayer group during World War II. He became a member of the group to form "The Powerhouse Five."

In 1944 Torrey persuaded Bob to move in a venture of faith to Seattle, Washington to set up Youth for Christ rallies in that city. Bob launched into his new job with great enthusiasm. Seattle was the main launching base in this period near the close of World War II for sending military men into the Pacific war areas. The knowledge that some of these men would die in battle and never return to their earthly homes greatly concerned Bob Pierce. How could he reach these men with God's gracious promise of an eternal heavenly home for those who would trust in Jesus Christ? Many of these soldiers and sailors

*Bob Pierce*

were not your usual church attendees, but indulged their fleshly appetites in pleasures to be found in the bars and brothels of the inner city.

So Bob rented a former burlesque theater on Skid Row because he knew that servicemen would come to that area. Churches cooperated so the theater, with the words "Entertainment Tonight" on the marquee, was filled every night. For some, it was the last and only time they heard the Gospel. Bob invited speakers who could reach the hearts of youth, such as Torrey Johnson from Chicago, Chuck Templeton from Minneapolis and Billy Graham.

From the first Bob seemed to possess the knack of handling an audience so the people's hearts would be prepared to receive the Gospel. He invited a former football star at the University of Alabama, Joe Weatherly, to be his understudy. Later Joe would take over the leadership of the Seattle Youth for Christ in the northwest part of America , then go out under YFC to India and Singapore.

## A Bible for the Generalissimo

Bob arrived in Shanghai in time to relieve David Morken (who was ill with dysentery) in speaking at the largest crusade in that city's history. He then went on an itinerant evangelistic tour of the Chinese cities, Soochow, Hangchow and Sian before traveling to Nanking for the Bible presentation to President Chiang Kai-Shek. The team was scheduled to have an interview with the President and Madame Chiang at which time Bob would formally have presented to him the inscribed Bible sent out by the young people of the Saturday Night Jubilee rallies in Los Angeles. However, the American ambassador to China arrived at an unexpected time and the President had to travel to Shanghai to meet with him.

So Madame Chiang and her staff graciously received Bob, David and the evangelistic team for tea and true fellowship in the Lord. She accepted the Bible on her husband's behalf. Her closing words, as a sad confession, pictured the situation in her homeland: "China's trouble is spiritual bankruptcy." After David led in prayer, he and Bob continued their itinerant evangelistic tour in Beijing, Chungking and Chengtu. Andrew Gih interpreted both for Bob and David in meetings throughout 1947. People responded to the Gospel far beyond what the missionaries and national leaders had ever seen before in China. The Lord supplied step by step. God kept testing Bob's faith, but he never once lacked funds for the next step. Bob would look back years later on those events as a major crossroad experience.

# THREE GREAT MISSIONARY ADVANCES

*1792 - 1946*

Patterns Still Applicable Today

# BACKGROUND

The more I have studied the history of world missions, the more I have come to realize how God has been at work to spread the Gospel since the days of the Apostles. The early apostles carried the Gospel beyond the ends of the vast Roman Empire. The apostle Thomas spread the Gospel into India where he was martyred near Madras.

According to church traditions, other apostles carried the message in all directions, even penetrating Spain, Russia, Africa, northern Europe and the Middle East. The Syrian church in the third century sent a Christian community into what is now called Kerala in India. In the seventh century the Nestorians settled in Sian, the capital of China. When Marco Polo reached this Chinese imperial city in the thirteenth century he found remnants of a Christian witness.

Yet for the most part, the peoples of Asia and Africa were without the Gospel. Focusing on India and China in particular, two great missionaries stand out. William Carey of England formed a missionary society to use "means" to reach the "Hindoos" for Christ. He also began translations of the Bible into the local languages. He tackled great social problems such as the burning of widows alive on the pyre of their departed husbands and the murdering of infant baby girls. He set up models of education and medicine that were followed by other missions. And he established a Baptist church. Many have acclaimed him as the father of the modern missionary movement, and many other church groups and missionary societies have followed in the trail he blazed to establish a Christian community in an idolatrous land.

But nearly 70 years later tribes and nations and peoples still existed in China without a gospel witness, since most mission groups concentrated on the coastal cities easily available to foreigners. So Hudson Taylor established the China Inland Mission (CIM) to reach those in the interior who had no touch with the Gospel. The CIM later targeted unreached tribes for the Gospel and had wonderful success in evangelizing such tribes as the Lisu, Miao and many others. My first wife, Lois, was assigned to reach one of these groups until China closed to missionary activities. So in my analysis, Hudson Taylor is a prototype for the targeting of unreached areas with the Gospel. The CIM also had other characteristics, such as being international and non-denominational, which we will consider later in more detail.

The first two great advances are generally recognized in modern missionary history. They were both British. I suggest that a third major advance stemmed from America when large numbers of American veterans of World War II volunteered for missionary service. This was by far the greatest missionary force ever sent out from a western country to a mission field.

At the close of World War II, General Douglas MacArthur immediately appealed for 10,000 new missionaries to come to Asia to help rebuild the countries devastated by war. Bible Schools and seminaries across America mobilized to answer the call. More than 10,000 new missionaries were sent out in the next ten years. More than 4,000 went to Japan alone, representing 145 missionary agencies*. Others flooded into China, Korea, Philippines, India and Southeast Asian countries. Although many of these were from traditional missionary agencies, a new type of missionary service arose from organizations like Youth for Christ, The Navigators, Pocket Testament League, Word of Life and later Campus Crusade for Christ and many others. Some called this a parachurch movement, but others objected to that designation. Whatever the title, it became a vital missionary force. The third advance, spearheaded by the veterans of World War II, stemmed from America. The Powerhouse Five were among the leaders of this third advance in modern world missions. These three advances are analyzed more closely in this section.

*Published in the Japan Missionary Directory of 1953

# Chapter 6

## THE FIRST ADVANCE

## In the Footsteps of William Carey
## (ENGLAND, 1790)

Every great missionary movement in later church history has begun with a spiritual awakening. In the eighteenth century God used John Wesley and George Whitefield to lead the first great awakening in England. Thousands of people listened to the Gospel proclaimed in outdoor meetings throughout the countryside of England and many sought the Lord in repentance for the salvation of their souls. A new awareness of spiritual things gripped the nation, especially among the common people.

Toward the end of this period William Carey (1761-1834) grew up in an Anglican home in an obscure village of Northamptonshire. He was born on August 17 in Paulers Pury to Edmund and Elizabeth Carey, but was raised by his grandmother. She had been influenced by the Great Awakening and eventually introduced him to the Scriptures.[1]

In his teen years through the persistent witness of a close friend, John Warr, Carey came to personal faith in Christ at a meeting of the Dissenters. That evening he decided to leave the Anglican Church and join the Non-conformist group in his area.[2] At this time in England these bodies were called Non-conformists or Dissenters because they did not hold allegiance to the Church of England. They held biblical views somewhat similar to the Baptists or Congregationalists of today. He was eventually baptized on October 5, 1783, and formally joined that group of Baptist Dissenters.[3]

## The Growth of the Missionary Vision

From his youth Carey had a keen interest in the study of the Scriptures. He also had an affinity for the study of languages; by the time he was 18, he was already able to do some reading in five languages, including Greek, Hebrew and Latin. His passion for geography and fascination with the world lifted him beyond the confines of his English environment. He worked as an apprentice to a cobbler. As his proficiency in both areas developed, he made a map of the world out of leather and diligently began to collect information on the population and religious status of each known country of the world. Is it any wonder, then, that God laid on his heart a great burden for missions?

As young Carey began to share his views with others, he met a few sympathizers, but most were skeptical. This enthusiastic exponent of missions argued that rather than expecting God to save the heathen without human effort, "means" should be used to introduce the Gospel in heathen lands. Carey felt particularly concerned about India, the largest and most populous of all the English colonies. But hyper-Calvinistic critics of his day argued that it was futile to send missionaries to Asia since God had obviously decreed that Europe was destined to be Christian and Asia to be heathen. At that time no known Hindu had embraced Christianity.

After a while Carey was invited to a pastors' conference of his denomination. There he took opportunity to press upon the ministers in attendance the necessity of sending missionaries to convert "the Hindoo." The leader of the conference, who was a hyper-Calvinist, put down this radical young man by uttering these words (which have since been carried into missionary folklore), "Young man, sit down. When God pleases to convert the heathen, He will do it without your aid or mine."[4]

Young Carey obediently sat down but did not stop arguing his case to the Christian community of his day. Someone has observed, "Greater than an enemy is an idea whose time has come" to put it into action. Carey, whose idea was a biblical concept ("idea"), refused to be silenced. In the spring of 1792 wrote his famous 87-page missionary book entitled *An Enquirey Into the Obligation of Christians to Use Means for the Conversion of the Heathens.*[5] This was God's time to arouse the hearts of some of the faithful toward their responsibility to take the Gospel to the ends of the earth.

The Scriptures contain specific commands and examples of sending missionaries throughout the world, but the verses God placed particularly on the heart of Carey are found in Isaiah 54:1-3.

"Sing, O barren, thou that didst not bear; break forth into singing, and cry aloud, thou that didst not travail with child: for more are the children of the desolate than the children of the married wife, saith the LORD. Enlarge the place of thy tent, and let them stretch forth the curtains of thine habitations: spare not, lengthen thy cords, and strengthen thy stakes; For thou shalt break forth on the right hand and on the left; and thy seed shall inherit the Gentiles, and make the desolate cities to be inhabited."

From this promise Carey believed that the desolate heathen would receive the Gospel and bear fruit abundantly. Therefore every effort should be made to expand the frontiers of Christendom to embrace the heathen nations whose new believers would in turn carry the Gospel to the whole world. Carey used this text to challenge a group of ministers at a Baptist Association meeting in Birmingham. Responding immediately, they decided to organize a new mission called the Baptist Missionary Society, and they elected Andrew Fuller as the first home secretary.

## India—the Early Years

Carey offered himself to the new society as a "suitable companion" to Dr. John Thomas, who was returning to India as a freelance doctor and evangelist.[6] He was immediately accepted and began making plans to go, which included trying to persuade his wife, Dorothy, whom he had married some 10 years earlier, to go with him. She defiantly refused to go. However, after a series of circumstances Dorothy Carey grudgingly agreed to go to India with her husband and family of four children, provided her younger sister Kitty would go with them. They set sail on a Danish vessel on June 13, 1793.

The Carey party arrived in India on November 19 of the same

year. The commercial East India Company, hostile toward anyone doing missionary work in their territory, tried to deport him. After many privations an East India Company official became their benefactor and protector by welcoming them into his home. That opening enabled Carey to obtain a position as a foreman in an indigo factory in Malda on the northern edge of the Bengali province.

In Malda Carey threw himself into a serious study of the Bengali language. By 1795 he established a Baptist church there with four members—all Englishmen. A number of Bengali people attended the services from time to time, but there were no converts among "the Hindoos." After seven tortuous years in India, Carey had yet to see his first "Hindoo" convert.

The Lord forced Carey out of Malda because of financial failure and his wife's deteriorating physical and mental condition. Although the East India Company still would not allow missionaries in the city of Calcutta, the Lord opened a wonderful haven for Carey in the Danish colony of Serampore, across the Ganges River to the northeast of Calcutta. The king of Denmark welcomed the advance of the Gospel within this small territory, and Carey was able to obtain a large house in the city. Soon new recruits sent out by the fledgling missionary society in England joined him. With the addition of able men like Joshua Marshman and William Ward, the missionary enterprise in northeast India took on a new dimension.

## The First Four Converts and Beyond

On New Year's Eve of 1799, right at the end of the 18th century, the missionaries held their first baptismal service for Hindu converts. For Carey it was a day of great joy, yet deep anguish. While four Bengalis were being immersed in the waters of baptism amid singing and praises to God, his deranged wife, Dorothy, was confined in another room. In yet a third room one of his children lay feverishly ill and would later die. Great indeed is the cost of missions: "Except a corn of wheat fall into the ground and die, it abideth alone: but if it die, it bringeth forth much fruit" (John 12:24).

After the initial breakthrough with the baptism of the first four

Hindu converts, the missionary enterprise made great strides forward. It had taken seven years of great hardships and setbacks before Carey witnessed the baptism of his first convert. However, in the next few years the ministry grew dramatically until about 3,000 people were attending the church services and classes. The missionary community, which included ten adults and nine children, all lived together in one large building on the missionary compound. This property was obtained through the generous help of the King of Denmark, a champion of missionary enterprises.

In the early days of the mission they shared all things out of a common pot. They held a family prayer time every Saturday evening to settle petty grievances that inevitably crop up when Christian workers live together in confined premises. For many years they lived together in unusual harmony and loving fellowship under the gentle guidance of Carey who had a tendency to minimize the faults of others and commend the strengths of the various members. He was quick to praise and honor his co-workers, especially his talented and diligent co-leaders Joshua Marshman and William Ward. They became known as the "Serampore Trio".

The team members combined their talents and strengths to tackle various types of missionary projects. Besides the work of evangelism and church planting, the paramount task was Bible translation. In his lifetime Carey translated the Bible into Bengali, Sanskrit, and Marathi—a mammoth undertaking! Assisted by his colleagues, Carey's missionary team eventually translated various parts of the Scriptures into some 40 languages.

Another important work was the founding of Serampore College in 1819 for the training of national evangelists and pastors. Even today this college still provides academic accreditation for some of the seminaries in India. The language skills of this great missionary, who had only a humble beginning, were recognized and honored with his appointment at Fort William College in Calcutta to the exalted position of Professor of Oriental Languages. Carey sought to use the prestige derived from this position as a means of extending the influence of the Gospel of the kingdom of God into the academic world. The influence of William Carey in India was augmented by his accomplishments in language, education and guiding the affairs of an emerging church.

He felt a great concern for the overall emotional, physical and spiritual problems of the people among whom God had called him to labor. He developed what would now be called a holistic approach to the ministry. He fervently attacked the evil practices of Hindu widow burning and infanticide to the extent that they were eventually abolished. Yet he recognized some of the excellent features of the Indian society and admired their ability to suffer submissively rather than retaliate. Within the culture were certain Christian-like qualities that needed to be tapped and cultivated. Since he had great respect for the culture of India, its people and its languages, he never tried to impose western substitutes on the Indian churches or society.

Carey's major goal was to build a church that would have Indian characteristics; he wanted to build an indigenous church by means of native preachers and by providing the Scriptures in the national language. It was to these things he dedicated his life.[7]

## Carey's Main Missionary Concepts

Here are some of the basic missionary tenets and practices illustrated by the example of William Carey which are still valid in our time:

1. Obedience to the Great Commission (Matthew 28:18-20; Isaiah 54:1-3). We should use "means," not wait for God to save the heathen without effort on our part; we are to go and make disciples.

2. The ropeholder concept and the missionary-sending society. Carey compared India to a deep pit filled with precious jewels, or souls, to be won to Christ. He would go down into that awful pit to rescue precious souls if those at home would hold the ropes of support through gifts and consistent, believing prayer.

3. Emphasis on translating the Scriptures into the language of the people. Carey and his colleagues translated and printed the Bible or portions of it into 40 different languages in his lifetime.

4. The formation of a local church made up of native converts.

5.  Wide-scale distribution of Bibles and Christian literature.

6.  Combating the social evils of a godless society. Carey is credited with bringing such pressure on the British government officials in India that they outlawed the practice of infanticide, the killing of female babies who were considered within the poor Hindu society to be an economic liability to the family. Carey also fought against the terrible practice of suttee, the burning alive of the surviving widow on the pyre of her departed husband.

7.  Bringing modern medicine and hospital facilities to India.

8.  The expansion of educational facilities, especially in establishing schools for women and people of the lower strata of society.

9.  Carey was a tentmaker during most of his career. He supported himself by teaching and other projects. Mission funds were used for evangelism and church extension.

10. Carey not only attacked the evils of this Hindu society, but also criticized strongly his own countrymen, especially for practices by the British East India Trading Company which exploited the people for company profit. He so angered the officials of the company that on numerous occasions they tried to expel him from India.

## Lasting Influence

Here are some of the ways in which Carey put into practice these tenets of missionary strategy:

The "means" became a missionary society made up of a few people in England, at first mainly from the various Dissenter groups. These became the "ropeholders" who took up the offerings and pledged to pray for the missionaries who would be sent out to the field.

Carey labored extensively to translate and publish the Scriptures in the languages of the people to whom the missionaries were sent. Carey began his translation of the Bengali Bible even before he came to Serampore. Now with the assistance of Marshman the linguist and Ward the printer, the three men cooperated in getting portions of the Scriptures translated into many different languages of India.

One of Carey's lasting achievements was the founding of the Serampore College in 1819 for training Indian evangelists and pastors. Even today the graduates of some of the leading seminaries in India receive their diplomas out of Serampore College.

William Carey became such an expert in Indian languages and dialects that he was invited to become the professor of Oriental languages at Fort William College in Calcutta. From this position of honor and influence Carey launched an attack against the terrible practices of suttee (see above) and infanticide which were so prevalent in the Hindu Indian society.

Carey, who began his life work as a cobbler, accomplished remarkable things during his amazing missionary career. His life motto, coined on May 30, 1772, was truly fulfilled and has been adopted by posterity, "Expect great things from God; attempt great things for God!" No wonder Carey has been called "the father of the modern missionary movement," for many of the principles he espoused 200 years ago are very much in practice today around the world. He was a visionary far ahead of his time.

ENDNOTES:
1. S. Pearce Carey, *William Carey*, New York: George H. Doran Company, 1923, pages 16-24.
2. Basil Miller, *William Carey, The Father of Modern Missions*, Minneapolis, Minnesota: Bethany House Publishers,1952, pages 13-21.
3. Ibid., page 21.
4. F. Deauville Walker, *William Carey, Father of Modern Missions*, Chicago: Moody Press, 1980, page 54 and Footnote 1.
5. The original title of Carey's tract, a missiological masterpiece and trendsetter, included: " . . . In which the religious state of the different nations of the world, the success of former undertakings, and the practicability of further undertakings, are considered," Ibid., pages 69-71.
6. Carey, op cit., pages 96-105.
   Factual data for the above paragraphs gleaned from Ruth A. Tucker, *From Jerusalem to Irian Jaya*, Grand Rapids, Michigan: Zondervan Publishing House, 1983, pages 118-121.

# Chapter 7

## THE SECOND ADVANCE

### In the Footsteps of Hudson Taylor
### (GREAT BRITAIN, 1865)

God graciously visited England with another great spiritual awakening in the middle of the nineteenth century. The Keswick movement emphasized the deeper spiritual life and a personal commitment to walk in obedience to Christ. The Lord raised up great preachers of the Word like Charles Haddon Spurgeon and F. B. Meyer and great men of faith like George Mueller and Hudson Taylor. God would then use Hudson Taylor as His instrument to open up interior China to the Gospel and give subsequent Christian history an example to follow in the matter of living by faith.

### The Faith Principle

One of the basic tenets that Taylor lived by has since been called the "Faith Principle." William Carey, operating initially with very few funds, was also a man of great faith. But Carey supported himself in his early years on the field by his teaching and printing, a forerunner of that which today is being called "tentmaking ministries." As time went on, however, Carey's work became more and more funded and directed by his denomination; so he became the prototype of the denominational mission. These major denominational groups of England and America would launch their missionary enterprises following this pattern in the early 19th century.

Taylor, on the other hand, insisted on the dictum, "God's work done in God's way will never lack God's supply." He decided never to make a direct appeal for funds, nor would he ever borrow money or go into debt. God tested him on these points many times before he ever left England, for one of the great promises claimed by young Taylor was Philippians 4:19, "But my God shall supply all your need according to his riches in glory by Christ Jesus."

God tested Taylor on his willingness to go to China and live by faith alone. On one occasion, he shared some of his inner struggles in a letter to his mother.

"To me it was a very grave matter to contemplate going out to China, far from all human aid, there to depend upon the living God alone for protection, supplies and help of every kind. I felt that one's spiritual muscles required strengthening for such an undertaking. There was no doubt that if faith did not fail, God would not fail. But what if one's faith should prove insufficient? I had not at that time learned that even 'If we believe not, yet he abideth faithful; he cannot deny himself' (2 Timothy 2:13).

"When I get out to China, I thought to myself, I shall have no claim on anyone for anything. My only claim will be on God. How important to learn, before leaving England, to move man, through God, by prayer alone."[1]

He continued his letter to his mother by describing in vivid detail how God had tested him in relation to his being willing to give all the money he possessed [about $1.00 US then] to save a poor woman's life.

"After concluding my last service about ten o'clock that night, a poor man asked me to go and pray with his wife, saying that she was dying. I readily agreed, and on the way asked him why he had not sent for the priest, as his accent told me he was an Irishman. He had done so, he said, but the priest refused to come without a payment of eighteen pence, which the man did not possess as the family was starving. Immediately it occurred to my mind that all the money I had in the world was the solitary half-crown, and that it was in one coin: moreover, that while the basin of water-gruel I usually took for supper was awaiting me, and there was sufficient in the house for breakfast in the morning, I certainly had nothing for dinner on the coming day."

"Ah, thought I, if only I had two shillings and a sixpence instead of this half-crown, how gladly would I give these poor people a shilling! But to part with the half-crown was far from my thoughts. I little dreamed that the truth of the matter simply was that I could trust God plus one-and-sixpence, but was not prepared to trust Him only, without any money at all in my pocket.

"My conductor led me into a court, down which I followed him with some degree of nervousness. I had found myself there before, and at my last visit had been roughly handled. . . . Up a miserable flight of stairs into a wretched room he led me, and oh, what a sight there presented itself! Four or five children stood about, their sunken cheeks and temples telling unmistakably the story of slow starvation, and lying on a wretched pallet was a poor, exhausted mother, with a tiny infant thirty-six hours old moaning rather than crying at her side.

"The poor father turned to me and said, 'You see what a terrible state we are in, sir. If you can help us, for God's sake do!'

"At that moment the word flashed into my mind, Give to him that asketh of thee. And in the word of a King there is power.

"I put my hand into my pocket and slowly drawing out the half-crown gave it to the man, telling him that it might seem a small matter for me to relieve them, seeing that I was comparatively well off, but that in parting with that coin I was giving him my all; but that what I had been trying to tell them was indeed true, God really was a Father and might be trusted. And how the joy came back in full flood tide to my heart! I could say anything and feel it then, and the hindrance to blessing was gone—gone, I trust, forever.

"Not only was the poor woman's life saved, but my life as I fully realized had been saved too. It might have been a wreck—would have been, probably, as a Christian life—had not the grace at that time conquered and the striving of God's Spirit been obeyed.

"Next morning my plate of porridge remained for breakfast, and before it was finished the postman's knock was heard at the door. I was not in the habit of receiving letters on Monday, as my parents and most of my friends refrained from posting on Saturday, so that I was somewhat surprised when the landlady came in holding a letter or packet in her wet hand covered by her apron. I looked at the letter, but could not make out the handwriting. It was either a strange hand or a feigned one, and the postmark was blurred. Where it came from I could not tell. On opening the envelope I found nothing written within, but inside a sheet of blank paper was folded a pair of kid gloves from which, as I opened them in astonishment, half a sovereign [$4.00 US then] fell to the ground.

"'Praise the Lord,' I exclaimed, 'four hundred per cent for a twelve hours' investment! How glad the merchants of Hull would be if they could lend their money at such a rate of interest!' Then and there I determined that a bank that could not break should have my savings or earnings as the case might be, determination I have not yet learned to regret."[2]

Dawson Trotman, 100-plus years later, also was greatly challenged by the example of Hudson Taylor's faith. I recall several experiences that Daws related to me of how God miraculously provided for his family's needs in the nick of time.

On one such occasion, Daws and Lila, whose home was always open for guests, had run out of money and food. After the Sunday services some servicemen had dropped in for fellowship and in the anticipation of a nice Sunday dinner.

Daws sent Lila into the kitchen supposedly to prepare food. The real reason was to pray, for there was not enough food to prepare any kind of a proper meal. Daws kept talking with the servicemen, but also praying earnestly in his heart. As the time for the dinner hour approached, there was a knock on the door. A couple of sailors entered carrying some large dishes of ready-cooked food. Lila rushed out to greet them and exclaimed, "Oh how nice! We will eat this together now rather than that which is in the kitchen."

## Inland—To the Regions Beyond

The second major emphasis of Taylor's missionary philosophy might be termed the "inland" concept. Following Carey's example various denominational groups had planted mission stations along the coast of China and all the major ports had been penetrated by various missionary enterprises. However in 1865 there were 12 inland provinces with some 300,000,000 people where there was no witness for Jesus Christ. Taylor's heart was burdened for the regions beyond, "not where Christ was named" (see Romans 15:20).

On a spring day in 1865 Taylor is unable to sit in a church where a thousand English believers are praising God for all the blessings that have been heaped on them. With a burdened heart he runs out of church and flees to a deserted area of the beach near Brighton, England. Thousands of Christians are praising God in services in England on this Sunday morning, but in China there are 12 inland provinces where the sound of the precious name of Jesus has never been heard. Taylor's heart is burdened for Chinese multitudes that have not heard the Gospel.

He cannot ignore the facts. The passage of Proverbs 24:11-12 comes to his mind as he is walking along the beach: "If thou forbear to deliver them that are drawn unto death, and those that are ready to be slain; If thou sayest, Behold, we knew it not; doth not he that pondereth the heart consider it? and he that keepeth thy soul, doth not he know it? and shall not he render to every man according to his works?"

He must respond to the commands of God. He must believe God and act by faith to send missionaries to these lands.

As he continues walking by the seashore, he remembers another Scriptural promise God gives to His servants: "And there shall be with thee for all manner of workmanship every willing skillful man" (1 Chronicles 28:21). He writes this promise with the date in his diary and in the margin of his Bible: "Prayed for twenty-four willing skillful labourers at Brighton, June 25, 1865."[3]

In his prayer Taylor asks for 24 willing, skillful missionaries, two for each province, who would join with him to take the Gospel to the 12 inland provinces of China. He asked God for 24 willing and skillful laborers, for some are willing but not skillful, while others are skillful but not willing.

God gave him those 24 promised workers. The first group of 16 missionaries (plus four children and two helpers) left London on the

*Lammermuir* on May 26, 1866, within a year of claiming this promise from God. Thus the China Inland Mission was born. On September 30, 1866, the *Lammermuir* arrived in Shanghai.

Taylor verbalized his plan in a pamphlet he had written prior to his departure for China: "Our great desire and aim . . . are to plant the standard of the Cross in the eleven hitherto unoccupied provinces of China, and in Chinese territory (Mongolia)."[4]

He also shared his vision in a letter to his spiritual mentor, the Reverend William Burns, the famous Scottish evangelist who had taken the young missionary under his wing after Taylor had first gone to China. He had traveled with him on extensive exploratory evangelistic trips by native boats into southern China as far as Swatow.

Burns had responded with a letter from Peking in January 1866: "Your plan of seeking to plant two missionaries in each of the unoccupied provinces is a noble one, and if, by the help of God, it is but half accomplished, a great step will have been taken in advance, and the necessities of China will become more visible and clamant in the view of all the Protestant churches."[5]

Taylor's party, which arrived on the *Lammermuir*, did not remain long in Shanghai, where there was already an established Christian community, but pushed on inland to set up a forward base. The party traveled for nearly four weeks by rented native boats via the Grand Canal system, established by the early Chinese emperors, until they reached their destination—Hangchow.

This historic city, located at the gateway to the Grand Canal system, which gave access by waterway into nearly all parts of central China, was a strategic location from which to begin their missionary enterprise. Because of the ravages of the prolonged unsuccessful civil war, known as the Taiping Rebellion, the area was undergoing unsettled times.

After due haggling over price according to Chinese custom, the party was able to rent a residence, formerly owned by a Mandarin official, which would house their entire group. Actually, the owner became afraid of losing this deal with his potential tenants when the missionaries refused to continue bargaining on Sunday; so he approached them on Monday with a very reasonable offer.

They immediately began to use part of their quarters as a Chinese chapel because this section opened out on the street. From the very first, Chinese visitors flocked to the chapel to hear the foreigners and their native helpers preach the Gospel. The Sunday services grew rapidly until from 50 to 60 Chinese attended.

Soon the opportunity arose to move some of the new missionary recruits to the neighboring town of Siao Shan, where, assisted by a trained local native evangelist, they opened another chapel on their premises.

This became the basic pattern of the mission's advance. First, move into a forward area with two or more missionaries assisted by a Chinese co-worker; and then rent quarters in the Chinese sector of the city where a chapel opening into a street could be set up for preaching of the Gospel. For the second step they scheduled a visitation outreach program in which they distributed tracts freely and sold portions of the Bible at a nominal price. After the work became more established, they often added a medical clinic and set up a program to teach illiterate women and children how to read and write.

## Blending with the Local Culture

A third important aspect of Taylor's missionary philosophy was to adapt and blend into the host culture. The CIM missionaries were able to move into the interior regions of China because they were able to adapt quickly to the various local cultures of that vast land.

Taylor took a radical step to alter his appearance to be more like the Chinese. He shaved his head and had some false hair plaited in with his own, dyed it all black and made it into a pigtail. This shocked the traditional missionary community. Yet Taylor found it much easier now to move among the people and preach to them the Good News of the Gospel. Proclaiming the Gospel within the culture of the people and planting churches with Chinese flavor, became an important goal of the China Inland Mission.

Many CIM missionaries were single women; the advantage of

using women workers lay in their ability to enter into the Chinese home without posing a threat to the family. Miss Jean Faulding describes her experiences:

"I think if you could see how the people love and trust us you would rejoice. It does so please them to see us liking to be like themselves in outward things. They express the greatest satisfaction, and are delighted especially that our shoes and style of hair-dressing should be the same as theirs. Instead of having difficulty in getting across to the people, they come here day after day saying,

"'Fu Ku-niang [her name in Chinese-"Miss Blessing"], we want you to come to our house and teach us about the religion.'

"A woman said to me the other day, 'Do come, my mother wants to hear. . . . '

"I sometimes long that my whole time could be spent in visiting, at others that at least half could be given to the school—for I do so long to see native preachers raised up there, and the boys want training. Then again, we need books so much that if I could spend several hours daily with the teacher I should be glad. The work just seems overwhelming taking this city alone, and how much more so when one looks beyond the provinces full of cities in which there is no missionary! And look beyond we must.

"My heart does so well up with joy that I am here, and here among the people to a great extent as one of themselves. . . . Nothing could be more encouraging than our position—so almost more than willingly the people listen. I should think when I go out I often speak to more than two hundred persons. . . . Yet I am never treated in any way rudely, but with all kindness. Sometimes, indeed, it is with difficulty I get out of having to smoke a pipe, while tea and lunch I frequently have to take."[6]

After the new missionaries learned the language and culture through intensive language training and exposure to the Chinese way of life, they were sent out in groups of two or more into interior provinces. To be permitted to reside within the wall of any Chinese city was a matter requiring much prayer and great patience. The Chinese called the foreigners *lan kuei* ["blue-eyed devils"] and mothers would sometimes snatch up their children to protect them against the foreigner's evil power. So the missionary must first live with acceptance among the Chinese people before having any hope of getting them to embrace the teachings of the Bible.

## A Love for Souls

The fourth major emphasis is a love for souls, a compassion to win the lost. The thrust deeper into the interior was spearheaded sometimes by men like George Duncan who, though not specially gifted or cultured, possessed grit, perseverance and a great love for souls. Although not a fast learner, he had led his language teacher to the Lord by laboriously repeating Bible verses by the hour and struggling to read the Gospels in the Chinese Bible until his tutor came to a knowledge of the Lord through the very earnestness of his student to make the Savior known. Taylor wrote in retrospect about Duncan:

"It is a great blessing when God gives a hunger for souls. A good many of our early workers had it. We get better people now in some ways, better educated and so on, but it is not often you find that real hunger for souls—people willing to live anywhere and endure anything if only souls may be saved. They were very often humble people. If they were to offer to our Mission now [1902], they might not be accepted—George Duncan, for example! But nothing can take its place, or make up for the lack of it. . . . It is so much more important than ability."[7]

In 1867 Duncan, this zealous Scottish missionary, who had been personally groomed by Taylor on some early journeys together into the interior, went to Nanking, the ancient southern capital of Imperial China with only a Chinese helper for his companion. No lodging was allowed to this foreigner, but he did find refuge with a kindly Buddhist priest in the Drum Tower of the city. The Taylors record the following:

"It was a miserable place! Few, very few Europeans would have thought it possible to live there at all. 'But we gladly accepted it,' wrote Duncan, 'and managed very nicely, though we have rather more rats than I like. At night they want to devour everything!' . . . 'I am not able to talk much,' he wrote, 'but God helping me, I will say what I can, and T'ien-fuh (the Chinese evangelist) makes them understand. Oh, to make everything conduce to the gathering in of precious souls and the glory of our Master!'"[8]

This is but one excerpt showing the heart of one man as he entered into an interior city of China. However, this can be multiplied many times by the stories of the men and women who went to China having caught the vision and practiced the philosophy of ministry of J. Hudson Taylor to the glory of God.

## Together We Stand

A fifth major emphasis of Taylor's missionary philosophy was the new idea of having people of many different denominations and nationalities working together in harmony as the evidence of their unity in Christ and commitment to the Scriptures. Taylor sought new missionary recruits for the CIM from Great Britain, continental Europe, Canada, Australia and the United States. Thus the CIM developed into an international, interdenominational mission, as a fulfillment of Jesus' last recorded prayer in Gethsemane. John 17:20-21 says, "Neither pray I for these alone, but for them also which shall believe on me through their word; That they all may be one; as thou, Father, art in me, and I in thee, that they also may be one in us: that the world may believe that thou hast sent me."

When I arrived in Shanghai in January 1949, I was invited to live as a guest at the CIM headquarters. Here I met the 54 new recruits of the Class of 1948. These missionaries were from a dozen different countries, from many different denominations. One of them, Lois Raws from New Jersey in America, would later become my wife!

## Ten CIM Principles and Practices

Here is a list of some of the main principles and practices of the China Inland Mission that subsequently have influenced many other missions and Christian organizations in the 20th century:

1. No direct appeal for specific amounts of money.

2. Emphasis on adopting Chinese dress and culture.

3. Importance of becoming proficient in the local dialect.

4. Sending out missionaries by two's to set up residence in hostile cities in inland China. Sometimes foreigners were not even allowed to spend the night within a walled Chinese city.

5. Planting "indigenous" churches with local national pastors supported only through local funds.

6. Emphasis on public preaching and distribution of Christian literature, including Bible portions.

7. Training local leaders through setting up Bible schools, lay training programs, and evangelistic preaching bands.

8. Setting up of schools and hospitals for assistance to the people intellectually and medically to aid in spreading the Good News of the Gospel of Christ.

9. Emphasis on spiritual warfare and the belief that victories are wrought through the concerted prayer of God's people on specific targets.

10. Creating an international and interdenominational mission to show the unity of Christians so that the world might believe that Jesus came from the Father.

11. Claiming the promises of God for all of life and specific situations.

The opening paragraph of the foreword to the book about Hudson Taylor and the China Inland Mission, *The Growth of a Work of God*, well summarizes the life and ministry of this man whom God used to lead the great Second Advance of his world mission in modern times. Professor Warneck has written:

"The founder of the China Inland Mission was a physician, J. Hudson Taylor, a man full of the Holy Ghost and of faith, of entire surrender to God and His call, of great self-denial, heartfelt compassion, rare power in prayer, marvelous organizing faculty, energetic initiative, indefatigable perseverance, and of astonishing influence with men, and withal of childlike humility."

ENDNOTES:

1. Dr. and Mrs. Howard Taylor, *Hudson Taylor's Spiritual Secret,* (London: China Inland Mission, 1935), page 23.
2. Ibid., pages 24-27.
3. Dr. and Mrs. Howard Taylor, *Hudson Taylor and the China Inland Mission: The Growth of a Work of God,* (London: China Inland Mission, 1927), page 32.
4. Ibid., page 69.
5. Ibid., page 69, footnote 1.
6. Ibid., pages 125-126.
7. Ibid., page 120, footnote 1.
8. Ibid., pages 121-122.
9. Ibid., page vii.

# Chapter 8

## THE THIRD ADVANCE

### In the Footsteps of the Veterans of World War II (AMERICA, 1946-1960)

#### Gospel Spreads After Pearl Harbor

The first two advances of the modern missionary movement grew out of the great awakenings that took place in England and Great Britain. The spirit of renewal that spoke to John Wesley and George Whitefield influenced William Carey. The deeper life teachings of the Keswick and the Volunteer Student Movements challenged Hudson Taylor's generation. The dynamic faith and optimism of the World War II American servicemen nourished the third advance.

The initial impetus of this third advance began with a lay movement among U.S. servicemen, particularly pronounced among those who traveled by ship or were assigned to duty overseas. Separated from the comforts of one's own culture and plunged into a great worldwide conflict that threatened to destroy the very pillars upon which America was founded, many servicemen experienced a new dimension of faith. A new appreciation for the relevance of the Word of God sparked this lay movement.

Prior to the attack on Pearl Harbor, God began a work in the hearts of some of the sailors stationed on the great battleships which were the pride of the U.S. Navy until devastated by Japanese carrier-based planes.

On the USS *West Virginia*, as well as some of the other ships, a few men who called themselves Navigators took a fanatical approach to the Scriptures. They not only read the Bible and observed a disciplined quiet time with the Lord before the wake up call, but they memorized lots of verses from the Bible which they could quote word perfectly. And even though chaplains were assigned to take care of the religious needs of the navy personnel, these Navigators took upon themselves to confront their buddies with the Gospel in order for them to make a personal decision for Christ. Those who responded were expected to begin a disciplined life of Bible study and prayer so that they also could witness to their buddies and lead some to Jesus.

Before the attack on Pearl Harbor, God had already planted His witnesses, about 125 strong just on the *West Virginia*. All the battleships and other vessels suffered a great number of casualties during the Pearl Harbor attack. Although not stationed on one of the battleships, I met Jim Downing of the *West Virginia* at a Bible class on December 6, the night before the Pearl Harbor attack. The challenge of the Navigators to memorize Scripture changed the course of my life.

Since the battleships damaged at Pearl Harbor were no longer able to maneuver, many of the sailors were transferred to other ships. So the Navigators were no longer concentrated in one spot, but God scattered the believers as He did in the book of Acts (Acts 8:4). Then these disciples began a new witness throughout the fleet. The movement spread to other branches of the service; also other Christian organizations and service groups joined in the harvest. It continued to accelerate throughout the conflict until it reached its zenith at the close of the war. Then thousands of these veterans began to prepare to serve again overseas in a missionary capacity. This time, the servicemen were challenged to a new kind of worldwide conflict that would take the Gospel to every creature, even to every human being in this generation. "And he said unto them, Go ye into all the world and preach the gospel to every creature"(Mark 16:15). This sounded the battle cry for the third advance.

## Influence on American Churches

Although the initial impetus of the spiritual awakening among the servicemen was basically a lay movement, the influence of these men, particularly as they returned to their family and community, began to have a profound impact on the local churches in America.

Tracing church history, America experienced hard times during the late 1920s and early 1930s, not only economically but spiritually as well. The skepticism and rationalism, which permeated the European continent and England in the 19th century, finally crossed over to America in the 20th. The validity of Scripture came under attack and "old-time" religion was ridiculed. Church attendance dropped dramatically and people rarely expressed their personal faith openly. For example, the manual for U.S. Navy personnel advised that "an officer and a gentleman" should refrain from discussing with another person any matters relating to religion or politics.[2] Those who still attended church seldom read their Bibles outside of church services, and the few people who engaged in personal evangelism were considered eccentric.

But during World War II the Spirit of God began to work in thousands of American servicemen in a way that profoundly affected church life and then world missions after that war. Unlike the attitude after World War I when the majority of veterans returned home as quickly as possible to forget the horrors of war and to isolate themselves from world involvement, many World War II military men had a life-changing spiritual experience during their tour of duty. It was a remarkable work of God through the moving of His Holy Spirit. At the heart of this mini-revival were the Scriptures, a new appreciation for the power of the Word of God to save and transform lives.

In large numbers American servicemen rediscovered their Bibles. Groups like the Gideons and the Pocket Testament League furnished New Testaments to every soldier, sailor, airman and marine. The Navigators, beginning with men in the U.S. Navy, encouraged the serviceman to read his Bible, study it, memorize it in systematic fashion and share its message of salvation with others in companies, ships, squadrons and on invasion beaches. Home churches found many ways to encourage these servicemen to maintain their newfound faith. Denominations printed special literature, and local churches worked together to set up Christian Servicemen's Centers wherever military people were concentrated.

## Influence on Missions

The first two advances in modern missionary history were based in the British Isles and were primarily aimed at establishing a local church through which the ministry could be extended. During World War II a new kind of movement took place—it did not spring from pastors or chaplains. This was a lay movement among servicemen witnessing to one another aboard ship or on the front lines.

Although various organizations were involved in this movement, The Navigators led the way. By the end of World War II, men on more than 1000 ships and stations were navigating for Jesus Christ as they memorized Bible verses and witnessed to their fellow servicemen.

Toward the end of World War II the Youth for Christ movement introduced Saturday night gospel rallies as an exciting new way to reach young people with the Gospel. Our Powerhouse Five missionary heroes became prominent leaders in this movement. Some of the servicemen set up Saturday night rallies in cities where they were stationed overseas in order to reach both servicemen and the local young people with the Gospel. These rallies sprung up in all directions— around bases in Guam, Japan, China, Germany, England—wherever servicemen were stationed. When the servicemen returned back to the States, many became involved directly with other Saturday night rallies that influenced young people in their hometowns.

An emphasis on missions prevailed everywhere. From its American base, YFC type meetings spread to the mission field. After the war, the victorious American military forces set about rebuilding the devastated war-torn areas both with economic and spiritual help. General Douglas MacArthur appealed to Christians in America to send out 10,000 missionaries to Asia. America responded with the greatest surge of new missionaries in history—more than 4,000 new missionaries and 145 new missionary groups and organizations entered Japan alone between 1945 and 1955. I was one of those missionaries, serving with The Navigators.

## YFC Goes To India and China

Hube Mitchell, with the help of Daws and their friends, had started the Los Angeles Rally. In January 1946 at a gigantic farewell rally the Mitchells were sent forth as missionaries to India. A group of pastors from various churches in Calcutta invited Hube to preach at an evangelistic meeting for youth held in a public theater during Easter week. The response to Hube's preaching was overwhelming and the YFC movement caught fire and spread to other cities of India.

When Dick Hillis returned from China he prepared the way for the team of David Morken and Bob Pierce with their Chinese counterparts to preach in public meetings throughout China. They preached in some of the largest halls and churches of the principal cities of China week after week for nearly five months. In those dramatic days of 1947, just prior to the Communist takeover, Chinese people of all classes responded in unprecedented numbers to the claims of Christ. Numerically nothing like this had ever happened in Asia, even in the great revivals of Evangelist John Sung. YFC recorded about 30,000 decisions for Christ in a one-year period, as multitudes flocked together to hear the Gospel.

In 1948, David moved his family to Shanghai where they set up a base for the Youth for Christ ministry. Then, joined by YFC national evangelists Andrew Gih and John Goo, they held another city-wide crusade in Shanghai during December 1948 at the historic Moore Memorial Church (*Mo En Tang*), across the street from the international race course. Some 800 people registered their decisions to receive Christ. This was my first missionary assignment: David and Dick handed me 800 decisions for follow-up on the day after I arrived in Shanghai in January 1949.

## YFC Goes To Japan

Youth for Christ took a prominent role in Japan by public preaching in the streets, in parks, and in public halls. In the national educational hall (Kyo Ritsu Kodo) within Tokyo's university belt, students in their black uniforms with white cuffs formed a queue over a block long for the regular YFC rally.

David Morken, Far East YFC director, with advice from Sam Wolgemuth and gifts from Bob Pierce, outfitted a trailer that could be transformed into a stage equipped with purple draw curtains, a

Hammond electric organ, and the latest sound equipment. With these fittings he held street meetings in first class style. This outdoor gospel unit appeared one time a week at each of the four busiest transport centers in the city of Tokyo, which were Ikebukuro, Shibuya, Shinjuku and Tokyo Central. In Shinjuku alone more than one million people changed trains daily.

The high-class music and gospel preaching program directed by David Morken attracted thousands nightly. Sometimes on a single night more than 100 people walked up to the front of the stage to register their decisions for Christ. The Navigators, in charge of follow-up, invited the seekers to join weekly follow-up classes and also put them in contact with local churches. More than 33,000 Japanese successfully completed the "Assurance of Salvation" Bible study and mailed it for grading to the YFC office, which was staffed by a dozen national follow-up workers and evangelists.

The Youth for Christ movement reached its zenith at the 1953 World Congress on Evangelism in Japan. Following a week of fruitful meetings in Tokyo, the 300 delegates from abroad formed small gospel teams that held 800 gospel meetings in 45 of the 46 provinces of Japan with more than 22,000 registered decisions for Christ. Never before—or since—has such a thorough public saturation evangelism taken place in that country.

I wrote the syllabus for counseling classes taught in 300 locations by follow-up staff and national pastors. After the meetings a staff of 15 workers coordinated the follow-up through a correspond-ence course and encouraged the seekers to link with a designated local church. Later, the Japanese pastors responded concerning the list of names supplied to them and reported that more than 4,000 of these seekers who had been referred to them had been integrated into their regular church services. This was considered highly successful. To form a bridge to link the new believer into a regular church fellow-ship was the primary goal of the follow-up department throughout the weeks of the Congress.

## YFC Goes to Taiwan

Yet the most dramatic story was still to come. What God did in Formosa (named "beautiful" by the Portuguese and known today as Taiwan) is remarkable in mission history. Bob Pierce visited Formosa in mid-1950, when it had been occupied by 1,500,000 Chinese nationalist soldiers and their dependents who had fled the mainland and its new communist masters with Generalissimo Chiang Kai-Shek. His armies had found refuge on this island and under these difficult circumstances experienced great need of spiritual help. Bob immediately contacted Dick Hillis. Even though Hillis felt emotionally and physically drained from having just left Communist China, Bob insisted that he go to Taiwan at once to minister to these desperate people.

When Dick Hillis and the YFC team entered Taiwan in September of 1950, the Presbyterian Church was the only recognized mission on the island and nearly all services were held in the local dialects. A veteran Presbyterian missionary couple, Jim and Lillian Dickson, opened the door for the YFC team to hold extensive evangelistic meetings throughout the island. Following in the wake of thousands of new converts, many other church groups quickly entered the field to reap a harvest both of Taiwanese and Mandarin-speaking people. The Southern Baptists, Lutherans, Methodists, Holiness, Assemblies of God and indigenous Chinese groups from Watchman Nee and others had established many churches by 1960.

The response to the Gospel was phenomenal. Dick Hillis and his Youth for Christ preaching teams systematically distributed Gospels of John to the 600,000 nationalist troops. General Chiang wrote a letter to his troops commending them to read the Bible, which he called "the rock of salvation in a time of need." Next, openings to present the Gospel inside the schools arose throughout the island. Later, gospel vans carried the message to nearly every village in the countryside.

During these times of tremendous response, approximately 10,000 decisions for Christ were recorded each month over an 18-month period. We sent a four-lesson Gospel of John follow-up correspondence course, which I designed, to every seeker. By 1955 more than a half million people on the island of Taiwan had completed one or more of these Bible studies. A follow-up staff of 25 workers served in the Youth for Christ office. Approximately five percent of the total population (one out of every 20 people on the entire island) responded favorably to the Gospel and began to study the Bible for themselves in a systematic fashion. The average Chinese dwelling at that time housed about ten family members. So there was an average of one new witness for Christ for every two dwellings. Such an all-out effort to evangelize a particular region has seldom been equaled in modern history.

All missionary groups and local churches greatly benefited from this movement. For instance, in 1950 at the start of this program there were only about seven churches in the capital city of Taipei. In 1960 the church directory listed 115 churches, an increase of well over 1,000% in a ten-year period.

## Principles and Practices in This Advance of God's Mission
The above are but a few outstanding examples of the impact Youth for Christ made on missions and the church in Asia following World War II. In a variety of different yet parallel ways these examples could be multiplied in missions worldwide, the majority led by ex-servicemen of World War II and later the Korean War. Some characteristics of the American-based Youth for Christ missionary movement in Asia were:

1. A bold, direct approach in public evangelism calling for a personal, open commitment to Christ.

2. An effort to give individual counseling and personal follow-up to every seeker.

3. An emphasis on individual Bible study, Scripture memory and a daily devotional "quiet time."

4. Cooperation among the local churches and missionary groups to obtain the largest possible hearing for the Gospel.

5. A break from traditional methods through the use of widespread advertising, ticket distribution and technical aids to draw a large audience.

6. The use of famous people, talented musicians and the best of sound and visual equipment to attract more youth.

7. Mobile, fast moving itinerant evangelistic teams rather than the standard "build a mission station" approach.

8. A spirit of abandonment and sacrifice for the Gospel's sake (home, finances, security were thought to be secondary issues).

9. Believing God for the impossible—willing to take a risk (travel without reservations, book public halls without money).

10. An atmosphere of expectancy and excitement (some really believed the world could be reached with the Gospel in their generation).


**Analysis**

In retrospect, that generation of post-World War II Americans were bold, proud, generous, enthusiastic, lovable and exasperating to their European counterparts. The American worldwide prestige and Yankee dollar were at their height.

True, the highest goals were not reached, but not since the first century had the Gospel been proclaimed worldwide with such effectiveness. God raised up laborers with sharp sickles to work in a ready harvest. Today, the evidence of that harvest remains in Taiwan, Korea, the Philippines, Indonesia, India, China and elsewhere in the world. This chapter concentrated on Asia because that was my field of ministry, but similar stories can be gleaned from the other continents as well. Hundreds of veterans went to Africa, Latin America, the Middle East, Western Europe and into clandestine works in Eastern Europe in the latter part of the 20th century.

The spiritual awakening, accompanied by a new appreciation for the power of the Word of God that took place among the servicemen of World War II, had tremendous impact on the advance of world missions. It was as great an advance collectively as those earlier ones under William Carey and Hudson Taylor.

The influence of Dawson Trotman touched not only the Youth for Christ movement, but was linked closely to that of the Wycliffe

Bible Translators. Its founder "Uncle Cam" (Cameron) Townsend invited him to serve on the Wycliffe board. Daws put the highest priority on the top trained "Navigators" becoming missionaries with other groups to the unreached peoples of the world. He called this Other Works[3] in his "Big Dipper Illustration." Throughout all of his years of ministry, he exhorted everyone he met and preached to every group he visited to get a world vision—to get on their hearts what is on God's heart—the world.

Daws "gave away" the men whom he had trained with unselfish abandonment. Kenny Watters, one of the earliest sailor Navigators, became a leader with Wycliffe Bible Translators. He spearheaded the program of their "jungle camp" training for all new recruits, which included an exposure to Navigator methodology for one's personal Bible study, a Scripture memory program and the devotional life.

A gifted Navy chaplain, Arthur Glasser, was encouraged to join the China Inland Mission, and would go to the Lisu people, following the footsteps of J. O. Fraser and Isobel Kuhn.

Each of the first five "original" Navigators (all Navy men), led to Christ through the spiritual lineage descended from Dawson Trotman, went to some field with another missionary organization:

- Gurney Harris went to Africa.

- Virgil Hook went to Tibet with the CIM.

- John Dedrick went to rural Mexico.

- Les Spencer went to rural America.

- Ed Goodrick went into Bible translation and scholarship.

Thousands of dedicated American ex-servicemen entered Bible schools, Christian colleges and seminaries immediately following the war, and many of them prepared for missionary service around the world. Missionary Aviation Fellowship (MAF) and Jungle Aviation and Radio Service (JAARS) were nearly entirely staffed by veterans of the war. The Far East Gospel Crusade (now called Send International) consisted of servicemen who formed a fellowship shortly after the war ended. Orient Crusades (now called O. C. Ministries) was founded by Dick Hillis as an avenue for public evangelism in

Asia. The Pocket Testament League and scores of other new missions were largely staffed by World War II veterans and later by GIs who had fought in the Korean War and could now see God's needy world from another perspective. Additional hundreds went overseas with denominational missions.

## A Summary of the First Three Advances

Each advance in modern missions overlapped the earlier one, building on the principles of its predecessor and adding new ones rediscovered from the study of the Scriptures and early missions history. The Protestant Reformation had restored the Scriptures as the ultimate authority to the church, but for the large part Protestant missions did not begin again until all the internecine conflicts were over and the era of the great revivals had come.

In the first advance Carey formed a missionary agency which sent faith and bivocational missionaries to make converts among the "heathen" people, primarily in India. The task began by translating the Scriptures into the local languages. Carey also attacked the evils of an oppressive society and sought to better the life of a downtrodden people with education, medicine and social reforms. His, then, was a "holistic" ministry (before the term was even used). Although Carey came from a dissenter background, he founded a church patterned on denominational lines.

In the second advance Taylor benefited by the foundations laid by the earlier missionaries to China. The Bible was already translated into the official Chinese language and churches were firmly established in the major port cities. Christian schools and hospitals were beginning to influence the minds and hearts of the people toward Christianity. Taylor felt burdened, however, to preach the Gospel where missionaries had not yet entered; the 12 unreached inland provinces of China at that time had a population of some 300,000,000 people.

So he founded the China Inland Mission with the aim of sending out resident missionaries, who would not only preach the Gospel but also train nationals, who in turn would further spread the Good News of Jesus Christ. He wanted to form a real Chinese church in contrast to a western-oriented church. But in fairness to the missionaries of the first advance, Carey had also trained nationals to lead the church and was thoroughly familiar with the local languages and customs. It was a matter of perspective and emphasis.

In the third advance the ex-servicemen of World War II and the Korean War used all kinds of methods to get the Gospel out to every person and ethnic group in the world. They sensed great urgency, for in those days atheistic world Communism seemed to be making an unstoppable march toward world conquest. These new missionaries also built upon the basic principles of the first two advances—for many of them translated the Scriptures, planted churches and served their mission groups in traditional ways. Yet the third advance included many lay people who used innovative ways to spread the Gospel and reach out to make friends among the unchurched people.

## An Interesting Historical Appendix

In light of the communist successes in the earlier part of this era following World War II, it is interesting to note how effective this third advance was in terms of what we know today since the apparent shattering of International Communism. Even China, with the inroads of capitalism extending into its still communistic governmental system, will never be the same. But the resurgence of the church in that vast land in the post-Mao Tse-Tung and Chou En-Lai era shows undeniably how the foundations laid by the missionary pioneers could not be destroyed. Although the Communist government forcibly closed the doors of every church in China during the Cultural Revolution, it rose from the ashes of the fiery trial—to live again.

Throughout the years of communist oppression and the excesses of the Cultural Revolution, the church survived. It not only survived, but it multiplied into numbers still not fully known today. Under God's guidance and the work of the Holy Spirit the missionaries, not knowing what the future held, did a tremendously effective work in preparing the Chinese church for its great "hour of trial." Even when Bibles were burned, some of the dear saints were strengthened by the Word of God implanted in their hearts.

In the later 1940s in the midst of the impending threat of communist armies advancing toward the great cities of China, both the local people and hundreds of refugees flocked to church services and church activity abounded. Both the denominational church and the house type church withstood the threat of the extreme Communist leaders who boasted that they would destroy the Bible and the Christian religion in China. From my conversations with other missionaries and my own personal observations, the conclusion is that the denominational churches were strongest in the cities, while the China Inland Mission and house type churches were strongest in the countryside.

History has shown that there are strengths and weaknesses in both approaches. According to historian Kenneth Scott Latourette, Christians in churches which had some roots and ties to the West were just as steadfast—sometimes more so—than the more indigenized national-planted churches. In fact, from the standpoint of remaining true to their roots, Latourette suggests that Catholics seemed to fare better than the Protestants.[4]

But the fact remains that in China today we find that God has greatly blessed the seeds planted by both the established church (TSPM) and the many "house" churches. From both groups many were sent out to forced labor communes and some died for the faith through those 40 years of intense persecution. There is but one Body of which Christ is the head.

ENDNOTES:
1. See the writings of Ralph Winter on this, particularly "The Two Structures of God's Redemptive Mission," *Missiology*, II, 1 (January 1974), pages 121-139; also note the doctoral dissertation by William A. Shell, "Partners in Mission As Servants," Fuller Theological Seminary, Pasadena, California, 1984.
2. United States Navy. Manual for Officers. (This manual is no longer in use by the U. S. Navy, is not in print, and cannot be found for a complete bibliographic entry.)
3. Dawson Trotman's "Big Dipper Illustration" includes the following ingredients of the Christian disciple's life and ministry:
   • THE WHEEL
   • THE HAND

- EVANGELISM
- FOLLOW-UP
- PACE SETTING
- OTHER WORKS
- WORLD VISION

These ingredients begin with The WHEEL, which is "The Christ-centered Life," part of which is the intake of The Word, which when we know it and obey it causes us to take part in Evangelism (the picture is now a scoop). When we Follow-up the fruit of our outreach we "close" the scoop. By our Pacesetting we show our disciples by our lives what they ought to be and do. In addition, we anticipate in harmony with other churches and groups (as Other Works) and culminate in all of us having World Vision to reproduce the process.

4. This data is gleaned from the following: Ralph D. Winter, *The 25 Unbelievable Years*, South Pasadena, California: William Carey Library, 1970, and Kenneth Scott Latourette, *Christianity in a Revolutionary Age*, Volume V, New York: Harper & Row, Publishers, 1962, pages 4, 15.

# THE POWERHOUSE FIVE
# LINK WITH
# YOUTH FOR CHRIST

*1946 - 1960*

Public Evangelism Plus Follow-Up Pattern

# BACKGROUND

In this section the Powerhouse Five join with the Youth for Christ movement to spearhead a huge public evangelism thrust into China. Hube Mitchell, who directed the great Saturday night rally at the double balconied auditorium in downtown Los Angeles, was sent off with much fanfare from Christian young people to become a missionary in India. In Calcutta he started a weekly Youth for Christ Saturday evening rally, where the young people of India responded with the same enthusiasm as those in California.

Dick Hillis arranged for David Morken to hold this type of evangelistic rallies in China. Even as he was on his way to China, he joined Hube in India for successful rallies. Upon reaching China David spoke to overflow crowds in evangelistic meetings in several cities in southern China. Then David was joined by Bob Pierce in Shanghai for a week-long gospel crusade in which nearly all the churches co-operated. During the next four months they preached to the largest crowds ever to attend gospel services in China. At the end of 1947 Bob reported to the YFC leadership that 30,000 people had made public decisions to receive the Lord Jesus Christ as their personal Savior.

The few national and missionary co-workers were overwhelmed with the response and could not begin to cope with the follow-up. So the Youth for Christ leaders urgently appealed to Dawson Trotman, founder of The Navigators, for help in follow-up. Later, Billy Graham would also make an appeal to Daws to set up a follow-up system for the Billy Graham crusades. Dick Hillis, already serving under the China Inland Mission, set up the YFC meetings throughout China. In the winter of 1947-1948 Dick and David also arranged for Daws to come to China. Daws spoke to missionary and church leaders in Shanghai, Beijing, Chengtu and other major cities on the importance of follow-up and the value of memorizing Scripture. They received his messages and examples of spiritual reproduction with great interest. When the YFC leaders urged Daws to send a man to China to serve in handling the follow-up of Youth for Christ meetings, I was honored to be sent out on this assignment.

In the beginning of 1949 the Communists began an offensive to capture all of China. I was with Dick and David in Shanghai when the city fell to the Communists. It took more than a year before the Hillis family with five children and the Morken family with six children were allowed to leave. I stayed on a few months longer because hundreds of young believers were continuing to memorize the Navigator memory cards of 108 verses. We even held special cooperative evangelistic meetings for the English-speaking young people with an American evangelist. Then John Goo, the local Chinese YFC leader, held two district crusades in certain parts of Shanghai. After I left Shanghai, this bold Chinese evangelist was put in prison where he died.

Generalissimo Chiang Kai Shek fled to the island of Taiwan with about 1 1/2 million refugee people of whom 600,000 were combat soldiers. The communists threatened to invade Taiwan, and the refugees fleeing communism were desperate for help. But Madame Chiang Kai Shek, an ardent born-again Christian lady, told Bob Pierce on his visit to Taiwan that their greatest need was spiritual help. Then her husband, Generalissimo Chiang Kai Shek urgently requested that a Gospel of John be distributed to every soldier under his command. He wrote a letter authorizing the Gospel of John to be presented by a Youth for Christ evangelist at every military installation in Taiwan.

This was a spiritual opportunity not to be missed. Bob said, "Hillis is the man to lead this." So Bob ordered a half million Gospels of John and pushed Dick to go to Taiwan to take charge of the program, even though he felt emotionally exhausted from the pressure of living under communism in China.

Dick mobilized gospel teams to take the Gospel first to soldiers, then to students, then the farmers in the countryside. The Taiwan harvest 1951-1960 is one of the greatest in missionary history.

Next David and Bob teamed together to launch outdoor gospel rallies at the great railway centers of Tokyo, Japan. The Americans were looked upon as benevolent heroes because they helped build back the devastated Japanese economy. For another time of golden harvest from 1951 to 1953, nearly 100 people a night came to Christ at these outdoor youth rallies in Tokyo held each week in the four great railroad centers.

# Chapter 9

## SATURDAY NIGHT YOUTH RALLY EXPORTED

In downtown Los Angeles in late 1945, Saturday nights were usually the Devil's night. On Spring Street and the adjacent areas the Devil indeed seemed to be in control. Thousands of servicemen returning from the Pacific theater of World War II, along with local youth, indulged themselves in the pleasures of sin.

### The Saturday Night Jubilee

At the same time on a typical Saturday night, however, just a few blocks away near the towering City Hall on Hope Street, some 4,000 young people would suddenly burst into their joyful theme song: "Christ for me, yes, it's Christ for me!"

On the platform of the spacious auditorium of the historic Church of the Open Door, a radiant Hube Mitchell with his accordion directed the Saturday Night Jubilee. People considered the combination of Rudy Atwood at the piano and Loren Whitney at the organ the best in California. The former, trained in classical music and a master of embellishment, transformed the simple tunes of the youth choruses into something like the Hallelujah Chorus.

Rudy, a close friend of Daws, sometimes visited for an evening in the Trotman home to the delight of all the Navigator staff who lived there. They gathered around him at the piano and sang their hearts out, as Rudy played by ear or improvised any song requested.

Loren, also a concert organist, often teamed with Rudy to perform on the radio and in various public meetings. When they blended together, each alternating in the lead, beautiful music filled the auditorium and lifted up hearts to the Lord.

In the Saturday night meetings, a mixture of robust singing of gospel choruses, short testimonies and well-prepared musical items kept the program moving at a lively pace. Gifted John Shearer often led the singing, and groups such as "The Old Fashioned Revival Hour" men's quartet provided special music. Dr. Charles E. Fuller featured Rudy, Loren and the quartet, broadcasting live from the Long Beach Civic Auditorium every Sunday afternoon in a gospel radio program followed by millions of listeners around the world.

The Saturday night program often began with one of their famous numbers, such as:

> "On the Jericho Road
> There's room for just two,
> No more and no less,
> Jus' Jesus and you."

After an hour of excellent music and audience participation, a dynamic speaker talked to the young people in an informal style. At first some in the audience didn't realize he was delivering the main gospel message for the evening.

His direct talk would hit home, for the power of the Gospel works in hearts to bring sinners to Jesus. At the invitation to come forward to make a public commitment for Jesus Christ, several hundred people — mostly youth — would make their way down to the altar, some coming from the first balcony and even the second balcony. Outside the church, special buses which brought the young people from outlying areas of greater Los Angeles would wait until all the seekers had been counseled.

The Bible says there is rejoicing in heaven over every sinner who repents and comes to Christ. So the Devil did not have control on Saturday nights over all the youth in the great metropolis of the Los Angeles area, and the choir in heaven would sing songs of praise for the many sinners who repented.

In this strategic era of history the Gospel was being communicated and men and women were being saved in great downtown gospel rallies, not just in Los Angeles but also in other major cities of

America. Saturday night in many U.S. cities and later in numerous cities around the world became known as the night of Youth for Christ.

How did all this come about? Hube Mitchell says the Saturday Night Jubilee in Los Angeles was born in much prayer. God had begun to answer the fervent prayers that were lifted up faithfully from "The Powerhouse." Meeting at 5:00 A.M. every Tuesday morning, Hube Mitchell, Daws Trotman, Dick Hillis, David Morken, Bob Pierce, Bob Munger and a few other dedicated men of God voiced their burden to reach the youth of Los Angeles. Later the first four enlarged their petitions to encompass Asia and eventually the whole world. This group of men not only prayed, but they acted in faith to bring young people together in downtown Los Angeles to hear the Gospel.

Simultaneously, the Lord raised up other leaders and rallies in the major cities of America. At first it was not organized for the movement just sprang up spontaneously as a result of importunate prayer and the working of a sovereign God. In addition, Christian Endeavor and the recently founded Young Life were active, particularly among high schoolers.

The Lord worked in the hearts of thousands of American servicemen during World War II. The Gideons provided them with Bibles or New Testaments; the Pocket Testament League and other groups also printed Scriptures and Bible helps. The Navigators taught sailors and soldiers to get victory over sin by memorizing many Scriptures. "Thy word have I hid in mine heart, that I might not sin against thee" (Psalm 119:11). Thousands of servicemen found Christ and a new living relationship with the Lord Jesus and the Word of God.

God was also raising up leaders in the great cities across America with a burden to reach the youth through gospel meetings. In New York Jack Wyrtzen, an able youth worker, started the Word of Life rallies in Times Square, in the very heart of the city. These later developed into the Word of Life youth camps on Schroon Lake in upstate New York. Word of Life Bible clubs flourished in Greater New York, and then formed summer camps overseas in a number of countries. "Hi BA" (High School Born Againers) became well known in Japan and other countries.

Percy Crawford called his Philadelphia rallies "Youth on the March;" he went on to become a famous youth evangelist. In 1952 he came to Japan at the invitation of the chaplains to hold a gospel rally in the gymnasium on Yokota Air Force Base (during the Korean War). Our Navigator team (Robertson, Scott, Crabtree) trained the counselors for that meeting. Percy stayed in our home and gave lectures to our staff on the role of the evangelist—stressing that the message always be the Cross and the Resurrection, as well as emphasizing the urgency and spiritual battle that takes place at the time of invitation.

His style was: "You! Get up out of your seat right now and come forward to receive Christ!"

When the seekers with their counselors came forward, it appeared in that gymnasium as if more people were moving than remaining seated. In actual numbers about 25% of the audience responded to the invitation to make a decision for Christ. Yes, it was a time of war, but men were serious about their spiritual conditions.

Chicagoland Youth for Christ was started and led by Torrey Johnson, a dynamic youth leader in that area. In these early days of this growing movement a young evangelist-preacher named Billy Graham ably assisted him. Torrey would later become the mentor for Bob Pierce.

These men collectively were each a dynamic leader of a regular weekly youth rally in a large American city, which created excitement and enthusiasm on a scale never observed before in American Christendom. They had the cooperation and involvement of most of the evangelical (Bible-believing) churches. All these men became prominent evangelists, mainly with youth, speaking at youth rallies and carrying on many other youth-related activities.

At first these Saturday night youth rallies sprang up independently of each other. Then in the summer of 1945, shortly before World War II ended, they loosely banded together with the name "Youth for Christ" (YFC) and elected Chicago's Torrey Johnson as president.

In the meantime, American servicemen started youth rallies in overseas stations such as Guam, China, the Philippines, Japan, Germany, England and France. Most started locally, but the local leaders eventually applied to Youth for Christ headquarters for a local chapter recognition.

Hube, director of Saturday Night Jubilee in Los Angeles, however, couldn't wait to get back to the mission field. At least once a month he spotlighted missions on the program. After returning to America with four motherless children, he had courted and married Rachel Edwardsen, a Norwegian, who had lived in India for 15 years and was fluent in the Hindi and Urdu languages. Although Indonesia was now closed, openings in India existed even in the midst of the turbulent struggle for independence. So Hube accepted the call to take his new bride and children to India as missionaries.

In January 1946 the Saturday Night Jubilee held a great farewell for Hube and Rachel Mitchell. With Hube playing the accordion, they sang together with their five children a medley of songs. On the eve of their departure to take the Gospel to a troubled India caught up in the overthrow of British rule, this lovely, talented family melted the hearts of the audience, similar to the Von Trapp family singers in the famous movie "The Sound of Music." The next day, the Los Angeles newspapers featured the story with photos of the great farewell rally for the Mitchell family.

Hube passed on the mantle for directing the Saturday Night Jubilee rallies to his brother-in-law, David Morken. Under David's direction the weekly youth meetings continued to prosper. Nearly every Saturday about 4,000 young people filled both balconies of the auditorium of the Church of the Open Door in downtown Los Angeles. Twice a year the Saturday Night Jubilee moved a few blocks away to the Shrine Auditorium which seated 7,000. A. Randolph Hearst, the newspaper tycoon, instructed the Los Angeles Examiner to cover the rally every Saturday night. Consequently, every Monday morning the front page of the second section of this well-known and influential newspaper featured pictures, articles and background stories on what God was doing in the lives of young people. Saturday night was no longer dominated by Satan in downtown Los Angeles.

In the summer of 1946 David and his associates took another

giant step of faith by inviting evangelist Percy Crawford from the East Coast to stage a gigantic Youth for Christ rally in the famous Hollywood Bowl of Los Angeles. In those days even the Los Angeles Symphony Orchestra or performances by top movie stars could scarcely fill it except on rare occasions. But the Spirit of the Lord worked mightily as Christian groups throughout the greater Los Angeles area cooperated in harmony and excited anticipation to gather what was then considered an unprecedented number of people to hear the Gospel.

The Los Angeles Examiner on July 1, 1946 carried many pictures and articles about the vast crowd: "More than 20,000 Southern California youth sat in the Hollywood Bowl, facing the beautifully lighted stage during the gigantic Youth for Christ Jubilee Saturday Night." The reporters told how far some of the youth had traveled to attend and printed many close-up pictures of the evangelist and some of the young people. The paper continued, "Percy Crawford delivered a moving message from the Bible. At the climax of the Jubilee his inspiring message brought more than 2,000 teenagers to the stage to make their decisions for Christ."

The Jubilee rallies no doubt set the stage for the launching of another young evangelist, whose crusades with their dynamic preaching and the great responses to the invitations to receive Christ have since caught the attention of the whole world. Billy Graham's spectacular God-honoring public career really began at a citywide tent campaign sponsored by the churches of Greater Los Angeles in 1949.

## Youth for Christ Penetrates India

The Hube Mitchell family did not go to India to set up YFC, but were sent out under the Go Ye Fellowship. This mission had been founded by the Mitchell family, Hube's parents, to take the Gospel to Asia; Hube later became the director of the mission. Rachel, a veteran missionary and skilled linguist, became head of the language school for missionaries studying Urdu and Hindi at a northern hill station at the edge of the Himalayan Mountains. But Hube was a gifted itinerant evangelist. The Indian young people responded to his radiant platform personality and were blessed by his preaching and music.

One day soon after getting his family settled into their new mission station in Karwi, in the northern part of India in the state of Uttar Pradesh, Hube had to take a trip to Bombay to claim his belongings sent out from California. Hube recalls what happened there.

"While in Bombay, I received a telegram from a group of ministers in Calcutta who planned to have a youth rally in the Tiger Theatre the Monday after Easter 1946. The telegram read as follows:

"'We would like you to come and speak at this Monday morning rally in the heart of Calcutta. Please let us know.'

"I really did not want to go because just a few weeks earlier there had been a great upheaval between the Hindus and Moslems in Calcutta and many thousands of people had been killed. However, Rachel and I decided that I should go, even though I dreaded it."

Hube was invited to speak at a youth convention in the surging, teeming, restless area of downtown Calcutta. He found Calcutta to be a city of great contrasts; in one section were the beautiful palace grounds and the famous royal university where William Carey had taught in the language department. In this section, the British had built magnificent parks, private clubs and cricket grounds.

However, the crowded, dirty, volatile central section ranked among the most filthy, chaotic and heart-rending big city areas of the world. In 1947 all of India was in the throes of violence and anger as she struggled to overthrow 150 years of British colonial rule.

Great contrasts were evident not only economically but religiously. India is the birthplace of some of the world's great religions: Hindu, Buddhist, Shintoist and Taoist roots all originated there. In addition, British-ruled India hosted millions of Islamic adherents who violently hated the Hindus. Calcutta was located in Hindu territory close to the Islamic homelands.

The first convert came to Christ in Calcutta in 1800, led to the Lord by "the father of modern missions," William Carey. Although the percentage of Christians was rather small, the influence of

Christianity during the 150 years of British rule was great in education, medicine, commerce and industry. Christianity also had its landmarks in church buildings.

"Not only was the Saturday Night Jubilee born in prayer, but Youth for Christ in India also grew out of prayer," reported Hube Mitchell. The William Carey Memorial Baptist Church was pastored by the Reverend Walter Corlett and the Anglican Mission Church by Cyril Thompson. Hube met with these leaders and some of their youth in prayer, but they had little idea what was in store.

So on Easter Monday 1946, Calcutta Youth for Christ held its first youth rally in a movie theater rented for the occasion in the downtown area. Some local leaders felt apprehensive about whether this kind of meeting would go well in such a volatile city, which was controlled by radical elements of Communism on one hand and the entrenched Hindu idol worshippers on the other hand. Less than one percent of the people identified themselves as Christian.

But when Hube arrived at the theater, so many people crowded around the entrance that he had trouble getting inside. As he studied the audience, he prayed for wisdom on how best to communicate to these young people of India. He began by quoting from his favorite book, the Gospel of John; he had committed this entire book to memory.

Can just quoting the Bible in the Authorized Version's Elizabethan English (KJV) communicate to young people in a country like India with its tragic poverty and emotional needs? Hube quoted the old, old story in its biblical form with heart and emotion. He began with the trial of Jesus, the Son of God, then recited the details of His death on the cross for our sins, and concluded with His glorious resurrection (John 18:12–20:31).

Most of the people there did not realize that he was quoting Scripture. They simply heard a story that penetrated their hearts, the story of the wonderful love of a man willing and able to die for the sins of others. Then Hube explained from other verses how to be saved and extended an invitation to the audience for individuals to come forward to receive the Lord Jesus Christ as one's personal Savior.

Many Indian young people filed down the aisles to receive the Lord Jesus. One of them was Winnie Bonner, an Eurasian. She had heard little of the Gospel before, but the message that night touched her heart. She grew rapidly in the faith, and eventually became one of the first staff workers for India Youth for Christ.

Hube contacted Christian leaders in other cities who had a burden for reaching their youth through public evangelistic rallies. On Wednesday, May 14, 1947, a Youth for Christ rally in Bombay featured David Morken as the speaker.

After his ministry in Bombay, David visited other cities of India, then joined Hube in Calcutta once again. David recalls, "We arrived in the 'city of riots' at 11:30 at night, utterly weary from many days and nights of speaking. Unable to get in touch with Cyril Thompson, YFC director and pastor of the oldest church in Calcutta, we boarded an airline bus to the main hotel in the city. Heavy steel mesh completely encased it as a shield against missiles thrown by the rioters.

"In the hotel lobby I slumped into a comfortable chair and half dozed when I heard someone shout, 'Hallelujah! Hallelujah!' It was Cyril Thompson. Short, sandy-haired, energetic, he had been a major in the British army and was now an enthusiastic preacher of the Gospel.

"'You must come to my church right away,' he declared.

"'Please, Cyril, not tonight,' I begged. 'Tomorrow.'

"'No, you must come now,' he said. 'We're having an all-night of prayer.'

"I shall never forget that scene. Young people of college age from various evangelical groups in the city were on their knees when we entered. Their prayers wrung our hearts.

"'O God,' one prayed, 'forgive us for our coldness and lack of interest in the salvation of souls.'

"'Do a new thing in our midst, Lord Jesus,' another requested.

"One after another, these young Christians poured out their hearts to God.

"On a Sunday night after that, I preached in the old mission church. I asked the pastor whether I would be at liberty to give an invitation, and he said, 'Yes, of course, although that practice has never been followed here.' That is not to say he was not a zealous shepherd of the flock, but only that his methods had been different from ours.

"At the close of the service, when the call was given, a dozen persons came forward to receive Christ, and we praised God for this evidence of the answer to the young people's all night of prayer. The following Sunday, however, something spectacular took place. The pastor himself preached, and for the first time in his experience, he invited his hearers to come forward as an indication of their desire to receive the Lord Jesus Christ. He thought perhaps another dozen would respond, but on this occasion many dozens came forward!"

## What About This "American" Approach?

Youth For Christ brought a new philosophy of evangelism into the traditional mission fields of Asia. Giving a public invitation to come forward to receive Christ is a rather common practice today, but it was not the strategy then used by British and European missionaries. For instance, in Hudson Taylor's 11 missionary journeys out from Shanghai at the beginning of his ministry there is no record of his making any public appeal for people to come forward. Rather, he invited people to come privately for counseling after the meeting closed; in that private session some would be led to Christ.

The prevalent idea of evangelism among most missionaries of that time was an educational process of teaching and a trial for up to six months before accepting anyone's conversion experience as genuine enough to receive that person into the church through baptism.

So the new "American" approach of "instant conversion" caused quite a stir in traditional church circles, both at home and abroad. Some heartily supported the idea; others were quite skeptical—even to the present day.

Of course, it was not really a new "American" approach. In fact God had previously used English evangelists like Wesley and Whitefield to call people to repentance and public confession of Jesus as one's personal Savior even before the birth of the United States of America. But more fundamentally, the apostle Paul had "instant" conversions nearly every time he preached the Gospel in all his missionary journeys. "And some believed the things which were spoken, and some believed not" (Acts 28:24).

So the public invitation is certainly not an "American" approach, but an old divine idea (see Acts 2) that had been lost in history. A careful study of the Scriptures will show that 120 Christian men and women had gathered together in Jerusalem to pray and to wait for the Holy Spirit. When that Day of Pentecost came, ten days later, and Peter preached his great Pentecost sermon, 3,000 people responded to his call to repent immediately and call on the Lord for salvation. The twelve disciples and 120 Christians began to encourage the new converts. The sudden increase from 120 to more than 3,000 was phenomenal.

Thus the impact of Youth for Christ's early meetings in India was very significant—just at the time of the overthrow of British rule and the radical changes occurring within the whole society of India.

# Chapter 10

## THOUSANDS OF VETERANS RETURN AS MISSIONARIES

Following the end of World War II America launched a great new missionary movement. Thousands of ex-servicemen, many of whom had come to Christ during the war, enrolled in various Bible schools and seminaries, preparing to go to the mission fields of the world, particularly Asia. Mission training schools, such as the Bible Institute of Los Angeles (BIOLA), Moody Bible Institute in Chicago (MBI), Wheaton College and Columbia Bible College were among some of the major mission-education centers. Many of the ex-servicemen enrolled in the missions departments of these schools.

After my five years of service in the Navy, extending from the Pearl Harbor attack until the end of World War II, I went to live in the home of Dawson Trotman in South Pasadena, California, for discipleship training. At that time (December 1945) the entire Navigator staff, with the exception of the Lorne Sanny family, lived in the Trotman home at 509 Monterey Road. Each work-day we rode together for 25 minutes in a three-car caravan to the Navigators office at 536 South Hope Street in downtown Los Angeles.

The Navigators office was in the Willard Hotel, adjacent to BIOLA, which also served as a dormitory for the Bible school students. "The Powerhouse" where Daws, Hube, David, Dick, Bob, and others met once a week for prayer was located on the roof of that 14-story hotel. Many ex-servicemen whose lives had been touched by The Navigators during the war were now enrolled as students in the BIOLA missions department.

During the war years Dick Hillis headed the missions program at BIOLA. However, as soon as China began to reopen in early 1946,

Dick traveled to that country as part of a survey team under the China Inland Mission (CIM). Shortly afterwards he moved with his whole family back to what the Chinese call *"Chung-Kuo,"* the central kingdom of the earth.

As a result, David took over as head of the missions department at BIOLA and also as the director of the Saturday Night Jubilee, which met at the Church of the Open Door (COD). Both BIOLA and COD were an outgrowth of the anointed ministry of the great evangelist and theologian, Louis B. Talbot.

One day I took a break from my morning work at the Navigator print shop, where I assembled Scripture memory packets and discipleship notebook materials, and slipped into the balcony of the main COD auditorium. On the floor below several hundred students listened to a lecture on missions by David Morken.

The singing, the prayer, the atmosphere of intense feeling about the enormity of the task of world missions stirred my heart, as David spoke with great emotion. What a privilege it would be, I thought, if I could be a part of the great missionary endeavor that is taking place. David closed his message with a poem from a missionary hymn called "Stir Me," and my own soul responded as I listened to the words:

> *"Stir me, O stir me, Lord, I care not how,*
> > *But stir my heart in passion for the world.*
> *Stir me to give, to go, but mostly to pray,*
> > *Stir till the blood-red banner be unfurled*
> *O'er lands that still in heathen darkness lie*
> > *Lands where the cross was never lifted high.*

> *"Stir me, O stir me, Lord, till all my heart*
> > *Is filled with strong compassion for these souls,*
> *Till Thy compelling 'must' drives me to prayer,*
> > *Till Thy constraining love reach to the poles,*
> *Far North and South, in burning deep desire,*
> > *Till East and West are caught in love's great fire.*

> *"Stir me, O stir me, Lord, Thy heart was stirred*
> > *By love's intensest fire, till Thou didst give*
> *Thine only Son, Thy best-beloved One,*

*E'en to the dreadful cross that I might live.*
*Stir me to give myself so back to Thee*
*That Thou canst give Thyself again through me.*

*"Stir me, O stir me, Lord, for I can see*
*Thy glorious triumph day begin to break;*
*The dawn already gilds the eastern sky*
*O Church of Christ, arise! Awake, awake!*
*Oh stir us, Lord, as heralds of that day,*
*For night is past, our King is on His way!"*

David, like Dick, could not continue to teach missions without himself responding to the call to return to the field. After Dick reached Shanghai with his family, he sent invitations representing the CIM and the missionary community to the leaders of Youth for Christ to come over to China and help reap a ripened harvest. Billy Graham and Torrey Johnson had accepted urgent invitations to go and preach the Gospel in Europe. China was still pending. Swamped with many speaking and teaching obligations in the United States, David felt inadequate for an assignment to such a great country as China, yet in his heart he desired to answer this "Macedonian call" from Dick and his colleagues: "Come over into China and help us" (see Acts 16:9).

Still David was not yet convinced that he was the one God wanted to call to China. He later wrote, "But one night after the Saturday Night Jubilee a businessman by the name of Lionell Mayell came up to me, and handed me an envelope. I barely knew him. He and his family had come to Los Angeles and had committed their lives to the Lord in one of the rallies. I stuck the envelope in my pocket and forgot all about it. We drove to our house in Atwood, near Placentia, and finally got into bed after a long hard day. Then I remembered the envelope, so I got up and opened it. Inside I found a check and a brief note, 'For your ministry in China.' Later Lionel told me that he had gone to the bank in order to borrow some money for his business as a developer; he was building large apartment buildings and houses in the Los Angeles area. At the rally that evening he believed that God placed it on his heart to give one-half of the money for my ministry in China.

"That was the turning point for me, for I realized that God did want me to go—not Billy, not Torrey, but I should be the one to go to China. The leadership at YFC headquarters immediately agreed, for they had been asking me to go there for a long time."[1]

So David responded to the urgent pleas of Dick in China as well as to Hube's invitation in India to preach the Gospel to the teeming youth of Asia. Yet he was led to go to the Orient by the long way, via the European route. In the spring of 1947 David went first to Europe with a team of budding young evangelists including Torrey Johnson, Bob Cook (who later became president of YFC) and Billy Graham.

At this time no one was well known outside his own area of ministry. However, in spite of being received somewhat critically by a suspicious European clergy and a fault-finding media, this Youth for Christ team of young American evangelists was used by God in a mighty way.

These enthusiastic Americans who wore bright-colored neckties and proclaimed a message of hope and salvation attracted many European young people who had passed through a devastating six-year war. The American evangelists divided into two teams and traveled first to Copenhagen, Brussels, Paris, Stockholm, Warsaw, then into Switzerland and Italy. When David reached Rome on May 8, 1947, he said goodbye to his companions and intended to set out to preach at youth meetings which had been arranged by Hube in India and by Dick in China.

But when he inquired at the KLM Royal Dutch Airlines about his flight from Rome to Bombay and then on to Hong Kong he heard distressing news. "Everything is fully booked for weeks. Don't you know that thousands of Dutch people are returning to Indonesia, and every flight is already packed full?"

"But God is leading me to speak at meetings in Bombay this week and I must catch the next flight," David pleaded.

After some lively discussion, the manager of the KLM office suggested that David might just go out to the airport and try his luck. When David reached the airport, the manager there introduced him to the pilot who had come into the airport.

When he heard David's name, the pilot looked at him quizzically. "Morken? Are you one of the two American evangelists who had an interview with our Queen Wilhelmina? It was in all our newspapers last week."

"Yes, I am!" David replied.

"Don't worry. Of course we will make room for you."

And so with thanksgiving and rejoicing, David boarded the plane for Bombay. At a stopover in Iraq all the passengers disembarked and were escorted into a customs area where passports were checked. To his dismay David realized that all the others had obtained visas for India before leaving Rome, but he did not have one. The officials treated him rudely and insisted he must travel to the capital city of Baghdad to obtain a visa and catch some other flight for he could not continue on this one.

David prayed in his heart and tried to explain his situation, but his pleas continued to fall on deaf ears. He heard the call to reboard the aircraft and watched with bewilderment as the others boarded the plane, leaving him behind. *Why, Lord?* he pondered in his heart. *I am sure You want me to be in Bombay for these meetings.*

While the engines revved up, another official approached David and said, "If you can stop the plane you are free to go."

David looked out and saw the plane already taxiing out on the runway. So he grabbed his bag and ran out onto the runway, waving his arm wildly. The pilot recognized the American missionary, stopped the plane, and opened the door for David to join them. As he entered the cabin, the other passengers cheered loudly.

"How much did you bribe the officials?" someone asked.

"I didn't give anything. It was just an answer to prayer!" David informed them.

It had never entered his mind to bribe them. The passengers and crew all laughed and talked and had a wonderful time as the flight continued.

When David arrived in Bombay, Hube failed to meet him

because he did not know on which plane he would arrive. So David checked in at a hotel in Bombay and after a brief meal strolled out on the famous Victoria Promenade overlooking the bay. In front of the imposing Taj Mahal Hotel he stopped briefly before a monument to Queen Victoria commemorating her royal visit to Bombay at the height of the British influence at the end of the 19th century. He proceeded along the broad Promenade walkway that followed the outline of the bay in the shape of a crescent extending for several miles.

In the late afternoon and early evening hours thousands of people strolled along the Promenade or sat on the benches overlooking the water to chat with relatives and friends. David wandered about trying to collect his thoughts and decide what to do next.

In the midst of thousands of people he suddenly heard someone shouting his name. It was Hube! They met on that Promenade, David was sure, only by divine appointment. Hube took him to Taylor Memorial Methodist Church. At the church, they had a wonderful time, weeping over God's marvelous leading and praying for the Lord to do a work among the youth of India.

David reported in retrospect, "These local people with whom we prayed that night had already started a ministry similar to Youth for Christ." David traveled with Hube across India from Bombay to Calcutta speaking at many missionary gatherings and youth meetings.

After Calcutta, David traveled on to meetings in Hong Kong and China, speaking in many places all along the way to eager and responsive people. He arrived in Shanghai in time for the opening of an eight-day YFC youth evangelistic mission, widely advertised on billboards and in theaters. The site was the building and grounds of the Moore Memorial Church located strategically near Nanking Road across from the racecourse in the heart of the largest city of the world in that day. David preached the first couple of nights to packed audiences and God gave a wonderful response. He felt elated, yet physically exhausted.

Yet help was on the way. The Youth for Christ leaders at the great Hollywood Bowl rally commissioned Bob Pierce to go to China. Bob's adventures have already been related in the chapter entitled "To China Without Funds". They will meet together in God's perfect timing in Shanghai.

Meanwhile Daws and Lila Trotman, who lived in their "509" Navigator estate home on Monterey Road in South Pasadena, made their house available to the YFC leadership. At that time I was one of six men and twelve women who were in training in the Trotman home. Sometimes the YFC leaders would visit the "Nav" home and we would hear fascinating reports of how God was working in reaching youth all over America and even in foreign countries. As the YFC leaders mobilized the youth of the Los Angeles churches in preparation for the Hollywood Bowl rally, there was an atmosphere of excitement— things were happening.

As part of my "Nav" training, I became Daws's companion and errand boy and accompanied him to many of the committee meetings. Who should be the Bowl speaker? Many prominent names were suggested. At that time I tagged along to a meeting where Daws put forward his suggestion for Billy Graham to come as the speaker. "He is young. He is not well-known, but he will preach a clear message and will not get sidetracked. God's hand is on him." Daws's suggestion prevailed.

On the night of the Hollywood Bowl rally the entire Navigator staff climbed into several cars to attend this historic event.

The crowd, the music, and the program thrilled me. Bob Pierce led this meeting, Daws took the offering by quoting Scripture on giving, Billy preached, and hundreds responded to the invitation. But there was no personalized counseling as yet. This greatly concerned Daws. He would later develop the counseling system that is still used today by the Billy Graham crusades. Under Daws's guidance, I would develop a similar system that was used by the YFC evangelists in Asia.

That night the Hollywood Bowl rally overflowed in attendance with much response to the Gospel and a strong missionary emphasis. From there, Bob Pierce went with a Bible as a gift of love from the YFC young people at Los Angeles to President Chiang Kai-shek in China.

# Chapter 11

## "BEFORE THE LIGHTS GO OUT"

"David, you are very sick with amoebic dysentery. There is no way you can preach again this evening. I am putting you into the hospital immediately. Someone else must preach tonight."

So on July 9, 1947, Dr. Paul E. Adolph, the senior medical doctor of the China Inland Mission, ordered David to halt his exhausting preaching schedule in the middle of a week of huge YFC Shanghai evangelistic meetings. Nightly, unprecedented crowds packed into the auditorium and overflowed onto a tennis court on the grounds of the historic Moore Memorial Methodist Church located in the heart of the city. The conservative British missionary community has joined hands with these innovative American YFC evangelists to make an all-out effort to reach the teeming young people of Shanghai before the light of the Gospel would be replaced by the impending darkness of Communism.

This is the largest "mission" ever undertaken in Shanghai. The word "mission" is the usual British term for a series of public evangelistic meetings. This project is solidly backed by the "G.D.," which is the nickname (spoken only in his absence) for Bishop Frank Houghton, the well-loved General Director of "The Mission"—which, of course, is the China Inland Mission (CIM). At this time The Mission has more than 1,000 missionaries in China. The CIM international headquarters is not based in England but rather in Shanghai, where God has provided a choice block of land in the heart of the residential area of the International Settlement section of the city. The gate at number 53 Sinza Road opens into a large complex of buildings and grounds that include mission offices, a hospital, a residence for about 170 missionaries, plus maintenance facilities and tennis and volleyball courts. The compound is like a miniature walled city, typical of many that have been built by French, English, German and Russian residents throughout the city.

Dick, who is on the CIM leadership council as well as China director of the fledgling YFC work, is using his talents for coaching and launching evangelistic teams with great effectiveness. Dick, with his widespread Chinese and missionary contacts, plus his respectability in the field of public preaching, has arranged for the American YFC evangelists to preach in major cities throughout China. This "Shanghai Mission" is the kick-off for a four-month blitz of public evangelism on a scale never before attempted by missionaries on a foreign field.

When Dick received the assignment to head up the YFC work in China, while still continuing his leadership role in the CIM, he immediately recruited the top Chinese evangelist, Andrew Gih, to work alongside him as the co-director for China. Dick knew that the missionary and the national working side by side with equal status and opportunity was the only way to get the job done effectively. He was ahead of his time in the understanding of the philosophy and strategy of missions. Without his knowledge of how to blend together the three cultures—Chinese, British, American—the whole undertaking would never have gotten off the launching pad.

Andrew Gih was a member of the original Bethel Band, a team of Chinese Christian workers committed to the ministry of itinerant evangelism. Other famous Chinese evangelists of that era were Calvin Chao, who worked with students both in China and in America; Leland Wang, known for the promise he made to God—"No Bible! No breakfast!"; Elder Hsu, who had been rescued from opium-smoking and spent the rest of his life working with the CIM among opium addicts in North China; Watchman Nee, author of many popular books on the Christian life and founder of "The Little Flock" movement; Wang Ming Dao, who ministered to university students in Peking (Beijing today) and labored with Dr. David Adeney in CIM's Chinese student work; Timothy Dzao, an evangelist who traveled throughout South Asia and founded the Ling Liang Tang ("Spiritual Food") movement.

The most famous evangelist of the Bethel Band was the great John Sung, a fiery preacher, whom God used in the 1930s and early 1940s to bring revival to the areas of Amoy and South China. Then he traveled extensively to preach among Chinese living in Vietnam and Indonesia which resulted in a great awakening and the founding of many new churches which still trace their roots today to the labors of John Sung. He has been compared to John the Baptist, particularly in his style of publicly denouncing a particular sin by name, then demanding that those who had committed this particular sin— adultery or stealing or whatever—to stand and confess it before God. He was loved by his friends and feared by his foes.

The son of a Methodist clergyman, John Sung traveled to the United States for his education, graduated with top honors, and tried to embrace the atheism of the academic world. But God reached down into his heart with a radical conversion. He became so obsessed with reading his Bible that he was placed in a mental institution for a time. When he was eventually released from that hospital and graduated from his university with the highest academic achievements, he set out to return to China. On the ship across the Pacific, he tore up his diplomas and letters of praise and threw them into the sea, determining to know nothing but Jesus Christ and Him crucified (see Galatians 2:20).

Within the Chinese culture there has always been a love for listening to stories, and professional storytellers, musicians and enchanters have entertained Chinese audiences for centuries. Many of these entertainers would also sell medicines to the appreciative audiences as a means of payment for their services. Piggybacking on this rich Chinese heritage the Bethel Band told their stories from the Bible as a means of proclaiming the Gospel in public places. This gave them ready-made audiences nearly everywhere they went.

But by the summer of 1947 John Sung had gone to be with the Lord and Dick asked Andrew Gih both to preach in his own meetings and also to interpret for the YFC evangelists. Andrew, who literally lived in the Bible, could quote more Scriptures by memory (in Chinese, of course) than any man I ever met, with the possible exception of Dawson Trotman. Sometimes an American evangelist in his excited exuberance might get the details of a Gospel story somewhat twisted—"two loaves and five fishes"—but never mind, Andrew would interpret it correctly—"five loaves and two fishes"—in Chinese.

Enroute to preach at the Shanghai crusade, David had arrived in Canton (Guangzhou), China on June 23, 1947. He launched immediately into a heavy schedule of preaching several times a day, in schools, or buildings or wherever opportunity afforded. An American military chaplain stationed in Canton decorated his large Army truck with huge banners and arranged to have a Chinese band march behind and beat on drums and cymbals in order to create a noisy clamor to advertise the meeting. The Chinese love noise and commotion, so they attracted large crowds. The main meetings were held at the YMCA, but the evangelistic team went to schools, churches, and even boarded a junk (a Chinese boat) to preach among the boat people (who may live a whole lifetime aboard the family junk).

Joined by Andrew interpreting into Mandarin and Daniel Cheong interpreting into Cantonese, the YFC evangelistic team traveled from Canton to Swatow, about 200 miles up the coast where a great number of people had registered their decisions for Christ.

In that city they spoke to more than a thousand high school students. At the invitation, more students wanted to enter the inquiry room than could be accommodated, so the evangelists dealt with one group of inquirers, then dismissed them and talked to another group. Yes, the follow-up was inadequate.

When the team traveled on to Amoy, another 120 miles farther north along the coast, the local pastors, due to poor communications, had not heard of their arrival. The team met a great deal of suspicion. Then suddenly one pastor recognized David as the missionary friend he had known when he served in a Chinese church in Sumatra, Indonesia. The two friends embraced and began talking excitedly to one another in the Indonesian language. After this incident, the other pastors gladly welcomed David and his team for special meetings in their area, with God providing great results.

These meetings where David ministered in South China, enroute from Canton to Shanghai, met with a response far beyond what anyone had ever experienced or anticipated. The YFC teams recorded more than 10,000 professions of faith in South China.

After these fruitful meetings in South China, the team took a plane from Amoy to Shanghai for the opening of the Shanghai Mission. Not only did nearly all Christian groups cooperate, but the mayor of Shanghai, K. C. Wu, with his dedicated Christian wife added their support. The meetings began on July 5th with many responding to the Gospel. David, with Andrew as interpreter, preached for four days to overflow crowds. Then David, drained physically and emotionally, became very sick. But, praise God, that very day Bob Pierce arrived and took over the preaching responsibilities.

So the largest crusade in Shanghai history continued without a hitch. David preached the first four nights, Bob finished off the week, and God gave the increase as some 1,200 people made public decisions for Christ. After the tremendous success of the Shanghai Mission, David emerged from the hospital, weak but eager to preach again.

So Bob, David and Andrew sat down with Dick Hillis to talk, to pray, and to plan what to do with the wonderful opportunities for large public evangelistic meetings that were opening up in major cities all over China. Dick had the strong conviction that God had brought them into the middle of an unprecedented harvest. The Communists were already invading the north and all of China would soon fall to this godless enemy. Many people desperately seeking God as never before thronged into their meetings. For the time Christian churches and factions were laying aside their petty grievances against one another and were united in their desire to proclaim the Gospel. They prayed and exhorted one another, saying, "Surely this is a God-arranged time of bountiful harvest. Let us make every effort now to buy up the opportunity to reap the harvest while it is still day, for the night comes when no man can work" (John 9:4).

So with joyful and expectant hearts the evangelistic team launched into four months of great harvest and blessing. These are some of the highlights of those four exhausting but wonderful months.


## Soochow

From Shanghai the team traveled up the Whang-po River to

Soochow (Suzhou), 50 miles to the northwest, a main base of the Southern Baptist missionaries. Some of the most gifted and dedicated Baptist missionaries, like Bertha Smith, had labored here faithfully for many years. Bertha, who spoke beautiful colloquial Chinese, would go into nearby farming villages to teach the Bible to women and children. On one occasion at the end of a hard day of travel and teaching she went to sleep on a bed that was the home of many bed bugs. When she discovered their presence, she prayed, "O Lord, I'm so tired. I have no other place to sleep. Please have the bed bugs stop biting me!" Later Bertha testified that the Lord answered her prayer immediately, for none of those bed bugs bit her that night.

No place large enough was found in that city to accommodate the enthusiastic crowds which came to the meetings. The team preached for five nights with many recorded decisions to receive Christ.

## Hangchow

The beautiful city of Hangchow (now Hangzhou), about 80 miles south of Soochow, served as gateway to the imperial canal system built by the Chinese emperors in previous centuries. Again there was inadequate space to handle the crowds. Some 1,500 people a night crowded into the hall, with about 200 recorded decisions each night.

## Nanking

Nanking (at this time the southern capital of China and main base for the Nationalist army fighting against the Communists), which was located about 140 road miles and 220 water miles northwest of Hangchow, warmly received the team. Premier T.V. Soong, whose mother-in-law was a Bible woman of great fire and dedication warmly received the team. Premier Chung, second in command to Generalissimo Chiang Kai Shek in Nationalist China, personally attended and supported the meetings. Again the team preached the Gospel to large and enthusiastic crowds with 471 recorded decisions for Christ.

## Sian

The largest evangelistic meetings in the history of China were held in the Episcopal Church courtyard in the center of the city of Sian (Xian today). This ancient Chinese capital was located about 600 miles to the west-northwest of the former capital at Nanking. Here Marco Polo visited the Chinese emperor to find that Christianity had already penetrated China with the Nestorians in the eighth century, and some vestiges of it still remained at his coming. Marco Polo then promised to send some missionary priests to China, but they were long in coming because of ongoing political intrigues at the Vatican.

Now the Gospel was being preached to the whole city by the visiting YFC team. The American military helped out by procuring a generator, so lights and sound could be provided. People packed the vast church grounds. How many attended that first night? One observer estimated about 25,000. No, argued another Chinese friend, "*San wan to*" ["more than 30,000"].

The crowd was brought together at a bargain price, as one missionary joked. "We gathered all these people for only 75 cents—the price of the gasoline to run the generator."

On the last evening of these great meetings, the big generator suddenly stopped. The whole area plunged into darkness. No lights! No sound! What could be done? Andrew Gih grabbed a battery-operated microphone and began to plead with the people in Chinese. "Do not go away. Come down here to the front and pray with us and invite Jesus to come into your heart . . . Believe in the Lord Jesus Christ . . . He will forgive your sins and give you everlasting life." As Andrew Gih continued to plead in the darkness, 340 people came forward to pray and to register their decisions for Christ, with the help of kerosene lamps and bullhorns.

But later that evening one of the missionaries remarked in a sober tone, "Tonight the lights went out." He continued, "This is symbolic of China's condition. Soon the Communists will come and the lights will go out all over China. Let us pray that God will bring many more to Himself before the darkness comes."

## Hsien Leng

This city lay not far from the battle zone. The Nationalist Chinese military feared there might be some disturbances because of the communist sympathizers and spies in the area. So after much discussion the military allowed the meetings, but posted soldiers with drawn bayonets to keep control over the crowds. This was a new experience for the Americans—a bit unnerving to preach under these conditions. Nevertheless, the crowd numbered about 15,000, and responded well.

## Tientsin

Tientsin (Tianjin today), a major northern city and the second largest in China, was situated 70 miles southeast of Peking [Beijing], and divided into foreign concessions (like in Shanghai), with many foreigners living there. The team placed a 15-foot cross with a sign advertising Youth for Christ written both in Chinese and English in front of the Methodist Church. Government radio broadcast the meetings on each of the four nights. Some 900 people made decisions to receive Christ the Lord into their hearts.

## Tsingtao

For two decades before the war it had been the favorite summer resort area for the trade, business, and diplomatic foreigners in China, probably the most European city architecturally in the Far East. It is located on the southeast edge of the Shantung peninsula some 350 sea miles north of Shanghai.

David had gone back to America and Bob continued on alone as the evangelist for a few more weeks. From Peking Bob bravely traveled on a railroad line that had been attacked by the Communists three days earlier. Central Shantung had been a haven for communist guerrillas fighting the Japanese during the war.

The Tsingtao area, a Christian stronghold where Lutherans had labored effectively for many years, having been a German colony prior to World War I, lay close to the fighting. It greatly saddened Bob to hear that when the Communists had taken over some of the northern areas a few weeks earlier, they killed many civilians there simply because they were Christians.

He preached to large crowds in the Lutheran Church and on the church grounds. But something happened in Bob's heart during those critical days, and by his own later testimony after this China trip his life would never be the same. Seeing the ravages of war around him, hearing the stories of contemporary Christian martyrs being slaughtered for their faith, and knowing of the many widows and orphans being left behind, Bob's heart overflowed with great compassion, and this would bring about the formation of World Vision and later The Samaritan's Purse.

## Tsimi

Bob received an invitation to go to a Lutheran school in Tsimi, a small town about 30 miles north of Tsingtao, located in no man's land, an area disputed by both Nationalist and Communist forces. While Bob preached to the 700 students still there, they could hear the sound of artillery booming in the distance. In this extremely emotional meeting, some 400 students, the highest percentage of response in all of their meetings in China, made a commitment to follow Jesus regardless of any coming consequences.

## Summary: Four Months of Harvest

The team visited other cities, such as Chungking in the west, some 900 miles southwest of Shanghai, and then they visited Canton again in the south. During this four-month-plus, all-out public evangelistic preaching tour, Bob and David preached to multitudes of people, many of whose hearts had been divinely prepared to receive the Lord as their personal Savior.

With great emotion Bob Pierce reported to the Youth for Christ leaders in America: "If I had the choice of laboring in any generation since Christ walked on earth, I would rather stand as a harvester in the midst of the present field of China than to have been Martin Luther,

Charles G. Finney, Dwight L. Moody or Billy Sunday in their fields at their ripest. In eighteen weeks of ministry, God gave us more than seventeen thousand recorded decisions!" How many countless others the Holy Spirit may have brought to the Savior is known to God alone.

It just could be that the seed planted in fertile soil during those dark and troublesome times, prayed over by a generation of western Christians, did bear fruit up to a hundredfold through the era of the post-Mao China and beyond.

# Chapter 12

## THE NAVIGATORS HELP YFC IN FOLLOW-UP

In the Spring of 1948 David Morken pleaded with Dawson Trotman, the follow-up specialist, to come and spend some time with him at Big Bear campgrounds above San Bernardino, so they could pray together about some important decisions he had to make. David had returned home completely exhausted from the extensive preaching meetings in China, but the call of the multitudes eager to hear the Gospel beckoned him back. Should he take his whole family with him to settle down in China? And what about the follow-up?

Daws and David went into the woods to pray; arm in arm they walked through the natural beauty of the trees. First David would pray with closed eyes while Daws would act as their guide, then they would reverse roles.

After a time of prayer, David remarked, "Daws, sometimes I cannot sleep. I wake up seeing in my dreams hundreds of Chinese people coming forward to receive Christ, but they need help to grow spiritually. They need follow-up. Daws, I don't want to go back to China unless you send someone to help us in the follow-up ministry."

Daws agreed to select one of his men and send him to China to help YFC in the follow-up of the thousands who were coming to Christ. Both David and Dick Hillis offered to give money from their own pockets to help financially; each gave $100. However, Dick sent a note with his check to Daws, which had been mailed from China, "Please wait until the end of the month to be sure I have enough money to cover it." Missionaries often operated on close margins.

So one day in early September 1948 I received this phone call from Daws in California while I was at home in Dallas, Texas, where

I was directing the local Navigator ministry, as well as working for my father who owned an automobile business.

"Roy, this is Daws . . . This may surprise you, and again it may not, but I want you to leave your home immediately and go to China to help YFC in follow-up . . . [pause] "

I remember asking only one question, which went something like this: "Yes, I know about the need. Do you really think I can handle it?"

Daws replied with something to the effect that he certainly would not be calling me if he didn't have confidence that I could do the job.

"Okay, then I'll go!"

"Leave as soon as you can. Try to reach Shanghai before the Communists do!"

As I remember, the whole conversation took less than five minutes. Money was never mentioned, nor the length of the time commitment. If my spiritual leader wanted me to go to China, I was ready to go.

Actually, whether Daws knew it or not, and perhaps he did, God had already prepared my heart to go to China.

While I was a Naval flight instructor in 1943 in Corpus Christi, Texas, three of us led a Bible class of about 125 men who were active in memorizing and studying the Word of God. Lieutenant Jim Farley and I, both flight instructors, taught the cadets at Cavanas Field the final steps of gunnery and formation attack maneuvers before their graduation.

Jim, who had more previous contact with The Navigators than I, started me on The Navigators "Topical Memory System" and the discipleship notebook. Kenneth Dial, a postman, had acquired the habit of reviewing Bible verses while walking from door to door delivering mail; by the time I met him, he knew a couple of thousand verses of Scripture. We were the leaders of the Bible study on the base.

We three decided to invite Daws to Corpus Christi for several days to speak to the men who attended the Bible classes. I was able to get leave for three days, and the group selected me to serve as host and to chauffeur Daws to all the functions. I picked him up at the train station and stayed with him constantly during those three days, driving him to all the meetings, arranging for all his meals, and booked myself in the same hotel. Daws was different from anyone else I had ever met. The Lord knit my heart to this man; he impressed me as a prophet of God. I talked with him for many hours as he explained biblical principles that were new and exciting. At the end of our time together Daws invited me to throw in my lot with the 'Navs' after the war.

Immediately after being released from the service in late 1945, I went to live in Daws' home in South Pasadena, California, to be trained by him for ministry. At the same time I continued flying fighter planes in the Naval Reserve. I also became a charter member of a new agency called the Missionary Aviation Fellowship (MAF). After a couple of years, the MAF invited me to join them to become a missionary pilot in Mexico and Peru.

To my surprise Daws opposed the idea. "I do not think that is God's will for you," he stated flatly.

I loved Daws, but I also loved flying. I felt a bit miffed and confused, and perhaps even a bit angry. *"Who is this guy who knows what God's will is for everybody?"* spoke my rebellious heart.

A few days later I went to the Christian Servicemen's Center in Long Beach. Daws had assigned me to live there on weekends from Friday to Sunday to handle the ministry of follow-up on the many men who were coming to Christ each week. I had succeeded Arthur Glasser, who was now on his way to China to work with the CIM among the Lisu tribal people.

A committee of Christian businessmen administered the Center and persuaded Daws to undertake the responsibility to provide adequate follow-up. Just a few blocks away at the Long Beach City Auditorium, the well-known radio evangelist, Dr. Charles E. Fuller, held his worldwide weekly live broadcasts called "The Old Fashioned

Revival Hour." On Sunday afternoons before a packed house, many servicemen, along with other convicted listeners, would walk down the aisles to receive the Lord Jesus Christ as their personal Savior.

My job was to handle counseling for the servicemen who made decisions. Then we would escort them to the servicemen's Center and encourage them to give a public testimony that very evening, as well as begin to memorize Scripture and do a Bible study once a week. Daws insisted on thorough follow-up.

But it was not all work, for there was a social life as well. Young ladies from the local churches would come to the Center to provide coffee and doughnuts, as well as a pleasing atmosphere. I was not beyond trying to impress the girls, and on one occasion an incident occurred that was to change the course of my life. This happened a few days after Daws had told me he did not like the idea of my accepting an assignment to become a missionary pilot.

On that particular Saturday when things were slow at the Center I said to Wes Jensen, a 220-pound high school football player whom I was discipling, "Wes, let's you and I go for a swim around Rainbow Pier."

After the long swim of about a mile, we returned to the Center to find a group of young people, including some girls. We boasted a bit about our swimming exploits, then began to do various stunts to impress our audience. In one stunt I stood on Wes's shoulders.

"Look, no hands!" I shouted as I let go of Wes's shoulders and stood straight up waving my hands in the air. Now I had done this trick often with my close friend Cecil Davidson, who also lived at the Navigator home in South Pasadena, and we had the signals and timing of the descent down pat. Not so with Wes, however.

I signaled to Wes that I was going to jump off and land squarely on the floor, but Wes missed my signal. As I started the jump, he thought I had lost my balance and grabbed hold of my ankles. Then as I reached for the ceiling chandelier, he let go of my ankles. I did a flip in the air and landed with the full force of my body on my right elbow on the hardwood floor. I saw all kinds of stars as I felt the pain, and my elbow was severely damaged—it was a compound fracture and my bones were crushed—requiring surgery and rehabilitation that lasted for more than a year.

This ended my flying career. I never piloted a plane again. I had scheduled a flight to Mexico with MAF for the following week, but had to cancel it and withdraw my application to that mission. I did learn some valuable, long-lasting lessons, however, albeit the hard way. As mentioned earlier, Daws had urged me not to go into missionary aviation, for he had perceived that God had more for me than a flying career. But I had resisted, even though I knew in my heart that he was right. The most valuable of these lessons that has guided me throughout my life was to learn to respect the advice of my spiritual leaders—Daws then and others since.

The Navigators sent me to the regional Veterans Hospital where I could get free medical care. At that time single staff workers were paid only $2.50 a week, plus room and board. Millie Hopkins, one of the staff women in the home, sent me both volumes of the life of J. Hudson Taylor,[1] nearly 1,000 pages of reading. In the three weeks I spent in the hospital I devoured these books, living with Taylor and his mission and their adventures by faith in China. This man, his incredible faith and vision, and his fascinating ministry in that vast Asian country greatly challenged my heart.

At the end of the three weeks and my hospitalization, I prayed, "Lord, You may not want me to go to China, but if You do want to send me to China or to any other mission field, I am willing to go."

## The Call

Daws called me one year later: "Roy, . . . I want you to go to China!"

That evening after the call my mother came home from her activities. A real southern lady, she collected antiques, belonged to the garden club and to the country club, and was involved in the social circles of Dallas. She later became active in church, but did not attend much at this time.

I said to her, "Sit down, Mom, I have something to tell you." As she sat down gingerly I blurted out, "Your son is going to China!"

"Son!" she screamed and jumped straight up in the air. But she already knew that my heart was set on serving God, so she gave me her assurance of support and blessing.

My father came home a little later. It would be harder to tell my dad about this because I was working for him in his automobile agency, as well as taking business courses at Southern Methodist University while leading the Navigator ministries in the State of Texas. I was his only son and Dad wanted me to take over the agency which he owned.

"Dad, I have something to tell you," I began, trying to make it sound important and reasonable. So I continued [. . . ahem . . . cough . . .], "A worldwide Christian organization has chosen me to be their representative in China!"

Dad was not fooled. He knew I was being sent out as a missionary. "Well, Son, if you want to throw your life away in China, I will not stop you."

So with his rather grudging blessing, I dropped out of school, turned my Navigator work over to my "Timothy," Ross Jennings, and boarded a train four days later for California, where I caught the proverbial slow boat to China. (The sequel on my dad was that his business failed three years later, and in future years he would introduce me with bravado to his country club friends as a hero, a foreign expert, and a personal friend of Billy Graham.)

The day before my departure from the States Daws called me into his bedroom for a time of instruction and prayer. When I first came to live with Daws and Lila at the close of World War II, nearly all the Navigator staff lived together in their large home in South Pasadena. That home, commonly and lovingly called "509," was rented to The Navigators at a special rate by Dr. Fuller's The Old Fashioned Revival Hour organization. When I moved in near the end of 1945, we had six men and twelve women living at "509." (Yes, many years later after my first wife died, I married one of those girls!) Daws and Lila had five children, the youngest of whom, Chuckie, was severely mentally handicapped, living out his entire life in bed.

Seldom would any of us visit that sanctuary bedroom where Daws and Lila, with Chuckie's crib nearby, shared their inner joys and sorrows.

After chatting about my assignment to China, Daws dedicated me to the Lord in prayer, which I later learned was based on 2 Kings 6:15-17. I will never forget those holy moments in that room.

"Oh Lord," Daws prayed, "open the eyes of this young man and lay upon his heart what is on Your heart."

What is on God's heart, I pondered as Daws continued, " . . . the world!"

Of course, God so loved the world that He gave His only Son . . . as Daws went on, "O God, give to this young man a heart for the world."

Then Daws repeated to me the objective to be sure I understood, "Roy, I'm not just sending you to China, but to the world." Then he claimed for me a promise which he quoted from Isaiah 43:19. "Behold, I will do a new thing; now it shall spring forth; shall ye not know it? I will even make a way in the wilderness, and rivers in the desert."

My job description was brief, "Roy, you go out to China and do what I have taught you to do."

## Follow-Up

For one thing, Daws had drilled me in his concept of follow-up. What is follow-up? The term was ordinarily used in business and sales to mean making additional calls on a client, but Daws defined it in a biblical context: "Follow-up is the process of helping a babe in Christ grow to spiritual maturity."

Here are some additional quotes I recall from Daws's teaching, exemplified by his life and ministry:

- "Salvation is an act. Follow-up is a process . . . it takes time."

- "You can lead a person to Christ in 20 minutes to a couple of hours, but it takes six months to a couple of years to bring him or her to maturity."

- "Decision is 5%; follow-through is 95%."

- "Every believer is born to reproduce."

Daws drilled into our very being that follow-up has to do with a person, not a program. It was not just some materials to be mailed out to new believers; it was the imparting of your very life to help another Christian grow in his or her faith toward spiritual maturity (see 1 Thessalonians 2:8).

Daws taught us that pastoral follow-up is vitally important. The apostle Paul urged pastors to feed the church of God "over the which the Holy Ghost hath made you overseers" (Acts 20:28). The apostle Peter exhorted elders to "feed the flock of God which is among you" (1 Peter 5:2) and promised that "when the chief Shepherd shall appear, ye shall receive a crown of glory that fadeth not away" (1 Peter 5:4).

But parental follow-up is also vital. Paul was not merely an evangelist, a preacher, and a teacher, but he performed the role of a nursing mother (1 Thessalonians 2:7) and a sensitive and loving father who gave individual guidance, discipline and comfort to his child (1 Thessalonians 2:11).

Blessed indeed is that new believer who has someone who will act as a spiritual mother and faithful father to give personal love, care and guidance as he or she grows in the faith toward spiritual maturity and spiritual reproduction.

Daws believed that follow-up was not just the duty of the pastor and paid staff workers, but that every Christian should be enlisted, challenged and trained to do this important work in the church. This is one of the vital Christian responsibilities that has been lost since apostolic times but is being rediscovered in the 20th century.

"If you know enough to be saved, you know enough to show someone else how to be saved," announced Daws to the counselors being trained in 1954 for the Billy Graham Crusade in London. "You don't have to know a whole lot to help another person grow spiritually. If you know how to pray, then show the new believer how he or she can pray as well."

Daws was especially sold on the blessing derived from committing the Word of God to memory. If you lived at "509," you had better keep your verses sharp, for at any time you might be called on to quote Scripture. Daws would never tell us how many verses he had memorized, but I heard from others that it was somewhere around 4,000. At the time he sent me to China I had systematically committed to memory about half that number.

Daws warned us, "I have never seen anyone get others to continue successfully in a memory program who did not do it himself."

## Daws Visits China

A year before I was sent out as a Navigator missionary, Dick and David with the blessing of the international YFC leadership had arranged for Daws to come to China. To a fascinated audience of missionaries and Chinese Christian leaders in some of the major cities of China, Daws presented such biblical concepts as follow-up, Scripture memory, consistent application-centered Bible study, the personal devotional quiet time, spiritual reproduction and born to reproduce.

Daws and Andrew Gih, both of whom independently had committed hundreds of Bible verses to memory in their respective languages, bonded together immediately as kindred spirits with a purpose. They challenged many missionaries and Chinese pastors to be more disciplined in their own prayer lives and in their personal intake of the Word of God. It is easy for any foreign missionary or Christian worker to get so immersed in the cares and problems of the church, not to mention the rigors of trying to communicate the Gospel in a resistant culture, that their own habits of daily devotions and extended times of prayer begin to slip.

"And when you neglect the Word and the Prayer spokes[3] of your Christian life," Daws would warn, "you begin to lose your power in ministry."

Daws arrived in China equipped with a mechanical wheel, engineered and built by Keith Flygare, an innovative member of his staff in Los Angeles, which he used to illustrate the basics of the Christian life. Daws would begin by showing his audience the rim of a mechanical wheel with no hub or spokes. Then with the flick of a finger the Chinese character for Christ would appear in the very center of the wheel as the hub.

"If Christ does not occupy the center of your life, you can do nothing," Daws would say, then quote, "I am the vine, ye are the branches: He that abideth in me, and I in him, the same bringeth forth much fruit: for without me ye can do nothing" (John 15:5).

Then Daws would explain to the fascinated Chinese audience, "Christ communicates with us Christians, who are represented by the rim, through the Word." Suddenly the bottom spoke would pop into place bearing the Chinese characters that are pronounced *shen ti hua*, The Word. "We, in turn, communicate with God through Prayer," and the top spoke would pop into place, bearing the characters *dao gao*. "The horizontal spokes, representing our obedience and witness throughout our lives and lips, are *shun tsung* ["following in Obedience"] and *tzo chien chung* ["doing Witness"], and he popped those spokes into place as he described each concept.

Daws would conclude, "These four basics are absolutely essential to a healthy, well-balanced Christian life."

Both Daws and Andrew were particularly interested in teaching the Chinese believers to devote time and effort to memorizing the Scriptures. Sometimes, for the sake of arousing interest, they would challenge anyone in the audience to quote a fragment of a verse or a whole verse they knew from memory; then Daws or Andrew would usually quote the verse in full, word perfectly, and give the reference location.

Andrew felt that The Navigators Topical Memory System[2] would be a great asset both to provide follow-up for new believers and to equip lay leaders. And if the communists were to capture all of China and confiscate all the Bibles, as they had in some of the captured areas in the north, then the Word hidden in believers' hearts would be the difference between maintaining a victorious faith or falling into despair.

So Andrew set out to translate the 108-verse memory system, composed of three sets of 36 verses each on small cards. In addition Daws designed a special memory card folder, made of heavy paper stock, with instructions on how to assemble it by hand. This provided a convenient way always to carry the cards on one's person so they could be reviewed at odd times during the activities of any given day.

An introductory packet, the *Chu hsin chi yao* ["essentials for the first step of faith"], was given to every person who made a decision for Christ.

The American version of the introductory packet was called the "B-Rations" or "Bible Rations" because it was developed during World War II when many commodities such as butter, sugar and gasoline were rationed. So the "B Rations" (years later renamed *Beginning with Christ*) were like a bottle of spiritual milk to help the new believer survive in his or her new spiritual life. The American packet had four verses in it (later increased to five), but the Chinese version was reduced to three. The original "B Rations," the *Chu hsin chi yao*, contained three assurances given to every new believer:

- Assurance of Salvation—John 5:24 "Verily, verily, I say unto you, He that heareth my word and believeth on him that sent me hath everlasting life, and shall not come into condemnation, but is passed from death unto life."

- Assurance of Victory—1 Corinthians 10:13 "There hath no temptation taken you but such as is common to man: but God is faithful, who will not suffer you to be tempted above that ye are able, but will with the temptation also make a way of escape, that ye may be able to bear it."

- Assurance of Forgiveness—1 John 1:9 "If we confess our sins, he is faithful and just to forgive us our sins, and to cleanse us from all unrighteousness."

Daws took Andrew's Chinese translations back to America with him and had the memory cards, the explanation information, and the folders for the cards printed in Los Angeles. Then several thousand sets were sent to Shanghai to be ready when the follow-up man would arrive. Some 5,000 of the *Chu hsin chi yao* were sent over as well to be given out to those who had made commitments to Christ. About 4,000 of the next step (the Topical Memory System, Step 1, the first 36 verses) were printed, with slightly smaller quantities printed for the other two steps of 36 verses each. A diploma was offered to any Chinese Christian who could correctly quote to another person all 108 verses word-perfect at one sitting. (The first person in China who qualified for the diploma was a 69-year-old grandmother who "wanted to learn all these verses before she met Jesus face to face.")

So the Youth for Christ leaders were vitally concerned with follow-up and made elaborate preparations to strengthen this department of their ministry. It was my privilege to work under these men of God to implement that ministry beginning in China.

## The Missing Strategy

Daws not only went to China, but at Hubert Mitchell's invitation went to India as well. Daws' messages touched many hearts on this world trip, but his own heart was touched also. After he returned to the States, he wrote the following letter to his prayer partners:

"To say God has done something in my heart is putting it mildly. I realize the past 15 years God has been preparing me for this hour and I must work and fight and press toward completion of the task at hand —the spread of the Gospel in this generation and giving every soul an opportunity to hear it.

"I saw in China, in India, in Holland, in France, in Switzerland, in Belgium a thing I suspected all along, but now I have seen it and talked to the missionaries and workers: they do not have adequate follow-up or even the beginning of it; they have neither been fully conscious of the need nor taught how to go about the job, and are ready to see something done. The people they reach are not getting down to business in personal work and would have no idea what to do with any who came to Christ through their ministry.

"Suppose even a few of the ten or twenty thousand missionaries in China in the past 150 years had understood what the Scriptures teach on follow-up, propagation, and multiplication . . . each generation in the past hundred years would have heard the Gospel. No, the cry today is, 'Send more missionaries,' as though that would do the job. The thousands haven't reached the hundreds of millions in many decades—how will additional thousands remedy this situation?

"The secret of fulfilling Mark 16:15 is in the last verses of Matthew—making disciples. My heart is set on this . . . I verily believe that within five to seven years we can double the number of souls won, to say nothing of the succeeding few years . . . There are two billion people in the world [this was 1947] and a big, tough job lies ahead—not too big, however. I believe we can get the Gospel to the ends of the earth in this generation.

"It thrills my heart to remember those early morning prayer meetings when all of us fellows prayed together and asked God to touch the whole world. Though spread apart by the diameter of the earth, we are working together with one heart for this thing that is upon the heart of our wonderful Lord."[3]

ENDNOTES:
1. These two books are classics of missiology: Dr. and Mrs. Howard Taylor, *Hudson Taylor in Early Years: The Growth of a Soul*, Volume 1 of 2, and *Hudson Taylor and the China Inland Mission: The Growth of a Work of God*, Volume 2 of 2, London: Morgan & Scott, Ltd., 1920.
2. The "Topical Memory System" in the United States today is composed of 60 verses divided into five topics of six verses each. It is available in most Christian book stores or directly from The Navigators, P.O. Box 6000, Colorado Springs, CO 80934.
3. Betty Lee Skinner, *Daws, A Man Who Trusted God*, Colorado Springs, Colorado: NavPress, 1974, pages 296-97.

# Chapter 13

## BEHIND THE BAMBOO CURTAIN

David Morken was speaking to the student body in the high school auditorium located on the Pao Shan Road just outside the city limits of Shanghai. Although this was a Christian school, most of the students were not believers but had been sent there by their parents who felt the school had higher educational standards than the government schools. Christian leaders had invited David to hold a series of special morning evangelistic services because they were afraid that Shanghai would soon fall to the Communists.

It was springtime, but no one felt relaxed; a tense atmosphere prevailed. As David spoke, the sound of artillery boomed plainly in the background. From Chinese New Year until April (1949) the Nationalist army had been able to halt the communist armies north of the Yangtze River at Nanking. The Communists had offered a truce to discuss peace. But in the middle of the talks, the Communists suddenly broke their promises and their armies poured across the Yangtze River, which was the last natural barrier that protected Shanghai. Now the communist armies rolled relentlessly toward China's largest city. Everyone knew that within a week or two the Communists would take over the area, and wherever the Communists had taken over, they oppressed and sometimes killed Christians.

That morning David pleaded with the students to put their faith in the Lord Jesus Christ. Usually many would openly respond to the invitation, but this morning not even one person would raise his hand or stand to his feet. Rumors had been circulated among the students that the Communists had infiltrated the student body and Christians who would declare themselves openly were in for trouble. Still David pleaded with them, but no one dared to move.

David decided to change tactics. "All right, if no one will stand for Jesus this morning, is there anyone who will say, 'I now renounce God forever and I turn my back on His Son Jesus Christ. I do not want Him as my Savior'?"

Heavy tension filled the auditorium and the roar of cannons in the distance seemed to get louder. I nervously looked around the auditorium, for I had come with David to handle the follow-up.

Then, toward the door in the back at the right, two girls with defiant looks stood to their feet clutching tightly to each other's hands. And now on the other side two more, then a few others—eight in all stood to their feet. An icy chill seemed to sweep into the auditorium on this beautiful spring day.

Then I saw something else: the student Christian leaders began responding. As soon as the meeting closed, these young people came to the front to pray, to weep, to ask God to grant a bold witness in standing for Jesus.

The students gathered at the front of the auditorium, crying and pouring out their hearts to God—for themselves, for their unsaved friends, for the city, for China. They continued to pray through the lunch hour, then throughout the afternoon. Some would leave for a while, but others would come to keep the prayer chain going. They decided to pray all night.

When David and I and the YFC team returned for the chapel service the next day, the Christian students had continued this chain of prayer for nearly 24 hours.

This time the service changed dramatically. The students sang exuberantly lifting up sincere praises to God. When David preached, you could feel the Holy Spirit penetrating into hearts. The Christian student leaders had boldly declared their stand. This time during the invitation a flood of students came forward to declare their faith in the Lord Jesus Christ publicly. I don't recall the exact number of seekers, but I remember that around 100 students declared their faith openly in the face of the impending danger.

I visited again and again to check up on the progress of the middle school students who had responded to the Gospel and who were studying the follow-up Bible study materials. I continued to teach a Bible study class at the Pao Shan Baptist School even after the Communists took over.

## The Ministry of Follow-up

When I first reached Shanghai I lived in the compound of the China Inland Mission (CIM) at 53 Sinza Road. Dick Hillis and David Morken, who also lived at the CIM headquarters, greeted me warmly and soon announced, "Here's your first project. Follow up on the 800 decisions that have been made the last few weeks!" These resulted from the recent YFC evangelistic meetings at the Moore Memorial Methodist Church (see Chapter 12). I didn't know any Chinese at this time, for this was my first day in China. But with the enthusiasm of youth I responded with a grin, "No problem!"

Actually, many things were already in place. Among them, the Topical Memory System packets in Chinese with instructions for new believers were available. When Dawson Trotman, interpreted by Andrew Gih, had presented the importance of follow-up in key Christian centers in China his teachings included the illustration of the Wheel, which gives the basics of the Christian life. He also illustrated the Word Hand, which gives the methods by which a young believer can get a grasp on the Word of God through hearing, reading, studying, memorizing, and meditating.[1]

I drafted a letter which was translated into Chinese to send to the new believers to attend a follow-up rally. About 300 people showed up and we divided them into about 20 ongoing follow-up groups. Each group was to be taught by some missionary or Chinese worker according to the follow-up syllabus which we put together.[2] I also taught one of the classes through an interpreter to discover for myself what things worked well in a Chinese context and what things didn't fit so well. Actually, to our delight, the materials and teaching were well received by the new Chinese believers. That which worked among American servicemen worked equally well among Chinese because it came mostly from the Scriptures, which are designed by God to transcend any culture.

## "The Liberation"

Every day the sound of gunfire drew nearer. Then one day in May my neighbor told me that this very night the Nationalist soldiers would be withdrawing and letting the Communist army come in and take over. The Nationalists had declared Shanghai to be an open city in order to spare the civilian population and buildings from useless destruction. Only the local police would remain behind.

After I had stayed for a few weeks as guest of the CIM, Dick found an apartment for me about a 15-minute walk from the CIM compound. It was located on Nanking Road, which is one of the main east-west arteries of Shanghai. The rent amounted to practically nothing (about 75 U.S. cents a month because prices were fixed although inflation at this time was astronomical). Some owners didn't even bother to collect the rent because it was so low. However, you had to pay "key money" (about U.S. $500) to the occupant for the privilege of moving in. In this case a China Bible Society missionary returning home to England invited me to take over the house and furniture where he was staying for only $500. This was a real bargain, especially since Dick Hillis paid for it.

When David Morken's wife and five children moved to China, Dick had also found them a nice house in a residential area for a bargain price. After "Liberation" in 1949, the number of Morken children increased to six with the birth of a son, whom they called "Shanghai John."

During the two-year period I lived in Shanghai, both under the *Kuo Min Tang* [the Nationalist Party] and the *Kung Chang Tang* [the Communist Party] nobody bothered to collect any rent.

On the evening of May 19, 1949, the Nationalist forces withdrew from the city that evening and the Communist forces invaded the city. I decided to watch the action from the comparative safety of a solid red brick apartment block. My apartment was in a rear section so I went over to a friend's apartment which overlooked the main thoroughfare of Nanking Road. We watched for several hours as the Nationalist army with their trucks and armor retreated west; then at about midnight we saw the vanguard of the Communist army coming in armored vehicles as they fired from machine guns into the streets.

I was a trained Navy fighter pilot, but I didn't consider this to be my war. So when some of the bullets ricocheted against the brick walls of the apartment, I felt safer by abandoning the window and lying on the floor.

The next morning I walked out on the street to greet one of the soldiers in a green uniform with a friendly "*Ni hao tsau chen*? [how are you this fine morning?]"

But he gave me a rather unfriendly answer; probably he was surprised.

When my missionary friends, who had remained behind the solid compound walls of the mission headquarters, heard I had seen some of the action and gone outside boldly to greet the communist soldiers the next morning, they were shocked. They probably considered this young American to be quite brash.


## "Walk—Don't Run"

A few weeks later I start out from my house to the CIM compound. It is a lovely day, so I start jogging. Suddenly I hear a soldier shout "Halt!" and he points his rifle at me. "Why are you running?" he asks.

I try to explain cheerfully in my limited Chinese that I am feeling good this morning and that I also like to jog as my exercise.

"In China we don't run, we walk!" he states firmly.

As I walked away less briskly, I thought that perhaps he had mistaken me for a thief. Then it came to me that the communists discouraged any expression of individual joy or freedom; it is a way to intimidate and control the hearts and minds of the people.

"Oh God," I prayed one morning during my devotional time, "if I am to face persecution, help me not to deny Your name. I am a Navy pilot and my squadron has been called into active duty to fight the communists. Oh God, if I am caught, and considered to be a spy, help me to be a courageous martyr and not deny my Lord Jesus Christ" (2 Timothy 1:12).

After serving as a Navy pilot throughout World War II, I had remained in the Ready Reserve, keeping up my flying skills at the Los Alamitos Naval Air Station near Long Beach, California. While serving as a missionary in China before the "Liberation" I had received my orders to report for active duty with my squadron.

When the last U.S. Navy warship left Shanghai just prior to the communist takeover, I went aboard to report on my situation. Of course the Executive Officer tried to persuade me to leave with him, but I told them that I had chosen to remain in China as a missionary. The United States and Communist China were virtually at war by this time; some former medical officers found to be in the "liberated" areas had already been arrested and jailed. If so, what would they do with a fighter pilot? But my life was in God's hands.


## The Heroic Missionary Ladies

The Chiang Wan Seminary, located downriver in a village eight miles from Shanghai, was run by two missionary ladies, Miss Ruth Brittain and Miss A. Wetherell Johnson. Miss Brittain had started a Christian school in 1914 to train Bible women and it had grown into a leading co-educational evangelical seminary with about 70 students who came mainly from the countryside. Dick Hillis, John Rhoads (see below), and several other CIM missionaries taught classes here, along with Yang Hsiao Tang, a Chinese pastor, and some able Chinese leaders. Later God greatly used Miss Johnson, the younger missionary, to get hundreds of women to study the Scriptures seriously. After her return to America, she founded, directed, and taught in the well-known and effective Bible Study Fellowship movement, now ministering both to women and to men.

When the communist soldiers first wanted to take over the school compound for a troop billet, the missionary women met them face to face at the gate and told them they were not allowed to come inside this women's school grounds. Impressive people, Miss Brittain and her colleague spoke fluent Chinese and customarily gave orders that were always carried out. These soldiers, mainly from the countryside with little educational background, still had the traditional Chinese respect for teachers. After that brief encounter, they backed down and went elsewhere to find quarters for their troops.

But one day the soldiers returned, entered the compound, and entered the seminary chapel with the excuse of wanting to get out of the rain. My missionary co-worker, Evangelist John Rhoads, present at the time, decided that this was a good time to preach the Gospel. So he got up in the pulpit with his interpreter and began to preach to the soldiers.

After a brief time, the leader of the group, who wore a patch over his eye, yelled out, "If this Jesus you talk about is so good, why doesn't He heal my eye?"

"If you will believe in the Lord Jesus Christ and receive Him into your heart, then maybe He will," John replied boldly.

They discussed this back and forth for a while with all the soldiers listening very intently.

Finally the leader shouted in anger. "My god is Mao Tse-Tung." And with that he ordered the soldiers out of the chapel into the rain outside.

Not long after this incident Miss Brittain, Miss Johnson, and their Chinese staff spent much time in prayer seeking the will of God for the seminary. They decided to close the school immediately and send all the students out into the countryside in small groups of two or three where they could continue to propagate the Gospel. A few weeks later, when the communist soldiers moved in to occupy the property, they found out to their anger that all the Bible students had gone. Only a small work among the orphan children remained.

## Dick Hillis—No Compromise

Dick Hillis served not only as my missionary mentor, but as my direct boss. He guided me in my early missionary activities and implanted in my heart the seed thoughts of the missionary philosophy and strategy that I would use over the next fifty years in serving under The Navigators and Training Evangelistic Leadership (TEL).

I would check in with him regarding my activities nearly every day and sometimes we would hold long discussions on various topics.

Dick went to the Honan province of northern China in 1934 (see Chapter 3), which was the year in which John and Betty Stam of the CIM were martyred by the Communists.[3] Dick himself had faced death on at least one occasion when bandits overran his mission station.

So one time I asked, "Dick, what is the best way for a Chinese Christian to deal with Communism?"

He explained that one of the main devices of the communists is to trick you into making some kind of compromise. Then they would play on your guilt. You would feel trapped, defeated and unworthy to resist any longer; thus your soul would become a prisoner of these ungodly people.

They also used the insidious psychological tactic of "brainwashing." Constant harassment and accusations would be thrown against you, until you admitted your errors and signed any confession they would place before you. In this way lies became the truth, and truth was no longer an absolute, for it became only relative.

The ways to deal with these tactics of the enemy has already been given to us by the Bible and its true record of history. The example of Daniel and his young friends who would not defile themselves is one such vivid record; these Hebrew young men would rather die than serve any other but the true God (Daniel 1 and 3). The Bible is full of other examples of men and women of faith who refused to compromise when threatened by the enemies of God. The list of courageous heroes of the faith includes Moses, Gideon, Jeremiah, Nehemiah and other Old Testament saints described so vividly in Hebrews 11:32-40, yet the supreme example is our Lord Jesus Christ. These and many others refused to compromise with the works of Satan, who is a deceiver and a liar (2 Thessalonians 2:9-10).

## The Works of Satan—Deceive and Divide

After the takeover of Shanghai the Communists set a goal to "liquidate" the existing church, educational institutions and business structures. This they called "liberation." The people didn't vote in favor of Communism. "Not even five percent of the people are in favor of Communism," confided one Chinese business friend to me. But having gained control by the gun, the communists would rule by intimidation and deceit. The works of Satan, whether under the guise of Communism or any other kind of false religion, are to deceive people into thinking that white is black, truth is a lie, and slavery is liberation.

How would the communists accomplish this? In the religious realm their first attack would be to isolate the Chinese church from the missionary. Whatever tensions may have existed between missionary organizations or whatever tension may have been felt between missionary and national would be subtly magnified and exploited by communist officials. They aimed to get the national to distance himself from his loyalty to historic missionary roots; it was the tactic of "divide and conquer!" Here are some of the accusations subtly planted:

"Our group is indigenous while yours is foreign-controlled!"

This controversy was already being debated before the Communists took over. The denominational missions, particularly, were accused of using money and foreign influence to gain followers. The Communists focused on this tension as an excuse to close many of the hospitals, schools and relief programs established by the sacrificial efforts of dedicated missionary societies.

"Your converts are all rice Christians!"

This attack was not so subtle, claiming that the Chinese Christians were not true believers in Jesus, but were "Christians" only because of the material benefits derived. So now, the Communists appealed to the people in the churches—you don't have to pretend to be a Christian any more. This accusation and the invitation to withdraw from the faith was a terrible lie from the accuser of the brethren.

"The Chinese church is better off without foreign influence!"

Even American Christians sometimes say that missionaries are no longer needed, for we should let the national church stand alone on its own two feet. The communists used such careless remarks as an excuse to expel all foreign missionaries from the country. The truth is that no church can ever stand alone and be separated from historic Christianity. When Christian groups are isolated from one another, it enables Satan to destroy them.

"Christianity is a foreign religion!"

This accusation came mainly from unbelievers, but when the national church went out of its way to try to distance itself from their historical and international biblical roots, it played right into the hands of the enemies of the Gospel. According to missiologist Ralph D. Winter and historian Kenneth Scott Latourette, the groups that tried to become most "Chinese" without any foreign roots or connections were the first to compromise with the Communists and lose their identity as the church. The Chinese Catholics, with their strong belief in the universality of the church headed by the pope, fared the best on this issue.[4]

"What's the use of preaching the Gospel to starving people!"

This statement forged a direct attack against the public proclamation of the Gospel and the honor of the Word of God, as well as being an outright lie, for evangelical missions have always been in the forefront of relief work in needy areas of the world.

"The missionaries want to control everything; it is time to turn all the work over to the Chinese!"

And so the Communists set out to do this forcibly. Again the historical record shows that most evangelical missions were already practicing an important missiological philosophy in planting churches that would, by design as quickly as possible, become self-governing, self-supporting and self-propagating. The communists borrowed this strategy and gave it a propaganda twist. The Three Self Patriotic Movement (TSPM) was set up to monitor the activities of the Christian church and to stress that the patriotic duty of the Chinese church was to make it completely Chinese.

Each one of these declarations (in the paragraphs above) has an element of truth in it, but can also be twisted in many ways to divide the missionary community. This is what the Communists did. Furthermore they sought to convince the local Christian leaders that they had been treated unfairly by the foreigners. This is never hard to do anywhere.

Then they would discourage the missionaries from fellowshipping with their Chinese brethren in the local church services. The Communists were diabolically clever in doing this. Instead of trying to intimidate the foreigner directly, thus making him a martyr, they set out deliberately to intimidate any Chinese who had social contact with that foreigner. For instance, after "Mr. Wang" [a made-up name] visited his missionary's house, Mr. Wang would be visited by the police and accused of illegal contacts with the "foreign imperialists."

Soon many missionaries became afraid to preach or encourage their Chinese friends. "I am not afraid to suffer for Jesus, but I don't want my Chinese friends to suffer," reasoned the troubled missionary.

What should the missionary do? The answer, as always, is surely found in the Scriptures, for Christians have suffered persecution and intimidation from the days of the apostles. In particular, Paul's second letter to the Thessalonian believers sets an excellent example.

(1) Love One Another—Paul pleads for love among the saints, for unity among the believers is his primary concern (2 Thessalonians 1:3).

(2) Be Worthy in Suffering—Paul exhorts believers to be counted worthy of the kingdom of God for which they also suffer (2 Thessalonians 1:5).

(3) Be Patient in Tribulation—God is righteous and He shall come to glorify His saints and punish with everlasting destruction those who do not believe the truth but have pleasure in unrighteousness (2 Thessalonians 1:6-12).

(4) Pray in Faith—God is sovereign, so pray that He will deliver you from unreasonable and wicked men in accordance with what is best for your growth and His glory (2 Thessalonians 3:1-5).

(5) Beware of Divisions—Do not associate with false brethren who come in to criticize and attack the missionary and pastoral traditions of your fellowship (2 Thessalonians 3:6). Don't pass on rumors and accusations.

(6) Follow Your Leaders—Follow the example taught in life and conduct by your founders. Do not denounce your roots (2 Thessalonians 3:7-15).

## Justice Under Communism

Many communist officials, especially the leaders, were anti-Christian and morally corrupt. Yet others were sincere people trying to better the lot of their countrymen. As in any form of government, even in a so-called democracy, we find good and we find evil. Not everything under Communism was bad and evil. The post office and railroads functioned far better than under the former regime. Crime was quite well controlled, albeit with cruelty and violence, so the streets were now relatively safe. The common people, at least, were less exposed to corruption, banditry, pornography, drugs and prostitution. So the Scriptures instruct the Christian to be "subject unto the higher powers. For there is no power but of God: the powers that be are ordained of God. . . For rulers are not a terror to good works, but to the evil" (Romans 13:1-3).

When Dick arranged for me to live in an apartment near the CIM compound, he also arranged for a cook from the Christian community in the countryside to be my servant. In China having servants formed part of the culture, built into the very system of life; it was a way of providing work and identity for millions of people who would otherwise have no meaningful work. And it was necessary considering the living conditions of that time. For instance, running hot water scarcely existed even in a middle class home. If you wanted some hot water for a bath, you would send your servant out to the hot water shop to buy a pail of hot water and transport it back to the home. All foreigners, including missionaries, had servants.

Now one of my valued possessions was a Royal portable typewriter which I had brought with me from America. Under the Communists no person, especially one who was a foreigner, was allowed to spend the night in any place other than his registered address without police permission. But one day a heavy rainstorm drenched the city and flooded the streets so that I was unable to get back from Dick's apartment on the CIM compound to my house. When

I reached home late in the morning of the next day, my cook waited at the door for me.

"Lookee master," he says in his broken English, "someone pushee door and steal master's machine."

"*Wei shen-ma ni chuh-chu a*? [How come you have to leave?]" I asked in my broken Chinese. Dick had instructed the cook never to leave the house empty. It was an old Chinese custom that no house was ever left without someone to watch things.

The cook explained that he had to go out to get some food to eat, and while he was gone—oh, so very briefly—someone came and pushed the door open.

"Lookee!" He demonstrates by first using the key to latch the door, then he gave the door a push and it flew open.

"*Hao, hao, mei yu kuan hsi* [Okay, never mind]"

I then went back to see Dick and get his advice on how to handle the situation.

When Dick and I return to my apartment we find that the police are already there. I had not called them, but the cook had called them to present his story and justify himself. The police are very polite to Dick who speaks fluent colloquial Chinese, but they do not believe the cook's story. One of the policemen opens the lock on the door and finds that the latch on the inside had been filed down so that it would no longer hold.

"Whoever filed this lock had to use the key first to open the door," announces the policeman. So they arrest the cook and take him off to jail.

"What do we do now?" I ask Dick, relieved yet worried about my cook. He was not a bad person, just a bit stupid, and furthermore, Chinese jails are awful.

"As Christians we must help him," declares Dick and goes alone to the police station, explaining to the authorities that the cook had come from the countryside and didn't understand the city. As Christians, we would take full responsibility for him and forgive him his faults. Dick explains the Gospel again to the cook, which he was supposed to have believed. So the police then release him.

We forgive him but decide that he should go back home to his village; we give him a couple of blankets, some food and enough cash to return to his home in the country. This thought then occurs to me, but without bitterness, *He's probably also keeping the money he got from selling my typewriter.* I particularly admire Dick's compassion, sense of fair play and sensitivity to both Chinese and Christian ethics.

## The Art of Personal Discipleship

The communists tried very hard to restrict the activities of the official church services, but they seemed quite unconcerned, at least in those early days, about Christians meeting informally to pray and to study the Bible. Officially they did not consider anything less than five people to be "an assembly." It need not be reported to the authorities. Herein lay one of the greatest opportunities of my entire lifetime. During the 18 months I lived under the communists, I met with individuals in my home, in tea shops, in the school canteen and elsewhere without anyone ever questioning me or apparently even taking notice of my activities. I also attended church services, but was not yet fluent enough in the language to be invited to speak in Chinese.

Yet through developing the "key man" concept—training a person to be equipped to reach others within his own circle of influence—and also by enlisting the cooperation of key missionaries and pastors who had Youth for Christ or Navigator backgrounds, we were able to develop a rather extensive network of discipleship.

At the close of this period I had the names and addresses of about 1,600 people who had finished some of our Scripture memory and Bible study lessons. These contacts were scattered in some 53 cities and 13 provinces of China. In Shanghai we had a relationship with students practicing their discipleship, which included a quiet time, Bible study and Scripture memory, in half a dozen universities and colleges. Actually I had performed almost the same kind of ministry when I led the Navigators ministry from Dallas, Texas, where

God had enabled me to develop some disciples in six universities. We were able to implement this same pattern in Shanghai.

My particular goal was to raise up faithful men in whom I could impart my life, so that they in turn would reach others. This is called the Timothy Principle.[5] "And the things that thou hast heard of me among many witnesses, the same commit thou to faithful men, who shall be able to teach others also" (2 Timothy 2:2). During my two years in China I paid particular attention to and spent special times of instruction with about 10 men, each of whom I considered to be a key man or a Timothy. Three were missionary kids and seven were Chinese friends who came to my home in small groups or for individual discipling.

Eric Wong, the son of a merchant whose family sold linen table-cloths and other articles made in Swatow, came often for discipleship training. One day he told me of the plan his relatives had arranged to smuggle him and three other family members by boat out of Shanghai to Hong Kong. They had money and they made it! Eric has remained a close friend. He would later attend my wedding when I left China and eventually came to Hong Kong. Still later he would become an active Christian businessman who would be elected president of The Gideons in Hong Kong.

William Hsu, meditative and artistic, had a much different personality than the friendly, outgoing Eric. But we also became close friends. He was able to get out of China and later had a job at the Kai Tak Airport in Hong Kong, where I continued to encourage him in discipleship.

Four of the seven were able to leave China, but three stayed behind. Wilfred Hsu, no relation to William, felt led of God to go into the countryside to preach and to pastor a church among people of his dialect.

Ted Ma was Eurasian. He had an American mother but his father was a Communist Party leader with connections to the YMCA. So Ted tried to cover up his American identity. At the time I met with Ted, he attended a government high school. He was a brilliant student whether doing Bible study or taking secular courses. He memorized many Scriptures diligently.

After he graduated with top honors in Shanghai, he was sent to the leading engineering university in Mukden, Manchuria (Liaoning Province today), an historic stronghold of the communist movement. When Ted and I corresponded, he would write in Chinese on the outside envelope bearing my Chinese name, but the letter inside would be in English.

At university he started discipling about half a dozen fellow students, using the Scripture memory and Bible study methods which I had passed on to him. For a while things went well.

Then one day I received a letter from him in which he said that the communist officials had called him in for questioning. Ted insisted that his group was student led, not controlled by foreigners, and as a student he just shared his personal faith as allowed by the Party, and he quoted from their own propaganda. After much discussion, they warned him but allowed the group to continue to meet for the time being. Even in the heart of a model communist school, there were some students like Ted Ma who dared to share their faith.

## Evangelist John Rhoads

One positive result from the Communist takeover was a greater unity among the various church groups. John Rhoads, a CIM missionary who taught at the Chiang Wan Seminary until it closed, became my closest friend. A graduate of Dallas Theological Seminary, he came to Shanghai with his wife and two children a few months prior to my arrival. His great heart and gift of preaching the Gospel in public meetings drew us together.

We were both assigned to work in a local church compound with English-speaking young people, the children of missionaries and business people. We decided to hold a special evangelistic rally for the youth group in our church, so we formed a team. John gave an evangelistic message, whereas I set up for the meetings. For our soloist I recruited Lois Raws, an attractive young missionary lady with a beautiful voice. Some were surprised when the gospel rally, molded after the YFC format, resulted in several of the youth, including some missionary kids, making public decisions for Christ.

Then John and I organized the Shanghai Youth Crusade, a week of youth meetings with the six English-speaking churches of Shanghai cooperating. This was an historic occasion—the first time that all these churches had cooperated in an evangelistic effort. We received a great response from the people of the Eurasian community of mixed German, Russian and Chinese background, as God wonderfully blessed these meetings in which some 30 young people made public their salvation decisions.

Two of the converts, Ilsa and Sam Emmamooden, a married couple, became the leaders of the youth in the Endeavors Church. Later they left Shanghai for Hong Kong, where they became pillars in the missionary prayer fellowship and active in providing shelter and aid for refugees of all races fleeing Mainland China.

## Evangelist John Goo

John Goo had been trained by Evangelist Andrew Gih, and I trained him for the YFC ministry under David Morken and Dick Hillis. After about one year under the communists most missionary groups felt that families with children should return home. Daws gave me the option to return to the States, but I wrote back 19 reasons why I should stay on to continue my ministry in China. I didn't mention a young lady who was reason number 20. When the Morken and Hillis families departed from Shanghai, John Goo and I went to the train station to see them off. After prayer and farewells, Dick yelled out the window as the train pulled away, "By the way, Roy, you are now in charge of YFC!"

We had successful combined English-speaking evangelistic meetings in church buildings with evangelist John Rhoads. Now we decided to hold regional evangelistic services among the Chinese churches with John Goo as the evangelist. Our plans were to encourage the cooperation of churches in the northern area, and then in the west. I gathered funds and provided the follow-up materials, but did not personally attend the meetings because as a foreigner I would have attracted too much attention. Before I left Shanghai we held two such regional crusades. In the last week of meetings, Evangelist Goo reported 125 public decisions for Christ.

A year or so after I left China, I heard through some of my missionary friends that John Goo had been arrested and thrown into prison. The communists had planted a gun under his mattress and falsely accused him of being an "enemy of the people" in his anti-state activities. Eventually Evangelist Goo died in prison, one of the countless Chinese martyrs for the Lord Jesus Christ—faithful unto death that many of their countrymen might be saved.

## A Time for Romance

Living under the communists might seem like an unlikely time for romance, but that was not so for me! Most of the 54 new CIM missionaries who arrived in Shanghai in 1948 were single. At that time, in fact, the CIM preferred that their new missionary recruits be single. The Mission's reasoning was practical. First, a single person adapted to the language and culture more readily; second, the Mission wanted each person, male or female, husband or wife, to receive the individual call from God to be a missionary in China under the CIM. Then once they arrived on the field, the missionary leaders encouraged each one to seek the will of the Lord as to one's future life partner. But the general rule prevailed that there be no marriage until after two years of language study and indoctrination.

Engagements were announced among the new missionaries as soon as the leaders had given their blessing; some of these leaders felt that it was their duty to engage in the revered Chinese custom of matchmaking. Therefore engaged couples were formally introduced from time to time to the delight of everyone—well almost everyone. So there usually was quite a bit of speculation and social excitement within the CIM family on the compound.

I was not immune to the love bug. When I was hospitalized for a week in the CIM hospital, Lois Raws, one of the missionary nurses and our soloist in the youth crusades, radiated a wonderful personality, godliness and much TLC [tender loving care]. She and I were also assigned to lead the young people's group together at the church, and she participated with us in the special evangelistic meetings. Extremely talented, she sang beautiful solos while I often led the congregational singing. Also, she attained the highest test scores in Chinese of any missionary in history. As the youngest person ever to graduate from Wheaton College, Lois obtained a four-year academic degree at age 19. Brought up in a royal Christian heritage, she was the daughter of Dr. and Mrs. Addison Raws, the director of America's Keswick.

Hey, she is the one for me, I thought. So I put in my bid, fully expecting her to swoon in my arms at the very mention that I would like her to be my wife.

Lois listened carefully to my proposal. Then she answered, "You are a nice guy, Roy. I like you, but I cannot marry you." And she ticked off the reasons:

(1) I am called to CIM—you are not!

(2) I am called particularly to China—you are not!

(3) I am called to work among the tribal people in Yunnan province— you are not!

The very next week a young suitor who happened to be from the CIM, called to China, and called to work among the tribal people in Yunnan explained to Lois why it was God's will for them to be married.

But she turned him down also, "Yes, we are called to work in the same place, but I am not sure I love you."

So the next week the "G.D."—Bishop Frank Houghton, the General Director of the CIM—called me into his office to talk about Lois. He said the poor girl felt confused. Although the bishop was sympathetic to me and had sponsored the YFC workers, he apparently preferred that their prize lady missionary stay within the CIM. He gave me specific instructions not to see Lois again in private until she came to a decision. However, I learned that my rival was free to develop his friendship with her.

So when I had written to Daws earlier about 19 reasons why I chose to remain in China, I did not tell him everything. Actually I had 20 reasons! I sought advice from my friend Dick. He was not only sympathetic, but forwarded his own matchmaking scheme by feeding me all kinds of tidbits about Lois's wonderful qualities—"All is fair in love and war."

Dick and Margaret even engineered to have Lois and me arrive at the same time for tea in their apartment. And others in the CIM family found subtle excuses to see that Lois and I were both invited to certain small social functions. No, missionary life is not without some fun, intrigue and excitement.

The sequel could only have been worked out by God Himself. Daws reached me by telephone in October 1950 with instructions to leave China as soon as I could. When I joined Dick, David and Daws on Taiwan, I heard the news that after some 100 years of service, the CIM was closing the field and ordering all their missionaries out of Mainland China. If any CIM missionaries had offers to go to any other mission group or country, they were free to do so.

So I sent a telegram to Lois pointing out that God had closed these doors to open the door for us to live and minister together. I concluded with, "LETTER FOLLOWS." David sent the telegram from Tokyo because Taiwan and China were not exactly on good terms. Later, David laughingly reported that a typographical error had occurred in the telegram. Thus "FETTER FOLLOWS" was telegraphed to Lois, changing the letter "L" to "F."

I traveled to Hong Kong to meet Lois at the China border. We were married in Hong Kong on March 7, 1951 at the St. Andrew's Church with John Rhoads serving as best man and my Chinese co-workers Eric Wong and others lending a hand. The CIM and Hong Kong missionary community rejoiced with us in God's leading.

ENDNOTES:
1.  The Word Hand Illustration is described in detail in Roy Robertson's *The Timothy Principle* (Singapore: The Navigators, 1986), pages 29-49, and illustrated below (from page 45 of the *Timothy Training Workbook*, which goes with *The Timothy Principle* and is included in it in some editions with separate pagination on page 53):

2. That syllabus is essentially what we now have in *The Timothy Principle* (above).
3. See *The Triumph of John and Betty Stam* by Dr. and Mrs. Howard Taylor (London: China Inland Mission, 1936).
4. See Chapter 8, End Note 4.
5. *The Timothy Principle*, Chapter 12, pages 91-94.

# Chapter 14

## THE TAIWAN HARVEST

In 1950, Communist leaders, drunk with success at having defeated Generalissimo Chiang Kai Shek and his armies in the arena of war, now set an agenda to wipe out the threat of Christianity to their system of government by closing the doors of all churches in China. They did this not directly, but deceitfully. While proclaiming outwardly the concept of freedom of religion, officials would visit a harassed pastor and demand an arbitrarily exorbitant amount of taxes to be paid immediately. When the Christians could not meet these conditions, the officials would close down the church claiming that the Christians were dishonest and unproductive. Then they confiscated the church building and generally turned it into some kind of factory. Thus the Chinese Communists launched their systematic program to close all churches, destroy all Bibles and intimidate all believers.

But a Nationalist Chinese remnant of about 600,000 troops plus 1,000,000 refugees managed to escape from the Mainland to Formosa (Portuguese for "Island Beautiful"), today called by its ancient Chinese name Taiwan. These refugees represented the leadership of old China, the cream of a 3,000-year cultural heritage. Thus a remnant, pledged to the preservation of the nation with its past glory and uncertain future, escaped the clutches of atheistic Communism.

In some ways it might be compared to the Jewish remnant of biblical history when those willing to leave Babylon behind, returned to Jerusalem to a life of hardship because there they could worship God and continue their Hebrew customs. This faithful Jewish remnant would eventually enable the nation to survive in history, through all the ups and downs of "world empires" (Daniel 2 and 7), till "the fullness of the time" (Galatians 4:4) would bring the promised Savior into human history to achieve the salvation of mankind. This Chinese remnant also hoped to preserve the nation's glory.

This is not to say that the followers of Generalissimo Chiang were all that righteous (nor were the Jews either), for some in both camps cheated and betrayed the confidence of their respective people. But the Generalissimo himself loved his people and in later years sought to follow Christian principles. When I lived in Taiwan, one of his staff who served as chaplain to the Generalissimo reported to me that this leader read the Word of God for 30 minutes every morning before he began his work. Some of his closest advisors and friends were keen witnessing Christians. Above all, his wife, Madame Chiang, was a great prayer warrior and witness for Christ.

## "We'll Do It!"

Subsequently, one Easter Sunday during my Taiwan ministry, the First Lady went on national radio to give her personal testimony and proclaim the gospel message to all her countrymen. Her subject was the resurrection of Jesus Christ. Some diplomats in the American Embassy scoffed at this broadcast and its evangelistic message, and some in the media reported that she was a better preacher than diplomat.

After all of Mainland China had been occupied by the communists, nearly everyone predicted that Taiwan too would also quickly fall to them. Gloom and terror gripped the island population. In this dark hour Bob Pierce visited Madame Chiang Kai Shek.

After tea and pleasantries he prepared to leave; as he was about to go, he asked Madame Chiang, "What can we do for you?"

This grand lady replied with a deep sigh, "I wish that every man in this army could receive a Gospel of John."

Bob replied immediately, "We'll do it!"

This promise began one of the most remarkable harvests of souls in modern history. Bob went to work at once. He visited Clyde Pearson, director of Every Christian Crusade, with a request for the printing of half a million Gospels of John in Chinese; he also ordered another half-million from the American Bible Society.

But who would lead this massive distribution? Only one person came to mind—Dick Hillis. Previously Dick had taught Chinese farmers in his ministry in the Province of Honan to form gospel teams (see Chapter 3). Laymen had learned how to witness and over the next four decades gathered a great harvest. Dick had helped set up the remarkable YFC evangelistic meetings in which David Morken and Bob Pierce preached to large audiences in the major cities of China just prior to the communist takeover. Dick and Margaret with their six children had recently returned to America from China, where they had been under tremendous stress while living under communist control. The ordeal had left them physically and emotionally exhausted.

But Bob knew that Dick was the man to lead gospel teams to reach the 1,600,000 nationalist refugees who had fled to Taiwan from the Mainland. Bob went to Dawson Trotman and enlisted his aid in persuading Dick to return again and minister among the Chinese people. Daws called an all-night prayer meeting with some of his staff. After prayer and feeling assured that this was indeed the will of God, he persuaded Dick to leave immediately for Taiwan. Then Daws called Shanghai to tell me that it was now time for me to leave the Chinese mainland and join him and Dick "on an island 400 miles to the east." He didn't dare mention the name Taiwan over the telephone.

I inquired whether this was a suggestion or an instruction. Daws replied that some of the Navigator staff had spent all night in prayer and were of one mind that it was time for me to leave Shanghai.

"Yes, sir," I replied. "I will come as soon as I can."

The procedure for leaving Communist China at that time required that a person have all his possessions inspected, then publish his name in the local newspaper for three weeks. If anyone had any complaints or charges against that person, he would not be allowed to leave. Having relatively few possessions and holding no official church position, no one accused me of anything. However, I had carelessly left a U.S. five-dollar bill in an envelope in some neglected file; the official inspecting my possessions found the $5 and reminded me that it was a crime punishable by imprisonment to possess any U.S. currency. I apologized profusely for my stupidity and assured him that I had forgotten about its whereabouts; besides, I pointed out, if I had been trying to hide money, I would have kept a fifty or a hundred dollar bill. He agreed that some foreigners are rather stupid.

After three weeks they allowed me to purchase a train ticket from Shanghai to Tsingtao, a port city about 360 miles to the north as the crow flies, where I could catch a Norwegian ship going to Japan. At the final inspection point I made a serious blunder that could have kept me in China as a prisoner or worse. Just before I boarded the ship, the communist officer at the dock asked me to hand him my wallet. I carried no U.S. currency, of course, but among the various cards in my wallet he found a credit card for the purchase of aviation gasoline.

He pulled it out and inquired, "What is this?"

My heart sank. How stupid of me not to have destroyed this card, I thought. Would this lead to the discovery that I was a Navy fighter pilot?

In fact, at this time, the aircraft carrier squadron to which I had been ordered to report as a reserve naval officer was bombing communist positions in Korea. A captured U.S. medical officer had recently been executed in China on trumped-up espionage charges. What would they do to a Navy pilot?

"Is this a military card?" the official asked severely.

"No, it isn't," I replied truthfully, for the U.S. military does not use credit cards.

After a few agonizing moments, he handed back my wallet and waved me aboard the Norwegian ship and freedom.

*Was he a Christian?* I pondered. I felt profoundly grateful to God for this man.


## Gospel of John Distributions

Dick Hillis received a letter from President Chiang Kai Shek (his new title) recommending that all the troops under his command receive and read the Gospel of John. Dick hastily put together a small team of gifted people and they rushed out to Taiwan under the sponsorship of YFC. The two major team members were Uri Chandler of Every Creature Crusade and Ells Culver of the Oriental Missionary Society; others would follow later. This joint project combined preaching, musical talent, Gospel distribution and follow-up. Jim and Lillian Dickson of the Taiwan Presbyterian Mission, who were close friends of Bob Pierce, sponsored the project.

Somehow this vast project had to be organized, funded and managed; but in a matter of a few weeks Dick had the whole program underway. President Chiang wrote a letter to all the troops under his command presenting Jesus Christ as the Rock of Salvation and recommending that every man in the armed forces read the Gospel of John, which would be given as a gift to them by Youth for Christ. The letter also commended the Bible as the foundation for moral righteousness and appealed to the Chinese military to begin reading Scripture. The men on Hillis's team, armed with half a million copies of the Gospel of John and a copy of this letter, set out systematically to visit each military camp and installation.

I tagged along with the American evangelist and his interpreter in the gospel van on one particular visit. After a preliminary conversation with the base officials, we go out to the parade ground where all the troops have been assembled.

"Attention!" the commanding officer shouts. The soldiers snap to attention.

"At ease, men!" the evangelist says, smiling. This is interpreted into Chinese and the soldiers relax a bit, but are still wary.

"We have a gift for you from the American people." The evangelist continues, "This is the Gospel of John [holding one up], a portion of the Word of God, a book of the Bible. Your great leader has recommended it to you." The evangelist does not use the full title of Generalissimo or President Chiang Kai Shek as that would be too forceful.

The evangelist continues, "Your great leader believes that the

Bible is the foundation for moral righteousness and he wants everyone here to have a copy of this portion of the Word of God. We will now distribute it through your leaders, one copy to each soldier."

As the Gospels of John are distributed, the evangelist takes about 15 minutes to explain the Good News (the Gospel) and the soldiers read a few selected verses together. He then invites those men who want to believe in the Lord Jesus Christ and receive forgiveness of sins and eternal life to fill out the decision slip at the back of each Gospel, tear out the page, then turn it in to us through their leaders.

A word of thanks, an assurance of love and support from the American people, and the invoking of God's blessing closes the brief meeting. The whole process takes less than half an hour and many soldiers seem eager to respond to the Gospel.

## And Now for the Follow-Up

On Christmas Day 1950 Daws and I are meeting with Dick Hillis and Jim and Lillian Dickson to discuss plans to follow up this great evangelistic opportunity. After Christmas dinner, we sit around a cheery fire built in their living room fireplace and discuss how the follow-up should be carried out. A huge stack of decision slips fill one corner of the room. We collected them from the soldiers at various bases and installations who had recorded their decisions to believe in Jesus Christ and receive Him into their hearts as personal Savior and Lord. All had been torn out of the Gospels of John distributed to the troops. The Chinese paper is thick and these stacks of decision slips, 6,000 in all, literally reach from floor to ceiling. To do any kind of effective follow-up on them looks to me like a hopeless task.

Alone with Daws for a few minutes, I remind him of the circumstances producing the decision cards. "These decisions are from soldiers, most of whom know very little about the Gospel or the Bible. They were collected en masse and there is a time lag of some weeks. I can't do any kind of adequate follow-up under these conditions."

Daws glares at me for a moment, then says softly, "Do what you can!"

My heart responds: *Why, of course! Yes sir! I will do everything I can to help these soldiers understand the Gospel and grow in their knowledge of the Word of God.* "Okay, Daws, I will do whatever I can," I assure him.

We go back to the living room to rejoin Dick and our host, Jim. Since each of the soldiers had received his own copy of the Gospel of John, I propose that we start with a simple Bible study that would explain the plan of salvation from verses found in that particular Gospel. We could mail this Bible study to each soldier along with a letter telling him how happy we are that he had received the Lord into his life as personal Savior. If he will answer the questions and send them back to us, we will grade the first lesson and send him additional lessons as Bible study helps.

The plan is approved and Dick offers the services of Elder Liu, a Chinese interpreter, to translate the Bible studies and the letter and see that everything is mailed out to the responding soldiers.

I went to work immediately and wrote a simple "question and answer" Bible study for the first lesson. The first obstacle I faced was how to give a clear plan of salvation using only John's Gospel. Daws had originally taught us a sequence of verses which we later developed into "The Bridge Illustration" using Romans 3:23, "All have sinned . . .," then Romans 6:23, "the wages of sin is death . . . ," and Hebrews 9:27, " . . . but after this the judgment." That's the Bad News.

Now for the Good News. The above three verses were followed by a passage that tells how Jesus had died on the cross for our sins (1 Corinthians 15:3-4 or Romans 5:8 or 1 Peter 3:18). But not one of these verses was in the Gospel of John. How could we give a clear plan of salvation using only John's Gospel? We had to find similar passages that taught these truths for the Gospel presentation.

As I studied and prayed over the first chapter of the Gospel of John, I noticed that the apostle teaches the fact of sin by showing that Jesus is the Light (1:7-9) and men choose to live in darkness because of their evil deeds (3:18-19). Soon we developed the same points of view on death and judgment based on the Jews' rejection of Jesus, who is the Light of the world (1:29). Then we brought out the facts of Jesus' trial, death on the cross, burial and resurrection (chapters 19 and 20). Finally it is by faith and receiving Jesus that one can become a child of God (1:12). The last question asked directly, "Are you a son of God? If so, when did this happen?"

Sixteen study questions and one application question were included in the first lesson, and each question, except for the last, could be answered by explaining in one's own words the meaning of the reference given.

Within a week the Bible studies and our letter were translated, printed and ready for mailing. Someone came up with the idea that we could print the return address on the back of the Bible study, so the soldier could mail it back without hunting for an additional envelope. The post office cooperated with us by allowing this procedure and we provided the return address written in Chinese:

> Bible Investigation Correspondence School
> P. O. Box 555, Taipei, Taiwan

## Harvests of Souls

Did it work? Someone ventured to say that if the return rate of completed Bible studies were just five percent (300), the project would be considered a success. After only a few days I received the good news that the post office box overflowed with completed Bible studies. For days they continued to stream in—hundreds at first, then 1,000, then more than 2,000. We received a phenomenal 33+ percent response from the first mailing of 6,000 studies.

So the work of follow-up grew. With my colleague Doug Sparks, sent out by The Navigators to take over the follow-up work, we prepared three other lessons from the Gospel of John, followed by a wide variety of discipleship studies. Dick Hillis and his teams, with the blessing of President and Madame Chiang Kai Shek, grabbed the opportunity to give gospel presentations to all the military camps. After this, Hillis' gospel teams went into the public schools of Taiwan and then invaded city auditoriums and basketball stadiums. Finally the gospel teams traveled from village to village throughout the length and breadth of the island. An opportunity to receive Christ as Savior and Lord was given at each public presentation, and those who responded were given follow-up materials, including a Gospel of John study on the plan of salvation.

After ten years more than 600,000 people had mailed back completed studies to the follow-up office. One estimate noted that this was five percent of the total population of Taiwan at that time. Approximately one out of every 20 people had not only responded to the gospel preaching, but had studied the Scriptures to affirm and seal their salvation experience. The average Chinese household at that time was comprised of about ten people, so the above figures meant that an average of one person per two households had turned to Jesus Christ. The Gospel had penetrated everywhere. It was an unprecedented harvest!

I had heard Dick Hillis explain his philosophy of the harvest on numerous occasions. In 1956 my family and I moved to the mission compound that had been purchased by Overseas Crusades (now called O.C. International). To save money, the mission bought a cheap plot of land in the middle of a large rice field and built four modern missionary cottages on it. From the main thoroughfare on the outskirts of the city a small gravel road, elevated above the moist paddy fields, served as the only access to the compound. Inside we were completely surrounded by rice fields.

"When the rice harvest comes," Dick would tell us, "everyone will drop everything to work in the harvest."

From our compound we watched the young and the old, mothers with babies on their backs, and every member of the clan work from daybreak till darkness. They had to gather the harvest quickly before the new rains came or other adverse conditions affected that crop.

From his study of Bible history and missions, Dick further believed and taught that nations also experience times of spiritual harvest. These do not come often, but during certain periods God brings a nation to a "ripened" condition to respond to God's messengers. In the Old Testament there were such times in the days of David, Hezekiah, Josiah and Nehemiah. In more recent times we had The Great Awakening in England and Colonial America and a Second Awakening in the 19th century in the newly formed United States of America. These were usually times of great adversity in which people called on God as their only hope of deliverance.

Now a small, proud remnant of one of the oldest cultures and most numerous people on earth had suffered terrible reverses and were threatened with destruction. Since all of Mainland China had fallen into the hands of the victorious communist armies, few people in the world expected the defeated nationalist remnant to be able to hold out for more than a few months against these overwhelming odds, for the 1,600,000 people who had fled to Taiwan opposed a China population of 750,000,000.

Yet the 1,600,000 represented the cream of the nation. Sometimes a Mainland family would select a favorite son or daughter, someone with high ideals, keen intelligence, and patriotic commitment to traditional Chinese values or their Christian heritage who would represent the clan in the new venture on Taiwan. "Straddle the issue by putting a foot in each boat and see which one survives," is an old Chinese saying. Among these people were some willing to flee, to fight, or to die rather than succumb to the imprisoning of the soul by atheistic Communism. Now this proud remnant had been brought to its knees in humiliation and despair. The Administration in Washington had issued a discouraging report on the situation and the news media had written off Chiang Kai Shek, his regime and Taiwan. Only the small missionary community and evangelical Christianity appeared to be giving solid support. So God now brought this people to a place where many were willing to call on the Lord for salvation.

The harvest on Taiwan began in November 1950 as Dick Hillis, Ells Culver, Uri Chandler and other evangelists, who came out for a short time, began to preach and distribute Gospels of John to the soldiers of the armies of President Chiang Kai Shek. By the time I arrived with Dawson Trotman at Christmas of 1950, there were already 6,000 signed decisions for Christ, so we began the massive work of follow-up. By February 1951, some 13 months later, more than 9,000 men in all branches of the military professed their faith through the completed first lessons of the Bible studies.

Now Dick, Ells and Uri, as married men with families, were eager to return to the United States to bring their wives and children to Taiwan and settle there for a while to continue work in the bountiful harvest. As a single man at that time I could stay on and handle the follow-up.

*Back row left to right:Uri Chandler, Roy Robertson, Ells Culver*

*Front row: Dick Hillis, Dawson Trotman*

But before they left the island, Jim Dickson, the head of the Presbyterian Mission on Taiwan, invited them to return to the island, not only to continue preaching to the military and refugees from Mainland China, but also to train laymen of the local Taiwanese churches in witnessing and discipleship. The outgrowth of their return would be the formation of a new missionary organization known as Orient Crusades (now called O. C. International).

Dick Hillis, a master in leading evangelistic teams, could find the right approach for any particular setting. He aimed not only to explain the Gospel to the people, but also to motivate them to respond to the invitation, thus preparing the way for the follow-up ministry. This would allow us to explain the Gospel more thoroughly through personal Bible study, then link them with a local church in their area.

After completing the project of distributing Gospels of John to the military, Dick obtained another half a million Gospels directed particularly at the student population, for they are the future of a country. Gospel teams entered both Christian and government schools with outstanding results. Again, the distribution of the Gospels of John was coupled with gospel preaching and public invitations to make decisions for Christ. The follow-up department had to be increased to more than 20 workers, in order to handle approximately 10,000 decisions per month during the next couple of years.

## "Venture for Victory"

In 1954 they inaugurated another exciting new project. A "Venture for Victory" basketball team, made up of Christian student athletes from America, played local basketball teams on Taiwan. A specific provision enabled the Americans to give their personal testimonies and share the Gospel during the half-time break. Thousands flocked to these games, as basketball ranked the number one sport on the island at this time. Again the arrangements had been made at the highest level, as the project had the personal endorsement of Madame Chiang Kai Shek.

"Venture for Victory" easily won the exhibition games as they toured from city to city. They climaxed that first trip with a contest between "Venture for Victory" and the top military teams in the country. Competition was keen, players on both teams fought hard, and the games were very close. The real victory, however, was the opportunity given the young American basketball players to share Jesus Christ with the thousands of Chinese young people under the most favorable of circumstances. They received Gospels of John and the Bible studies when they responded to the message and to the invitation at the basketball games.

Even though Orient Crusades and "Venture for Victory" officially sponsored the project on Taiwan, the Chinese name, *Ching Nien Kuey Chu* [Youth for Christ], was displayed and known everywhere. Even non-Christian people were familiar with the spread of the Gospel in army camps, schools and sports arenas through the YFC meetings during that wonderful decade of the 1950s.

Did everything go smoothly all the time? Of course not! Were mistakes made? Certainly! Although we must be aggressive in preaching the Gospel, we should be careful to respect government authorities and not offend cultural sensitivities unnecessarily. At the height of the "open door" among the military, one evangelist, who did not belong to Dick's group, insisted that the soldiers lay down their rifles and kneel on the ground. Military leaders who were not sympathetic to the Gospel used this incident to hinder further distribution of the Gospels. Also, an evangelist from another group told school children not to salute their national flag, causing severe repercussions. Such extremists can halt the full flow of the Gospel. Insensitivity to the culture hinders the harvest. We are commanded in Scripture to proclaim the Word and the Gospel fearlessly, but we are to do it with humility, grace and respect for the authorities of the land.

## Into the Countryside

The last great evangelistic thrust on Taiwan in the late 1950s linked with local churches and targeted peasants in the villages, native Taiwanese, rather than the Chinese mainlanders or the educated urban Taiwanese. Weldon Culver, the older brother of Ells, led the project. Weldon's team would begin by spending a week training the people in some rural Presbyterian church. Then they would join with the Orient Crusades gospel team to testify and preach in all the villages in that area and to do counseling and follow-up.

Dick Hillis systematically planned each of these rural ministries. He often repeated his battle cry, "No one has the right to hear the Gospel twice till everyone has heard the Gospel once."

Dick determined to do everything in his power to make sure that the Gospel was preached at least once in every village of Taiwan that appeared on the huge wall map in his office. So as not to spread themselves too thin, they tackled the northern half of Taiwan first. The Gospel came to each village in similar fashion to the biblical record that Jesus went into all the villages in the countryside of Galilee (Matthew 9:35-36). Not all might choose to listen, but all would get the chance to hear.

In 1957 Weldon Culver showed me the map with a pin over the name of every village in the northern half of Taiwan. So having completed that job, the teams were already working in the southern half of the island. This kind of hard work can be done in any part of the world at any time. All we have to do is train the local people in an area, then send them out as preaching teams to reach their neighbors.

This aggressive all-out preaching of the Gospel and training of lay people for evangelism affected the Christian communities in the big cities as well as in the countryside. At Christmas 1950, when I first came to Taiwan, the capital city Taipei had only seven churches. At the end of the decade, by 1960, I found 115 churches listed in the telephone directory . . . 15 times more than before . . . a phenomenal church growth rate by anyone's estimation.

## Principles in a God-given Harvest

What are the lessons we can learn from all this? Here are some suggestions:

1. We must continue to evangelize. Every generation is responsible to evangelize the people of its era of time.

2.  We should work together. God gives maximum blessings when groups and people with various gifts work together. No church or group can do it alone; we need partnerships. Dozens of churches and organizations joined together to participate in the great harvest on Taiwan.

3.  We should send more missionaries. God commands missionaries to go to foreign cultures and countries. Seldom does anything dynamic happen without a missionary catalyst; someone has "to light the fire." The missionary cannot do it alone, however: but neither can the national. The commercial world calls it "a joint enterprise." God commands, "Go ye . . . ," and we do it together.

4.  We need the help of all nationalities. We need men and women of faith regardless of nationality. These are people who believe God and will use all kinds of legitimate means to proclaim the Gospel. Who will be the Dick Hillis of the next generation?

5.  We should blend with the culture. We need people who will respect their host cultures and do everything they can to learn how to function with them, so that they can communicate the Good News most effectively to its people.

6.  We should respect the host governments. We need men and women who will respect the host governments and be willing to work within any restrictions with humility and faith.

Therefore when a harvest comes again—a ripened harvest of souls—every effort should be bent to recruit as many laborers as possible into that harvest, wherever it might be. The harvest period historically is generally short. Jesus reminded His disciples that the night was coming when no one could work.

For everything there is a time (Ecclesiastes 3:1-8). For years missionaries might work in a given country with little or no fruit. The government might be oppressive, the people's hearts might be cold, and the doors might not be fully open. Then suddenly a government leader might open the door wide—General MacArthur in Japan, President Chiang in Taiwan, King Cyrus from his palace in Shushan in Persia, Pharaoh and Joseph in Egypt. For these reasons and for many others, such periods provide short times of spiritual harvest, as seen in the early days of the apostles of Jesus. The China Inland Mission's J. O. Fraser came to the Lisu people in southwest China at the turn of the century,[1] but the harvest would not come to them till many years later and in the ministry of Isobel Kuhn many decades later.[2]

In such blessed times people will respond to God in great numbers and we must lay aside all other trivial pursuits to join in the reaping of the harvest God has brought about in His time.

Dick Hillis was God's vessel to recruit many laborers for the harvest in Taiwan half a century ago. Today there are signs of a coming harvest in various places in the world. Open doors and responses to the Gospel seem to be approaching or already upon us in the moving of the Holy Spirit in certain countries where hearts are open and people are being saved. The need remains the same—prayer for more workers to enter into the harvest (see Matthew 9:36-38).

ENDNOTES:
1. Mrs. Howard Taylor, *Behind the Ranges, Fraser of Lisuland in Southwest China*, London: China Inland Mission, 1944.
2. Isobel Kuhn, *Ascent to the Tribes*, London: CIM, 1956; In the Arena, London: CIM, 1959; *Nests Above the Abyss*, London: CIM, 1947; and *Stones of Fire*, London: CIM, 1951.

# Chapter 15

## THE GOSPEL PENETRATES THE LAND OF THE RISING SUN

A gospel van pulling a large trailer prominently displaying the words *Seinin o Kiristo e*, meaning "Youth for Christ," maneuvered through the crowded Shibuya *eki* [Shibuya railway station] and parked in front of one of the world's busiest railroad stations. In the Spring of 1951 an estimated 1,500,000 people changed trains daily at the Shibuya *eki*, the connecting link of the major train lines of the Yamate and Chui systems which serve Greater Tokyo, the capital of Japan. What a choice spot to reach the multitudes with the Gospel of Jesus Christ! How did all this come about?

David Morken had moved with his family to Tokyo after they had finally received permission from the communist government to leave China. Those experiences during the communist times had been stressful, yet had afforded some of the greatest opportunities he had ever known in preaching the Gospel. Arriving in Japan in the fall of 1950, David eagerly launched an all-out evangelistic blitz to reach the Japanese people through the public preaching of the Gospel.

And God had prepared a prominent leader who would open the door that no man could shut. Just as God had used King Cyrus to open the door for the remnant of Israel to return to the Promised Land (Ezra 1), and God had used President and Madame Chiang Kai Shek to open up a magnificent harvest in Taiwan (Chapter 14), so God used the status of General Douglas MacArthur to send a wave of new missionary recruits to Japan and to other countries of Asia. The Japanese people revered the General not only as the military genius who had defeated them but as a man of great compassion and justice in the way he treated the conquered people. Immediately after the war ended, he set in motion a program to rebuild the shattered infrastructure and economy of Japan. The Japanese historically had been taught to regard their emperor almost as a god, so when Imperial Japan lost the war, the Japanese people looked on this man as a conqueror and benefactor at the same time. Crowds would stand in line daily in front of his military headquarters on "A" Avenue, located just outside the Imperial moat, in order to cheer the General when he left his office for the day.

General MacArthur insisted that Japan be rebuilt not just economically but in moral values as well. He made a famous speech calling on the American churches to send out 10,000 missionaries to the Far East. Evangelical America was greatly stirred by this appeal, and across the land from the Atlantic to the Pacific leading Bible schools and seminaries were flooded with students, primarily ex-servicemen from the recent war, preparing for missionary service.

Missionary yearbooks reveal that 10,000 new missionaries did reach the Far East in the decade that followed World War II (1945-1955), but many of them returned home after a short time because of difficulties that included getting along with one another and with the nationals, adjustment to the language of the host country, living in an alien culture, and traditional missionary policies. Some 4,000 actually reached Japan, but only one-quarter of them remained after a few years.

Some mission groups, both denominational and interdenominational, did not look favorably on the Youth for Christ approach of preaching to large crowds through organized crusades and calling for instant responses. They preferred to stress the traditional approach that church planting had to be done with a handful of people who would be instructed in the faith over an extended period of time. The debate over the effectiveness of reaching the Japanese people through crusades and large public meetings still goes on today (2002).

It was my privilege to coordinate the counseling and follow-up of English and non-Japanese languages in the 1994 Billy Graham Crusade in the Tokyo Dome, home of the Yomiuri Giants baseball team.

On the final Sunday afternoon more than 8,000 people, out of the 34,000 who came to the stadium, left their seats to come down to the playing field to record their commitments to Christ. This turned out to be one of the highest percentages of inquirers per total attendance (23.5%) of any meeting in the illustrious history of the Billy Graham Crusades. So Japanese do respond at public meetings when the message is clear, the Holy Spirit is working and the conditions are right.

## The Spotlight on Japan

When David first reached Japan in 1950, great excitement prevailed about the wonderful opening to reach the Japanese people with the Gospel of Jesus Christ.

General MacArthur and his staff were cooperative and favorable to Youth for Christ leaders, and David was able to get permission from local authorities to preach in public places such as the Shibuya *eki* area.

*We don't want someone just standing on a corner and hollering at a crowd of people,* thought David. *We want a first-class presentation of the Gospel, with the best of music, sound equipment and program format.*

David was highly experienced in organizing and controlling large evangelistic meetings, first through his directing of the Saturday Night Jubilees in Los Angeles (1946-1948), where 3,000 to 4,000 young people gathered each week in a huge double-balcony auditorium downtown. Second, he and Bob Pierce had handled crowds in China reaching 30,000 people. David sensed that now many of the war-weary, disillusioned Japanese young people were ready to respond to the message of Christ. For Japan, the harvest was now (1951).

As David prayed and dreamed, the thought came to him to build a stage and transport it to places like Shibuya *eki* and the other large railway centers of greater Tokyo. In the fall of 1950 Sam Wolgemuth from the YFC headquarters in Chicago took a gospel team on a world tour visiting various YFC fields in Europe and Asia. Hube Mitchell arranged meetings for the Wolgemuth team in India; Dick Hillis made arrangements on Taiwan, as well as in South Korea at the urging of Bob Pierce. Bishop Sam Wolgemuth, whose family owned an automobile parts business, came up with the right specifications for a trailer that could be converted into a gospel platform. Bob Pierce enthusiastically helped raise funds in America for the project; so the portable stage was built. The well-equipped trailer had its own generator to provide high quality sound and light.

David's dream had come true. In early 1951 the first meeting was held at the Shibuya *eki* and a large, curious crowd gathered in front of the stage platform on a cold winter evening.

*"Nan desu ka?* [What is this?]" someone asked his companion.

Suddenly there rang out a clash of cymbals and the purple drapes parted to reveal a beautifully decorated stage. A group of young musicians broke into song, accompanied by the wonderful sounds produced by an electric Hammond organ played by the talented Paul Goerke.

*"Subarashi desu nee!* [This is wonderful!]" someone else remarked loudly.

David Morken stepped up to the microphone, greeted the crowd through his interpreter and explained their purpose and the program to follow.

This was no ordinary street meeting. The program followed the format of the highly effective Saturday Night Jubilee rallies in Los Angeles. What appealed to the young people in America also appealed to the crowds, mostly young people, on the streets of Tokyo. The program included singing, testimony interviews, choir arrangements and a gifted Japanese soloist who sang about God's love before David as the evangelist gave a straightforward gospel message. That wintry night David preached from the Gospel of John to an audience that listened well. He quoted from memory the principal parts of the Scriptures used in his message.

At the close he invited those who wanted to receive the Lord Jesus into their hearts to raise their hands for prayer. Then he invited these people to make their way through the crowd and stand in front of the platform. This is not easy for the Japanese to do. Any preaching to a street crowd in a non-Christian culture encounters spiritual warfare. One could sense the tension, emotion and heart conflict taking place in individual lives. On this particular winter evening snow covered the pavement of the *eki* grounds; the chill in the air was matched by the coldness in the hearts of some of the listeners. Satan, no doubt, busily whispered in the ears of those who had been pricked in their hearts by the message from the Word of God, saying: "After all, we are Japanese. We don't need a foreign religion."

Some openly displayed their cynicism by their expressions, some merely laughed, while others just started to walk away. The majority always considers the preaching of the cross to be foolishness.

Yet the Spirit of God worked in some individuals. A trickle of people made their way forward, one woman obviously in tears, others following seriously and silently. Still others seemed to be coming more out of curiosity. Who can ponder the depth of the heart? An interesting feature was that there were more men than women among the seekers; most were young people. The Japanese had been taught from their youth to kneel before their emperor, but now David told the seekers to kneel before a holy God, acknowledging the Lord Jesus Christ as their personal Savior. After an intense inward struggle some proud Japanese men knelt in the snow. They were followed by the women, some dressed in the traditional kimono (the Japanese formal dress), then many students still wearing their school uniforms.

The Japanese counselors began mixing and speaking with the seekers; each counselor had a follow-up packet which included a Gospel of John, a "Bridge" explanation of salvation, the Gospel of John Bible study, memory verses on assurance and an invitation (with a map) to attend a special follow-up class in downtown Tokyo which would meet on Tuesday nights. The counselors explained the follow-up materials and prayed with each seeker.

My interpreter, Tsumo Tsukamoto, helped monitor the process. He and I dealt with the more difficult cases which were beyond the abilities of the counselors. This night was a fruitful meeting with more than 100 people registering their professions of faith, most of which were first-time decisions.

This type of meeting was conducted four times a week in a major *eki* [railway] center in the Tokyo area. David had been able to reserve space at the Tokyo, Ikebukuro, Shibuya and Shinjuku stations. This presented a marvelous opportunity to contact masses of Japanese people with the gospel message.

"We average more than 100 decisions a night at these outdoor meetings," David reported to the YFC leadership. "Send us more workers. Many Japanese young people feel guilty and helpless; their dreams have been shattered. They are disillusioned and ripe to receive the Lord Jesus Christ."

We held the follow-up meetings every Tuesday night in the auditorium located on the fourth floor of the *Asahi Shimbun* ["Rising Sun Newspaper"] building. The people attending were divided into three groups. The first-timers, usually about 15 to 20 people, went to a class that explained the Gospel and confirmed one's salvation commitment; Scripture memory was introduced and emphasized. The second-timers attended a class which also emphasized assurance of salvation and gave an introduction to a life of discipleship, which stressed a time of regular prayer and Bible study, as well as continuing to memorize Scripture. Coming to these follow-up meetings for the third time, the new believers joined a 10-week rotating series of classes.

Ten subjects were taught along with assignments for Scripture memory and Bible study. If anyone missed a particular teaching, he or she could make it up the next time around. Those who attended all the lectures, completed all their Bible studies and quoted all the memory verses correctly to their pastor or teacher were awarded diplomas. Those who faithfully attended the follow-up classes nearly always found their way into valuable service in their local churches.

Some time later we started an advanced Bible study class on Thursday nights in our home. Some of those who attended eventually became YFC staff members who helped in the evangelism and follow-up departments. After some weeks the local YFC staff grew to about 16 people, nearly all of whom had attended the YFC gospel meetings and the YFC follow-up classes. The follow-up staff served more than 30,000 people, who had finished at least one of the Bible study and Scripture memory courses. This momentum also supplied scores of fulltime workers for the churches and other Christian organizations. During this time period most young Christian workers you would meet anywhere in Japan would tell you that the YFC ministry had a positive influence on their lives.

Someone connected with the American military donated a huge circus-size tent to YFC, and David Morken decided to use it for a gospel tent meeting near the U.S. Naval base in Yokosuka, Japan for both Japanese civilians and American servicemen. After the large tent had been set up with the aid of some of the sailors from the base who had volunteered their off-duty time and the meetings had been widely advertised, news came that a strong typhoon was heading straight for Yokosuka. We were advised to take the tent down, but it had already rained so heavily that the tough tent was thoroughly water-soaked. To take it down in this condition would ruin it; furthermore, the meetings were scheduled to begin the next day. The team initially did not know what to do, so they did the only thing Christians are to do—they prayed —fervently and effectually.

We gathered our workers and volunteers together to pray and to determine the will of God. The prayer meeting began in the afternoon and some of the people remained to pray through the night; Warren Myers, whom Dawson Trotman had just assigned to Hong Kong,[1] was with us in Japan at this time for training and orientation for ministry in Asia, and was with us for this prayer meeting. We asked the Lord to turn the typhoon around so that we could begin the planned meetings. We were desperate yet confident that God would answer our prayers His way and to His glory.

Meanwhile, Jim Downing, one of the early Navigators and the captain of the USS *Patapsco*, was in the area with oher Navy ships on a special mission during the Korean War. He had received orders to take his vessel out of the path of the typhoon, but around midnight "an astonishing phenomenon was occurring," Jim wrote in his report. The typhoon, instead of altering its direction somewhat as it headed straight for Yokosuka, suddenly turned completely around and headed back out to sea from whence it had come, rather than curving to the north as these storms usually do. One of the weathermen at the Fleet Weather Central on the base remarked that he had never seen this happen before in all his experience. It also puzzled Captain Downing until Warren Myers told him that the YFC team and American servicemen were praying that night and beseeching the Lord to turn that typhoon around.[2]

The professional weathermen may not have understood what had happened, but we who prayed together in the tent that night firmly believed that God, who is the Lord of His creation, had turned that typhoon around.

So the meetings went on as scheduled amid great rejoicing and a wonderful spirit of expectancy among both the American military and Japanese communities. The tent had no floor, so we used traditional sawdust to cushion the ground and absorb the dust. The atmosphere resembled the great revival meetings in America nearly a century ago when sinners walked "the sawdust trail" to come forward to register their decisions for Christ. Every night unusually large crowds came into the tent and many responded to the invitation. We set up a dual system of counseling with the American servicemen going into one area and the Japanese civilians into another.

### Trophies of God's Grace

David Morken recalls one story: "One night, when the servicemen had filled one of the counseling rooms and the Japanese the other, as we were singing the last verse of the invitation hymn, I saw a street girl coming down the middle aisle. She looked like an old hag, for she was the most pathetic human being I had ever seen. I remember turning to one of our women interpreters and saying, 'Yamamoto-san, would you please lead her to Christ, and while you are doing that we will be praying for you.' And she did, as this awful-looking call-girl, by the name of Yashiro, was wonderfully converted and the angels of heaven rejoiced."[3]

She was only 25 years old. We learned that she had been sold by her parents into prostitution in order for the family to survive economically; she had been on all kinds of hard drugs. We did not know what to do with her, so we prayed; we asked everyone to pray—

team members, missionaries, Christian servicemen, Japanese Christians. Then a barber and his wife, who lived above their barber shop near the front gate of the Yokosuka Naval Base, invited her to stay in their home. This was a fantastic act of mercy to me, for the Japanese are so proud as a people and careful about their reputations; to invite this woman of ill-repute into their home went against every cultural norm. They did not even know whether she was terribly diseased or had any other serious physical or mental problems.

I recall how during that night every member of the team awakened to pray for that woman. When we gathered together the next morning, all of us shared our concerns for Yashiro-san. The following day we brought her to the Seventh-Day Adventist Hospital, and the doctor there was amazed to find that she was free of all diseases. So God had delivered her physically as well as spiritually. She was later baptized, served on the YFC staff, and went on for seminary training and full-time Christian service. She is one of the many trophies of the amazing grace of God.

Billy Graham has often observed, "The Gospel is preached to thousands, but people come to Christ one by one." Many other wonderful testimonies emerged out of those meetings. Yumiko Senno, who became the manager of our follow-up department, testifies that she received Christ at one of the YFC meetings in front of a railway station when she heard the Gospel for the first time in her life.

One late afternoon a young man came to my house and introduced himself as a graduate of our Bible study course; in fact, he had his diploma with him which identified him as Tsuchiya-san. He was a convert of the YFC prison ministry. He had just been released from prison and had no work nor a place to stay. Could he stay in my house? Now I had a family with two young daughters. A former prisoner stay in my house? Several verses, including 2 Corinthians 5:17, immediately flashed into my mind. "If any man be in Christ, he is a new creature: old things are passed away; behold, all things are become new".

"Dozo [please] come in, Tsuchiya-san, and I will introduce you to my family."

Tsuchiya-san stayed in my home that night. The next morning I took him with me to the follow-up office and put him to work, where he labored faithfully. After staying in my home for a few weeks, he found a place with other Christian brothers. He took on more and more responsibilities in the office, and he set up a special ministry for those in prison. Some years later he came to me and asked me to represent him as his father at his wedding, for his own father had died some years before. He married a lovely Christian staff worker in a local Baptist church, where he later became a deacon. Tsuchiya-san—another trophy of God's abounding grace!

## The Hi-BA Auditorium Youth Rally

The street meetings outside the railway stations and the tent meetings in Yokosuka were successful, but David Morken also wanted to see if the Saturday Night YFC Rallies in an auditorium setting would also work in Japan. He was able to book the *Kyoritsu Kodo* [Education Hall] in the student belt of downtown Tokyo for a Saturday night rally, inviting his friend Bob Pierce to be the main speaker.

The Hi-BA movement in Japan joined this venture with its leaders very enthusiastic in backing the project. The Hi-BA organization, "High School Born Againers," had been founded by Jack Wyrtzen of the Word of Life ministry in New York and had spread abroad to several countries, including Japan. The Hi-BA staff members went into the high school grounds in the central Tokyo area and distributed thousands of handbills announcing the teenage rally. College students in the university belt also were invited, but the meeting was particularly aimed at the high school population. The doors were set to open at 5:00 P.M. and the meeting was scheduled to start at 5:30, because once the students had gone to their homes from their schools, they would not return to the heart of the city.

At 4:30 P.M. John Rhoads and I ventured out into the streets to see if the students were coming. John is an evangelist and has been a colleague of mine for many years in all of Asia. About two blocks before we reached the auditorium we saw students already in line waiting to get in; the queue reached all the way around the block and down the next street. After a great musical program and special interest items for teenagers, Bob spoke with his usual passionate heart about Jesus and the Gospel. At the invitation that night more than 250 students came forward to receive Christ. Our YFC follow-up workers and the Hi-BA leadership joined together in the counseling and follow-up ministry.

The auditorium youth rallies would continue for several years, about once a month or whenever a Youth for Christ speaker would be visiting Tokyo. Many high school converts would find their way into the Hi-BA fellowship groups and into the local churches where they would become active.

## Youth for Christ World Congress, 1953

The high water mark of public evangelism in Japan was the enormous undertaking of the YFC World Congress in 1953 to saturate the whole nation with the Gospel. So every *ken* [province] of Japan was targeted for a series of cooperative evangelistic meetings. Japan has 46 provinces.

We were involved in intensive preparations for these meetings for six months. I recall that at one stretch I traveled for 40 days by train, city by city, staying in some local *kyokan*-style hotel and sleeping on *futon* [mats] on the *tatami* floor (no beds or furniture in a typical Japanese inn), enjoying the hot *ofuro* [bath] daily, eating mainly rice and fish. I traveled with Tsukamoto-san or Ito-san (my co-workers attached to the YFC staff) or occasionally with an American staff worker. We generally met with a group of pastors and lay leaders in a given city to discuss strategy and plans for the coming evangelistic meetings. We also introduced our counseling and follow-up procedures; we promised a team made up of three to five gifted westerners would provide the preaching, teaching, and music. We would bring our own interpreters.

We also discussed finances. The westerners would pay their own way, but we would take up a public offering to pay for local crusade expenses, so all funds would stay in the locale where they were given. We would *sodan* all the issues together. (The concept of *sodan* is a typical Japanese cultural form of group decision making in which the members discuss and suggest alternate proposals until a general agreement is reached; members may not oppose another person's viewpoint, but talk around it. The closest English term for this process is "consensus." Christian groups would add prayer to their *sodan*.)

This kind of evangelism was new to most of the Japanese pastors and church people. We learned that the evangelical church in Japan was very small, with 30 members being considered a large church. Yet we never went away empty-handed; we were always invited to come and conduct these meetings. Then after a long evening of *sodan* and a night in the inn, we would board the train next morning for the next destination.

My team and I worked mainly in the southern *kens* while YFC staffer John Rhoads and his team worked the central and northern *kens*. We operated on a tight budget. Sometimes to conserve money we slept on trains between cities to save hotel bills. It was a weary and tiring ministry away from our families, but we were kept going by the anticipation of the Gospel being preached simultaneously in every *ken* of Japan.

More than 600 delegates came to Tokyo in August 1953 to attend the Youth for Christ World Congress on Evangelism. After a thrilling week of preaching and teaching in Tokyo, the delegates were assigned to gospel teams to preach in every one of the 46 *kens* in the country. (Eventually only Kumamoto-ken canceled out because of recent devastation by floods from a typhoon.)

This was the largest and widest gospel thrust ever attempted by the Youth for Christ movement, and from my observation one of the most successful. It proved to be highly effective through the prayers, work, and faith of many Christians, Japanese and American.

I believe the follow-up for this massive project was the most thorough we had ever attempted. Our Navigator staff arranged all the materials for teaching counselors and for the follow-up. We prepared the way months in advance by organizing 300 groups of counseling classes extending to every province in Japan; all participants were taught the four-lesson counselor course. So trained counselors were ready for every meeting.

All seekers were to be given a Gospel of John, the Gospel of John Bible study and Scripture memory packets on assurance. They would then send in the completed study to our office in Tokyo, where 15 trained follow-up workers were assigned on a full time basis to grade the returned lessons.

Simultaneously we arranged that the decision cards would be assigned to a particular church in an area, and its people would be responsible to follow up each seeker. Then we encouraged the pastors in their follow-up efforts and asked them to let us know which of the seekers actually linked up with their church. We were delighted with the response of the pastors, which accounted for thousands of individuals who made the transition from a decision to receive Christ in a public place to a participation in the regular services of a local church.

In crusade evangelism we always hope for some of the seekers to make this transition, but in this case we have records that more than 4,000 actually found their way into a local church fellowship. It was a great reward for all the faithful labor of many people, both Japanese and American. Most of these more rural people had come from a background of idolatry, so to get 4,000 out of the 22,000 who made decisions (18.2%) is a very high percentage of fulfillment in this kind of ministry of public evangelism with adequate follow-up.

## Characteristics of YFC Work in Asia

Levon Melkonian, loaned by The Navigators to Youth for Christ in India to handle the follow-up work there, had prepared a list of the characteristics of the YFC work in Asia in that era. These observations would apply to the work of YFC in Japan as well.

- Enthusiasm

- Strong national and regional leadership

- Vision by predecessors (usually western) and on-the-job-training

- Strong interest by everyone in evangelism, follow-up and investing in the lives of new believers

- No barriers between national and foreign workers, even in their living quarters

- Women being incorporated into leadership positions and taking responsibility

- Openness in sharing among the leadership, both national and foreign

- Concern for the established churches and keeping good communication with them at all times

- Strong emphasis on prayer and prayer groups

- Mass rallies to train the leadership and to reach out to the cities and to the nation

- Minimum of casualties among national workers

- A strong yet humble national leader (Victor Manogarom in India)

- Foreigners willing to make themselves dispensable and willing to work alongside and under national leadership

- Strong interest in working harmoniously with other churches (local and denominational) and other groups through training pastors and leaders and seeing talent developed in different areas

ENDNOTES

1. At this point in time (1952-1953) Dawson Trotman and The Navigators had sent some of their key men to work with other organizations and asked me to give them orientation and training before they went to their new fields. I did that in the midst of the YFC meetings in Japan. These are the five men sent out for orientation and then to other Asian fields:
   - Doug Cozart to South Korea
   - Levon Melkonian to India
   - Nate Mirza to India, then Iran
   - Warren Myers to Hong Kong, then Vietnam
   - Marlin Nelson to South Korea
2. Taken from Jim Downing's forthcoming book, presently in manuscript form, Chapter 15, page 3.
3. Reported in a private interview with Roy and Phyllis Robertson.

*Planning for World Congress on Evangelism in Japan, 1953.*

*Kenny Joseph, Frank Ineson, Dale Cryderman, Roy Robertson, Ken Swanson, Andy Huff, A.E. Mitchell, Paul Goerke, John Rhoads, David Morken, Sam Wolgemuth*

# Chapter 16

## FAITHFUL TO THE END

### David Morken

After the 1953 YFC World Congress, David, who had been out in Asia for five-and-a-half years, went back to the United States for a while with his family to get his older daughters enrolled and settled in college. One attended Wheaton College and the other went first to Moody and then on to Wheaton College. Then he received an invitation to speak at a pastors' conference in Germany arranged by Dr. Bob Evans, the European YFC director. After that engagement, Billy Graham asked David to come to London to meet with the pastors there in preparation for the coming crusade to be held at the Harringay Arena.

The Billy Graham Crusade in London developed into the largest and longest cooperative evangelistic crusade ever attempted up to that time. It continued night after night for 12 weeks and still stands as the longest crusade in Graham's ministry. It became the launching pad for the phenomenal international crusade ministry that God enabled Billy Graham to have over the past four-plus decades. The Navigators follow-up staff alone comprised 14 people headed by Dawson Trotman and Lorne Sanny, and included the secretary who later became my second wife after Lois' death. Phyllis, in fact, recalls an inspirational message David gave on the subject of "wooing," retaining a deep first-love relationship with our Lord Jesus Christ.

It was my great privilege to serve on that follow-up staff from February to June 1954. After the other staff left, I remained in England for an extra month to coordinate a district by district visitation program. During the Crusade counselors had talked face to face with the more than 34,000 people who had registered their decisions for Christ at the Harringay meetings and the larger numbers at Wembley Stadium. Graham went on to have many crusades with a much larger attendance, but few with this intensity of preparation and follow-up. With the anointing of God, this crusade shook a city and a nation to get right with their God, their Maker and Redeemer.

During the crusade the people of London became so caught up with this "new" approach to evangelism that a common question to ask any stranger that you met on the street was, "Have you been?" Everyone understood that to mean, "Have you been to Harringay Arena to hear the message of personal salvation through Jesus Christ preached by Billy Graham?"

While in London, David felt that God wanted him back in Asia to preach in crusades that would include more thorough preparation among church people and more complete follow-up of the seekers.

David recalls, "But I didn't dare tell anyone. The only man I could tell was Daws. We were at Glen Eyrie [The Navigators headquarters in Colorado] and spent some time talking about my vision. I had a train to catch shortly so I said, 'Daws, I still have to talk to you.'

"We were going up to Denver to catch the train, so I said, 'Daws, will you come with me on the train so we can talk?' He agreed, so he and I sat together and I told him the burden on my heart—to have crusades in the large cities of Asia with proper preparation and effective follow-up. Daws had a way about him all through the years, that when I would share a vision with him, he would never pour cold water on my ideas. He always entered into my dream wholeheartedly and encouraged me. I think he's the only man I have ever known with whom I have felt free to share any vision that I had, knowing that if there were any corrective measures needed, he would be free to suggest them. But the main thing was his capacity to see the big picture right along with me.

"Daws said, 'David, we will provide secretaries for you; we will provide anything you need; and we will work right alongside with you!'"

So David returned to Asia and planned crusades in some of the area's major free cities. Daws sent me from Taiwan, where I had been assisting Dick Hillis, to help David in the follow-up work of four city-wide crusades in Indonesia. We held these in sports centers or stadiums of four major cities on the island of Java—Jakarta, Surabaya, Solo and Bandung. In each I taught counselor classes and rejoiced to see nearly 1,000 seekers come forward to receive Christ in each of these predominantly Muslim cities during the crusades.

This kind of crusade, where people come forward not for the hope of healing or receiving some kind of gift, but simply to believe on and receive the Lord Jesus Christ for personal salvation, had never before been seen in Indonesia, according to local church leaders. In addition, the individual counseling which seekers received regarding their decision for Christ was new as well.

In fact, when I met with pastors to arrange for the counseling classes, they usually asked, "What is your gimmick? What sort of special advertising will you use to get people to come . . . Healing? Pop singers? Movies?"

"No," I would reply, "We will just preach the Gospel and urge people to believe in Jesus for salvation."

"They won't come to hear the Gospel," was the opinion of most.

But they did come! I have observed time and again in all my experiences in public evangelism in Asia that the message of salvation by grace through faith does attract crowds when the right preparations have been made and the Spirit of God is at work.

I stayed in Indonesia for an extra month, not teaching classes, but in a hospital bed with a severe case of hepatitis. I could scarcely stand when I returned to my home in Taipei. The intense physical and spiritual pressure of crusade-type living, coupled with Asian food and the tropical climate, took its toll even more severely on David's body.

With the full cooperation of President and Madame Chiang Kai-Shek, Dick Hillis set up a major citywide crusade for David in Taipei, the capital of Taiwan. Under Dick's leadership the crusade committee built a temporary tabernacle, seating several thousand, right across from the President's building. David preached in the tabernacle every night for four weeks. During the first two weeks the meetings were interpreted into Mandarin, then interpreted into the Taiwanese dialect for another two weeks. With strong endorsement by government leaders and all the churches, the meetings were extremely productive.

At one of the meetings a man came forward to receive Christ who was known as "The King of Pickpockets." He not only experienced true conversion, but went on to become an evangelist for the Lord. After the meetings in Taipei David went to central Taiwan as the main speaker (for the sixth time) at the Sun Moon Lake annual missionary conference. When he returned to Taipei, he was physically drained. He had lost 50 pounds and the doctors could not diagnose the problem. Astonished at the appearance of his fellow-worker, Dick exclaimed one day, "David, you look like a ghost!" To those of us who knew him well, he did indeed look terrible.

Jim Dickson asked David to speak at the 90th Anniversary of the Presbyterian Mission in Taiwan, but because of his illness David declined and returned to Hong Kong. Jim made a special trip there to plead with David to reconsider. This was the first time in many years that they had invited a missionary to be the main speaker, and, furthermore, Jim stated, "You are not even a Presbyterian missionary!" David consulted his physician, Dr. Sam Rankin, who finally gave his permission if David would remain in bed resting while not speaking. So he went back to Taiwan.

Bob Pierce stopped by in Taiwan around this time to visit the work and found David at the Presbyterian conference. At this point David was all booked for two years of evangelistic crusades and conferences, but Bob spoke up immediately and emphatically, "David, you must cancel every one!"

Despite David's scheduled trip with Bob to Korea, Bob quickly arranged for him to go straight to the Mayo Clinic in Rochester, Minnesota.

After weeks of tests, they determined that David had tropical sprue, a disease in which some of the body's digestive juices have dried up and the victim is unable to digest his food properly. His days of intensive front line evangelistic effort in Asia were over. Like John the Baptist and many other prophets and evangelists before him, David had burned himself out preaching Jesus to the multitudes. But what an evangelist! God had raised him up in a strategic time in history to carry the clear message of the Gospel to multiplied thousands in Asian countries.

In later years David would review his calling into different kinds of cultures and in a variety of circumstances:

"When I first went out to the mission field, I felt burdened to go to the ends of the earth. I listened to the challenge for missionary work among the jungle people living in darkness and Satanic oppression and that night I heard the heart cry of God saying, 'Let My people go that they may serve Me!'

"Now I realized that they belonged to God by every known law of proprietorship, but they did not know Him. They were separated from Him by sin, by ignorance, by superstition, by everything.

"And God was saying to me, 'David, I want you to go and open their eyes and turn them from darkness to light, from the power of Satan to God, that they might worship Me' [see Acts 26:18], and that's why we went.

"But when we left China to go to Japan, the great burden then was to lay the claims of Christ before this proud, educated people . . . just the simple claims of Christ . . . and here are the evidences!"

David would also recall how Daws's influence changed his life toward the importance of memorizing and meditating on the Word of God.

"When we came back from Sumatra the family had memorized certain Psalms and prayers, but I felt that this memorizing the Word was the weakest part of my whole life and ministry. As Daws and I talked one day I said, 'Daws, I really can't memorize!'

"He replied, 'Yes, you can!'

"As we went back and forth on this, he finally asked, 'Do you know your name?'

"And I said, 'Yes!'

"So he declared, 'You memorized it!' Then he asked, 'Do you

know the alphabet?'

"Again I said, 'Yes!'

"'Well, you memorized it! Do you know your times tables?'

"'Yes, I do,' I admitted.

"'Well, you memorized them!' Then he began to remind me how I memorized these things by repetition in first grade and second grade and even before that.

"After a while he stated, 'If you will do that with the Scripture, just committing it to memory and reviewing it over and over again, it will be written on the table of your heart.'

"And that was one of the turning points in my life, for Scripture memory became part of my whole being. It became a foundation for my Bible study, not a substitute for it. Scripture memory gave me a tremendous foundation for meditation on God's Word, whether it was the study of a book, or a chapter, or a paragraph, or the cross-reference for a verse. I owe so much to Daws for changing the direction of my whole ministry."

At 91 years of age David Morken still speaks at Bible conferences and church services. He resides in Lodi, California.


## Hubert Mitchell

Hube, David's older brother-in-law, remained in close contact with him throughout the years. David had followed Hube into the jungles of Sumatra where he joined him in the ministry to the Kubu people.

Hube, a great man of prayer and praise, also became a close friend with Dawson Trotman as they met together before daybreak weekly for morning prayer during the war years. Each added a dimension to the spiritual life of the other. Sometimes as they prayed earnestly together, Hube would lift his great resonant voice in a shout, beseeching God to hear their cry. Daws, on the other hand, might pray in a barely audible whisper to sense the intimacy of a caring God. These men were so different in their backgrounds and learning, yet so close in heart and purpose.

Hube's zeal for evangelism inspired Daws, and Daws's discipline of memorizing the Word of God in a regular and consistent manner challenged Hube.

I recall an occasion when Daws took some of his staff to visit the families of Hube and David on a festive holiday occasion. What a joyous time of singing and sharing and feasting! While the ladies cooked a sumptuous meal, the men talked and planned future activities. After a heavy meal and an extended time of conversation, someone asked Hube if he wanted to retire for some rest.

"Rest?" shouted Hube. "We've got all eternity to rest! Let's get on with the plans and do the work of God!" So with a chuckle and renewed enthusiasm the planning continued.

The indomitable spirit of Christ drove Hube forward enthusiastically to carry the gospel message into the very heart of territory claimed by Satan—into the jungles of Sumatra, into the dead-end streets of Los Angeles, into the heart-rending filth of Calcutta, or into the luxurious inner offices of executives in modern America. Wherever he went, he gave a bold, enthusiastic witness for Jesus Christ.

Hube used to say, "Whenever you are tempted by the Devil, give a bold public witness. That will give you victory over the sins of the flesh."

After he became committed to Scripture memory, he would often quote, "Thy Word have I hid in mine heart, that I might not sin against Thee" (Psalm 119:11).

Challenged to memorize by Daws, Hube eventually learned by heart the entire Gospel of John, the Epistle to the Hebrews, and the Book of Revelation. When he preached publicly, he often quoted long portions of Scripture from memory. "When you get the Word into your heart," he would often say, "you can get your heart into the Word."

After Daws's death in 1956, Hube exhorted Lorne Sanny, the new director of The Navigators, not to let go of the foundations on which the lives of Daws and his men were built, namely, memorizing and claiming the promises of God. Even while in his 80s Hube maintained a telephone ministry with government leaders in Washington, D.C. He would call many of them daily and pray with them over the telephone regarding their personal needs.

The Lord called Hubert Mitchell home to his eternal reward at the age of 89 on October 27, 1995.

## Dick Hillis

Next to Daws, Dick had the most direct impact on my missionary life and vision. While Daws was my mentor in the Word and in discipleship, Dick was the one who introduced me to the basic ideas and concepts I hold to this day concerning missions. When I arrived in Shanghai as a "green" missionary who knew nothing about Chinese languages and culture, Dick took me under his direction and guided me step by step into becoming a knowledgeable missionary. Dick had reached into his own pocket and sent the first $100 to provide for my missionary passage to China.

Not only did Dick tutor and train me when I arrived alone in Shanghai, but he introduced me to the China Inland Mission compound and its residents, provided me with a place to stay, and subsequently helped me find a place of my own. Through his eyes and ears I could interpret the momentous flow of events that overthrew centuries of Chinese traditional ways of thinking as the Communists swept to power in that vast land.

Dick worked as a servant-leader who raised up and trained evangelists, both national and missionary. An opportunist, he sent out gospel teams into the abundant harvests of mainland China and Taiwan. He set up the meetings for Bob Pierce and David Morken which met with such phenomenal success first in China, then on Taiwan. He was so approachable and relaxed that anyone meeting him for the first time did not realize his importance or influence. In his humility he always gave credit to every other worker but himself.

He was an encourager, a "lifter-upper," and one who blended with the Chinese as easily as he did with western missionaries. He was one of the very few missionaries whose Chinese pronunciation was so perfect that he could even fool a native Chinese over the telephone as to his nationality. Once this linguistic gift saved his life when Chinese bandits challenged him in the dark and he passed for a Chinese farmer.

In the field of missiology Dick taught me everything I know. In the field of follow-up Dick apparently considered me to be a disciple of Daws, the "expert," so he backed me fully with time, energy and money in everything we ever proposed or tried to put into practice. From my own perspective and experience never has a missionary leader backed his field people more fully than did Dick Hillis.

Dick also established a mission—Overseas Crusades—that has had such outstanding success in Taiwan and great effectiveness since in all of Asia. Then he returned to the United States to send out missionaries around the world through the mission that he had founded, today called O. C. International.

So at the end of this great era of public evangelism the Lord chose to leave Dick here on earth to start and direct a worldwide mission for the glory of God and the spread of the Good News of salvation to the ends of the earth.

## Dawson Trotman

As mentioned in Chapter 4, Daws nearly drowned in a lake as he tried to rescue a young lady when their canoe overturned. This near brush with death helped him to seek the Lord for salvation.

God then gave him 30 years of an exceedingly fruitful and reproductive ministry. The other men in this book, particularly David Morken and Dick Hillis, looked to Daws as their spiritual mentor. In due course of time God used Daws to found the work of The Navigators and to be a major influence on all of Christendom by emphasizing the importance of Scripture memory and follow-up of new believers. He is the only man I think I ever met who really believed that a given generation of "down-to-business" Christian disciples could reach the whole world for Christ. And he had a clear plan for accomplishing this—continue to preach the Gospel faithfully in churches and in public meetings to reach the masses of people who do not attend church; and in addition, to apply the principle of spiritual multiplication in the teaching and training of the follow-up ministry.

Daws called it "born to reproduce."[1] Each Christian should disciple another and train him or her to raise up another faithful man or woman who would then teach others also (see 2 Timothy 2:2). If every Christian were faithful in reaching just one other person with the Gospel, then training him (or her) to reach another person to repeat the process, then the world could be reached in 33 or 34 reproductive cycles. If each one reached and equipped another over a period of one year, the world's population could be reached in the lifetime of one generation.[2]

Thirty years after God saved him out of the water, Daws was speaking to a Navigator conference at the Word of Life Island on Schroon Lake, New York in 1956. It was a conference grounds directed by Jack Wyrtzen. Jack took Daws and several of the conferees on a motorboat ride out on the lake. As they climbed into the boat, Daws asked the conferees if anyone could not swim. One young woman said she could not, so Daws sat next to her just in case.

In the middle of the lake the motorboat took a sudden sharp turn and Daws and the young woman were thrown out of the boat into the water. Daws grabbed hold of her and began to tread water rapidly. Although never a good swimmer because of his underdeveloped legs and heart condition, he held her up, pumping furiously, till the motorboat circled back to pick them up. Only a few minutes later, hands pulled the girl back into the boat and other hands reached out to grab Daws. They took hold of his thick bushy hair, but lost their grip, and Daws sank to the bottom of the lake, which was 40 to 50 feet deep at that spot.

A diving crew recovered his body the next day. His wife, Lila, thinks that he probably suffered a heart attack during his all-out effort to save another person.

Was this a preventable accident or was it God's perfect time for this dramatic homegoing of His faithful servant? We know that "our times are in His hands." *Time* magazine gave prominent coverage to the death of this Christian leader with the very appropriate caption:

"Always Holding Someone Up!"[3] He died as he had lived—giving up his life for others.

## Bob Pierce

One of my vivid memories of Bob Pierce was when he stood on the platform speaking to the delegates of the Berlin World Congress on Evangelism in 1966, which was sponsored by the Billy Graham Evangelistic Association. This great missionary statesman had spent his life for the cause of missions and the worldwide advance of preaching the Gospel. He had been criticized severely and suffered much, but was dearly loved by the thousands of people he had helped— missionaries, national leaders, the orphans, the poor and the afflicted. As we listened to this weary missionary statesman, he was speaking about death and sacrifice.

"The success of any missionary enterprise is built on the graves of those who have tried and failed." Bob was speaking the truth out of the experience of a broken heart.

While in Japan, earlier in his life, Bob had written inside his Bible cover, "Let my heart be broken with the things that break the heart of God." After that day Bob always spoke out of a broken heart. Franklin Graham reports that this was still Bob's prayer very near the end of his life.[4]

Bob also challenged the delegates, who came from all over the world to Berlin, to be servants of one another. He said, "There are ten men eager to stand on the platform to speak for every one man willing to build the platform!"

Not only was Bob a great compassionate speaker and doer of missions, but he was a platform-builder as well. He provided the means for many others to stand on the platform and preach the Gospel as well as go to the mission fields of the world.

He not only poured hundreds of thousands of dollars into missions through the World Vision organization, which he had founded, but he was also the main person representing the overseas YFC work to the American home base. He had complete faith in God to provide help to meet the physical and emotional needs of his co-workers.

When David Morken needed a trailer to bring the Gospel to the Japanese railway centers, Bob appealed to his constituency in America who then provided the funds. When Youth for Christ in India needed tents for their evangelistic meetings, Bob furnished them with five tents each seating 1,000 people. When YFC in Japan needed an office building in Tokyo for their massive follow-up ministry, Bob gave them the money to purchase a two-story building in the student area of the city. Bob's God-given talent to raise funds supported 20 out of the 25 staff workers in Japan and 22 YFC national staff in India. He purchased a "Crossroads" center for The Navigators' college work in Taipei, and behind the scenes financed many innovative evangelistic and follow-up projects in Asia and around the world.

Not only did he support many national workers and projects, but he also took special delight in entertaining missionaries. He would never take them to an ordinary fast-food noodle house, but would rent a banquet room in a luxurious hotel and invite his friends, the front-line missionaries, to bring their spouses to a banquet of loving fellowship and fine food that would be completely "out of sight". For many a hard-pressed weary missionary couple, it was a little foretaste of heaven.

"This is a special gift from some of my friends who want you to know that they appreciate the love and sacrifices of our beloved American missionaries," Bob would explain in such a way that everyone would feel comfortable.

It wasn't just a time for eating good food, for the evening would include testimonies, singing, sharing of prayer needs and victories, and a special chat when Bob would share his heart and give insights on the overall missionary picture.

No one has yet replaced this servant of God who brought together so many diverse groups of missionaries just to fellowship with one another and with the Lord, without pushing any kind of organizational agenda. He brought to near-perfection the interdenominational cooperativeness begun by Hudson Taylor over a century ago.

In an interview that my wife, Phyllis, and I had with Lorraine,

Bob's wife, she shared with us her reminiscences on what her husband was like: "What thrilled and excited Bob was God's great plan. God sees the future and allows us to see just a glimpse of what He is doing."

Part of Bob's philosophy of ministry was to discover where God was at work, then jump right into the middle of it. The wonder and awesomeness of God at work fascinated this man, yet he trusted God to provide those ordinary things with which we need to do His work.

Lorraine went on: "In these modern times with TV and the other media there does not seem to be much need to trust God explicitly. Today, people get a budget and go. They sit down with scripts and put together polished programs.

"Bob was pure compassion. He was not polished or sophisticated. He didn't want to be. He wanted to be 'a people person.' There is a needy, hurting world out there and we have the answers. The human heart needs love, and we, through the Holy Spirit, can supply that love. Words spoken under the power of the Holy Spirit save and comfort. There is no need to be professional, for God uses people to reach out and touch those who are hurting."

Lorraine recalled further: "He died with his suitcase packed and a folding wheelchair by his bed as he said, 'Don't tell me the world is evangelized. Only a drop in the bucket. Don't tell me there are not cries in the night. The children are still crying and there is a job to do. Though we have been doing it almost 2,000 years, we still need to do it.'"

Lorraine concluded our interview with: "He was ready to go when he died at 63. He had a peculiar calling and talked about having a great missionary special on a TV program called 'The Morning Coffee Hour.' He and I would sit at the breakfast table and talk about missions when people dropped in.

"He did not take care of his body. His annual exam revealed leukemia and he was told to take it easy. He didn't like to see the doctors because they would only try to stop him. His hope was that he would die in his task and not in a hospital bed. Pat Robertson once asked if they might tell the people to pray for him on The 700 Club.

'No,' Bob replied, 'God knows my time; my times are in His hand. There are many friends in heaven I want to see. When the job is finished, I want to sit down with Jesus and my friends.'"[5]

God called Bob Pierce to his heavenly home on September 6, 1978. His friends were not only in heaven, for his friends here and Christian leaders from around the world came to his memorial service to pay homage to a great missionary heart.

These five men—David Morken, Hubert Mitchell, Dick Hillis, Dawson Trotman, Bob Pierce—were knit together by a common vision and a heart burden to get the Gospel out into the whole world in their generation. Most of them at one time or another met together in weekly sessions at five o'clock in the morning for extended prayer, and there, at the Mercy Seat of Almighty God, they learned to love and honor one another. They were all strong individuals and quite different in gifts and personalities. Even though each became a leader in his own particular group, in any crisis they would cling together and encourage one another.

These heroes of the faith—David, Hube, Dick, Daws, Bob—gave their lives in seeking to get the Gospel out to the whole world in their generation, and they inspired many American servicemen who had come to the Lord in World War II and the Korean War to join in the effort. These men were the catalysts and those whom they trained have kept the mission going to the present day.

Now as a new generation enters the 21st century we believe God will surely call others to pick up the torch and carry the gospel light to the multitudes living in spiritual darkness. We must renew our efforts as we follow in the footsteps of all those who blazed the trail before us, for Jesus said, "Occupy till I come" (see Luke 19:13).[6]

ENDNOTES
1. See Dawson Trotman, "Born to Reproduce", a conference message originally given at the Back to the Bible Broadcast, Lincoln, Nebraska, Spring 1956; printed by Back to the Bible Broadcast, 1956, and NavPress, Colorado Springs, Colorado, 1975.
2. This is the mathematics of geometric progression: If you win one person to Christ and train him for a year, you now have two; if each of

you reproduces, then at the end of two years you have four, then 8, 16, 32, 64, 128, 256, 512, and in 10 years you'll have 1,024; at 20—1,048,576; at 30—1,073,741,824; and at 33 years you've reached the whole world!

3. *Time*, July 2, 1956, page 58-59.

4. Franklin Graham and Jeannette Lockerbie, *Bob Pierce: This One Thing I Do*, Waco, Texas: Word Books, 1983, pages 77 and 220.

5. Roy and Phyllis Robertson interview with Lorraine Pierce during the Youth for Christ International Reunion in Chicago, Illinois, October 21, 1988.

6. The Powerhouse Five

   a. David Morken, active in Youth for Christ for many years. He still preaches at Bible conferences, and lives with his wife, Wilma, in California.

   b. Hube became Director of "Go Ye" Fellowship, the missionary agency founded by his father, A.E. Mitchell. Hube went to be with the Lord on Friday, October 27, 1995.

   c. Dick, Founder of Overseas Ministries Inc., with headquarters in Colorado Springs, Colo. He prayed in thousands of dollars that went to send the Gospel by radio into Communist China. He and his wife, Ruth, live in California.

   d. Daws. Founded The Navigators which has beautiful headquarters and conference center at Glen Eyrie, Colorado Springs. Drowned on June 18, 1956. Scores of Christian leaders including Dr. Billy Graham came to his funeral at Glen Eyrie to give honor and thanks to God for his productive ministry.

   e. Bob. Founded World Vision and also the Samaritan's Purse. Went to be with the Lord on September 6, 1978.

# BUILDING UPON
# THE FOUNDATIONS

*1960 - 2002*

Discipleship and Training Pattern

# BACKGROUND

In part III we traced our five missionary heroes and their outreach and influence toward the great missionary advance in carrying the Gospel particularly into the largest countries of Asia. These men had a burden and a plan to reach multitudes through the vehicle of public evangelism that called for an open profession of faith linked with the importance of individual follow-up to preserve the fruit. In just 15 short years, 1945-1960, the Gospel made great inroads into the key cities of Asia.

Having begun a great evangelistic thrust, the movement needed to develop through discipleship and training patterns. In the section covering about 40 years (1960-1999), both the missionary and national leaders sought to build upon these foundations. The apostle Paul charged his followers with these sober words—"According to the grace of God which is given unto me, as a wise masterbuilder, I have laid the foundation, and another buildeth thereon. But let every man take heed how he buildeth thereupon. For other foundation can no man lay than that is laid, which is Jesus Christ" (I Corinthians 3:10,11).

So the building process has begun and still continues. Every man's work will be held accountable. We must not build shabbily but solidly, because the work will be tested by fire.

The new converts and emerging Christian leaders, both missionary and national, must be discipled using the eternal spiritual materials called gold, silver and precious stones. And then they must be equipped and trained to continue to penetrate the world with the glorious Gospel of salvation.

In this section notice how the Lord gave a variety of plans and methods that were adopted to fit the different cultures.

# Chapter 17

## A FAITH WALK

*Singapore is only 16 miles across; I can walk it in one day,* I thought.

On that particular Sunday morning, November 11, 1962, I stood in front of the memorial that honored men killed in action during World War I. I counted the four steps that circle the monument, a reminder of the four years that Great Britain had fought in the war. Carved on the side of the memorial were only 162 names, not many because World War I was fought mainly in Europe. Still, 162 men had fought and died for the British crown, which no longer ruled over independent Singapore.

*Lord,* I thought, *if these men were willing to die for an empire that is already diminishing, surely there should be those in this land who will give their lives to follow the Lord Jesus Christ to receive an incorruptible crown that will never pass away.*

I recalled again the verse of Scripture that had brought me to the monument: "Arise, walk through the land in the length of it and in the breadth of it; for I will give it unto thee" (Genesis 13:17). In the tradition of Hudson Taylor and Dawson Trotman I have been taught to claim the promises of God. The Lord not only fulfilled His Word to the prophets and apostles of old, but He fulfills them now to anyone willing to walk by faith in the footsteps of these saints.

I had recently moved to Singapore with my family to open a work sponsored by The Navigators. God soon laid before me this promise which I claimed for Singapore island, which is not so large geographically. It stretches about 22 miles in length from east to west. There are few connecting roads to get through the rubber trees, small farms, and mangrove swamplands so it would be difficult to walk in the east-west direction. But from south to north it is just 16 miles from this World War I memorial at the gateway of Singapore harbor to the causeway bridge on the north side that leads into Malaysia. So I decided to make a faith walk of 16 miles to fulfill the blessing of this verse.

Looking out over the harbor as I strolled around Elizabeth Walk, now known as "The Esplanade," I saw hundreds of ships bound for all parts of the world. Singapore is the major crossroads for all of Asia. Ships traveling from Europe, Africa, and the Middle East to the Far East must pass through Singapore and in reverse as well.

I prayed silently, *O Lord, please send forth committed disciples and missionaries from Singapore who will go into every country where these ships unload their cargoes.*

I stopped to read some passages in my Bible, then quoted some verses from my Scripture memory pack as I continued the walk. Passing through the business center, I prayed again that the Lord would raise up strong, witnessing lay leaders.

The main thoroughfare leading north is Bukit Timah [Tin Hill] Road which is marked in the old British system at regular intervals by a series of milestones—large cement blocks several feet high on which are written in English the number of miles from the heart of the city. Passing by the fourth milestone, I came to the University of Singapore campus, a strategic place to claim for God. I recalled that Joshua walked around the walls of Jericho seven times, so I decided to make the circuit at least once while praying that God would raise up many disciples from the main university in Singapore.

Completing my circle, I crossed King's Road, passing within 100 feet of the house the Lord would give us in the future for our first training center. Near the 10th milestone I came to a traffic circle and chose the road that would take me to the border. About two miles from the border I came to Kranji Memorial, a large park with a memorial dedicated to those who gave their lives fighting against the Japanese who overran Singapore at the beginning of World War II. This memorial honors not just a hundred plus like those who died in World War I, but records more than 22,000 names of those who perished resisting the Japanese invaders.

As I reflected on the enormity of this sacrifice, I was stunned. And they died in a losing battle under an empire that is no longer ruling over Singapore.

*O God*, I pleaded earnestly, *O God, if 22,000 soldiers were willing to die for this kind of cause, temporary at best, I pray that you will raise up 22,000-plus men and women in Singapore who are willing to give their lives to serve the Lord Jesus Christ—true disciples who will witness faithfully for You—and let some of them go forth from Singapore as ambassadors for Christ into all the world.*

I then noticed the inscription carved on the monument, a paraphrase from Revelation 14:13, indicating that though these 22,000 are dead, " . . . they died not in vain, for their works do follow them."

*"Lord,"* I continued to pray in my heart, *"those who die for Jesus, shall bring forth fruit—thirty, sixty, a hundred fold—and receive an everlasting crown in glory".*

I reached the border just before sunset, reflecting on God's unchanging faithfulness, and returned by bus to my home.


## An Open Door in Singapore

Daws Trotman had taught his men to serve others first. So instead of setting out immediately to build a Navigator ministry targeting the prestigious University of Singapore, I first made myself available to serve different local churches and other Christian organizations within their own context.

Dr. Benjamin Chew, chairman of the Youth for Christ Board and an elder in the large Bethesda Katong Brethren Assembly, had sponsored my visa into Singapore. At his invitation, I began to teach a special discipleship course for young men who had finished the basic Cambridge system of education but had not yet entered the university. Another friend, Ben Sawatsky, a missionary under the Evangelical Free Church, arranged for my family to take over his apartment while he moved his family into their newly acquired church property. He invited me to teach a discipleship class in his Evangelical Free Church which he had recently planted.

The Singapore YFC national director, Liew Kee-Kok, asked me to help nurture new Christians at the Newton Life Presbyterian Church, so I chose the Book of Romans for this class. People got excited about learning and discussing the great doctrinal truths found in this magnificent book, and the class grew from 13 to 70 in a relatively short time. I also accepted a class assignment in the Baptist church.

So in my first year as a missionary in Singapore, I found my Sundays filled from morning to evening as I taught four different courses in four different denominational churches; and hopefully each group considered me a loyal part of their program.

Also during that first year Dr. Ernest Poulson, head of the Singapore Bible College told me that he urgently needed a teacher for courses in missions and personal evangelism. He had been a missionary in the Dutch East Indies, but was caught up in the political tensions between the Christian and Muslim Javanese factions during the turbulent days of the establishing of the newly independent Republic of Indonesia. Banished from Indonesia, Ernie Poulson moved to Singapore and founded this Bible college. He started with a dozen students, and by the time I arrived enrollment had grown to several hundred. So I consented to teach these classes as well.

When Youth for Christ needed a sponsor for one of their clubs, I agreed to be that person. To all of these activities, I added a Bible study class with my key men. One week my diary revealed that I had taught 16 classes—exhausting, yes, but what a blessing to have the opportunity to nurture and train so many eager and faithful young people and to have such favor from so many different Christian groups.

## A Man Named Joe

The major reason for all these opportunities and blessings may be found in the wonderful foundation laid earlier by Joe Weatherly and the Youth for Christ movement. It had swept across Singapore, influencing thousands of young people to make commitments for Christ. Joe's comparatively brief time in Singapore was something like the ministry of John the Baptist, who in biblical times was a blazing light that shook up the pillars of the religious establishment and called hundreds of people from all walks of life to make an open, public confession of faith in the coming Messiah (the Christ). Then when He came, John told them to follow Jesus.

In September 1956, at the time of Joe's coming, the Christian church population was listed at 3%. Although this city had large church buildings and Christian schools, the main denominations seldom gave open invitations for public commitment in either church services or school meetings. Very little church-sponsored gospel outreach existed in the city and in the government schools, so most new believers came from the children of church members. For one student to witness to another would be considered unusual, and the term "follow-up" simply was not used in a Christian context.

Today, some four decades later, the Christian population in Singapore is listed as 15%. The secular newspaper, *The Straits Times*, reported in a 1996 survey that one out every three students graduating from the English stream of education claimed to be a born-again Christian. More than half of the members of the medical profession are professing Christians. Discipleship is taught and practiced in nearly all the evangelical churches. Singapore has the reputation of being a safe, clean, moral, orderly and evangelized city—perhaps more so than any other city in Asia.

Dr. Benjamin Chew, a prominent Christian clergyman, commented that the ministry of Youth for Christ under Joe Weatherly changed the whole face of evangelism and discipleship in Singapore. Before he came few churches did much evangelism in the Sunday School and youth services. Through the influence of YFC this later became the accepted practice.

God used His servant Joe Weatherly to begin the process of this change. An All-State football player in high school, Joe attended the University of Alabama on a football scholarship and became a star player until he suffered a serious knee injury. So instead of pursuing a sports career, he went to Moody Bible Institute in Chicago where he met his future wife, Bernice. After their marriage, they moved to Minneapolis where he continued his education. While Bernice worked as secretary to George Wilson, a leader in the early YFC movement and later in the Billy Graham Evangelistic Association, Joe continued his schooling at the University of Minnesota. Later YFC tapped him to become one of their speakers. He remained active in the Minneapolis YFC ministry until transferred to Portland, Oregon to head YFC work in the Northwest area that included Alaska.

When Bob Pierce returned to Portland with a movie which he and Ken Anderson had made in China, it greatly challenged Joe's heart. Joe showed the film, "The China Challenge," to audiences all over the Northwest. The film so stirred him that he volunteered to take his family and work with China YFC alongside David Morken.

By then, however, the communists had overrun Shanghai. Instead of going to China, Joe and Bernice with their son Buster set up a YFC work in Bombay, India, right about the time that Hube Mitchell and his family returned to the United States on furlough.

Joe quickly organized an aggressive program of public evangelism in India. He acquired a huge circus tent and recruited Joe Stump, an English evangelist and close friend of Billy Graham, to hold large public meetings in many parts of India.

Joe Weatherly also had developed a special relationship with Daws who allowed him to reprint The Navigators "Topical Memory System" (TMS) in India. This was the only exception Daws ever made to allow someone else outside The Navigators to control this memory system. Joe had also learned from Daws the concept and ingredients of follow-up, so he developed some indigenous materials for new believers in India and a system for training counselors in that country.

Joe also realized the importance of training a national (a "Timothy") who would become a future leader, one who could take over the YFC work when he and other westerners might have to leave India. Once when Joe had gone to South India for some meetings, he was impressed with his young Tamil interpreter, Victor, who worked for a Christian book store.

"Victor," Joe told the younger man, "you ought to become an evangelist. You should work under YFC."

Through Joe's encouragement and help, Victor Monogaram, developed a YFC ministry among the Tamils in Madras, later becoming the YFC India Director. By the time Joe left for furlough after five years in India, the YFC ministry there had expanded into four major cities with about 32 national staff workers.

After furlough, Joe traveled with some YFC friends to other cities of South Asia looking for a new base. When he arrived in Singapore he met Gordon Scott, an elder of the Bethesda Katong Brethren Assembly, who invited him to speak to the large youth group in his church. After catching something of Joe's vision and talents, Gordon and the other elders, including Benjamin Chew, invited YFC to come to Singapore.

On reaching Singapore, Joe literally hit the ground running as he launched immediately into a very aggressive and high profile program. All the things that Joe had learned in leading YFC ministries in America and India—how to attract teenagers to hear and receive the Gospel, how to motivate them for undertaking new projects, and how to train them in turn to reach other teenagers—these Joe brought with him to Singapore. In addition, he made adaptations and innovations never before attempted.

After his arrival in Singapore, Joe's first priority was to start a weekly YFC club. Beginning with the Bethesda Katong Brethren Assembly leaders and the young people behind them, he recruited someone who lived near a high school to open his home for the kids to meet together before or after class. The students later were able to get permission to meet on their school campuses. The general format consisted of refreshments, games, quizzes and singing. Usually a short gospel message followed with an invitation to make a public commitment to receive the Lord Jesus Christ as one's personal Savior. In some clubs they garnered decisions for Christ nearly every week. Through this highly successful new plan the ministry soon grew to 23 YFC clubs, which blanketed all parts of Singapore.

The weekly YFC club meeting laid the foundation, but the Saturday night rally provided excitement and unique identity. Victoria Theatre, Singapore's most beautiful and prominent building, was newly decorated and housed a famous huge clock—easily the most distinguishable spot in all the city. Joe prayed that this theatre could be used to reach the youth of the city with the Gospel. With the help of influential friends, he booked it permanently for a semi-monthly rally on every other Saturday night of the year.

Secular performances seldom filled the 900-seat theatre, but usually every seat was taken with standing room only for the Saturday night YFC rally. Sometimes the crowd was so great that police locked the doors so no one would get hurt trying to squeeze inside or outside. This happened to me when I visited a YFC rally on one such occasion; it seemed quite strange to be locked up inside a gospel meeting.

Those who came forward at the rallies were counseled and followed up after the pattern Joe had inherited from Daws and The Navigators. New believers were introduced both to the Topical Memory System and to personal Bible studies.

## Keen Teens

Joe Weatherly had another novel idea. During the school holidays, he wanted to hold a youth camp and couple it with a teen-age gospel crusade. School buildings were usually empty during the holidays, so he obtained permission to use the Serangoon Garden Estate school for a week to house the students.

One floor became the boys' dormitory and another floor the girls' dormitory. They used the bottom floor for eating and for meetings. He filled the morning hours with teaching sessions and workshops. In the afternoon all the kids visited the homes of neighbors that surrounded the school inviting them to attend evening gospel meetings to be held outdoors on the school grounds.

The "Keen-Teen Crusade" generated great excitement as the teens were keen to give skits, songs and testimonies. On the first night about 55 people responded to the gospel message and came forward to receive Christ. It was a good start. During the week many others made public commitments to Christ, and this revival stirred up the neighborhood. The first Keen-Teen Crusade and similar ones to follow are still remembered fondly by those involved.

At the end of his first full year of YFC activities in Singapore, Joe reported that more than 7,000 kids had made professions of faith. The YFC movement that swept across Singapore on a grand scale had shaken the religious foundations of this very conservative city-state.

### *"Something to Die For"*

Yet the multi-talented Joe Weatherly had still another innovation in mind—a gospel film ministry. Joe had already witnessed the power of films to motivate young minds when he took *"The China Challenge,"* shot by Ken Anderson with Bob Pierce, to an American teenage audience. Since a movie had so powerfully influenced Joe to volunteer for missionary service, he met with the leaders of the Gospel Films ministry just before going to Singapore and arranged to obtain their new movie just being produced entitled *"Seventeen."*

Joe recalls that the film had to be "prayed in." With a highly advertised national premiere booked for a Sunday night, the film did not arrive in Singapore until Saturday afternoon, and YFC leaders had to obtain special permission to pass it through customs without it being reviewed first by the officials. So God, who has control over all governments, had His friendly emissaries stationed in the right places. I still remember that when I first saw *"Seventeen,"* I wept along with many others. It displayed God's love and forcibly portrayed the Gospel in a modern setting, as one teenager sacrificed his life to save a friend.

Then Joe invited his close friend Ken Anderson, who wrote the script of *"Seventeen,"* to come to Singapore with his production team to film a gospel story in this local setting that would appeal to teenage youth everywhere. The film, *"Something to Die For,"* with its original script from Ken's creative mind, used local YFC club members and staff in all the important roles except that of the villain. This tremendously successful film was followed by Ken's production of other films in various countries worldwide, including the American teenage peer pressure culture. Hundreds of teenagers in Asia, America and around the world have come to Christ through these gospel films.

## Building on Excellent Foundations

Building on this excellent foundation I arrived in Singapore in August 1962 with my wife, Phyllis, and our four children—Janet, Susan, Keith, Leonard. Later, our twins, Lee and Lila, were born in Singapore. With the help of Benjamin Chew, all my children were eventually placed in the Singapore local school system instead of the expensive American school which was far beyond my budget.

By the time I arrived, Joe had already trained and left in charge of the YFC work a talented young Singaporean, Liew Kee-Kok. Benjamin Chew's son Jim, who had a part along with his future wife, Selene, in the filming of "*Something to Die For*," had also been trained by Joe with the help of Warren Myers and Don Hardy of The Navigators to handle the follow-up.

My assignment as a missionary of The Navigators was to teach and demonstrate the concepts of discipleship and disciplemaking while serving YFC, the local churches and the Bible college. I negotiated with Liew Kee-Kok to transfer Jim Chew to work under my tutorship, and he would later become the director for The Navigators' work in Malaysia and Singapore.

The ideal formula for training future leadership in any part of the world is called "The Timothy Principle." It is found in 2 Timothy 2:2, "And the things that thou hast heard of me among many witnesses, the same commit thou to faithful men, who shall be able to teach others also." Besides "mentoring" Jim Chew, who had already been discipled by others, I "adopted" Su-Kim Han as a "Timothy," a spiritual son in the faith.

Su-Kim was only 16 years old, just out of middle school, when I invited him to live in my home because his widowed mother was physically unable to provide adequately for him. He lived with my family for four to five years while I trained him in my ministry and helped him through Singapore Bible College. He became one of the answers to the promises claimed on my "Faith Walk" to send forth missionaries to carry the Gospel from the shores of Singapore into other parts of the world. Su-Kim was the first fruits. After he faithfully served with me in the local ministry, The Navigators sent him to Japan as their first missionary to be sent abroad fully supported by local funds.

Another "Timothy" was Tom Lee. He was actually a spiritual grandson because he was trained by Harold Palmer, in whose life I had invested hundreds of hours while I was living with Dawson Trotman at The Navigators' headquarters in South Pasadena, California. Harold then married and took his young wife to teach in a Methodist high school in Singapore. He latched on to Tom and wrote to me that he had passed on to Tom, who was a keen disciple, everything that I had taught him. So when I reached Singapore, Tom eagerly waited to meet with me.

Tom's dad ran a small grocery store and coffee shop which was attached to his house in a typical "Chinatown" neighborhood. He worked long, hard hours and struggled to support his wife and three children. Tom, the oldest son, helped his dad at the store after school and early in the morning. Since it was a neighborhood store, the customers dropped in at all hours, usually to buy something they had forgotten to pick up at the main market.

So in order to get time with Tom, I would drop by his store to buy a few items, particularly kaya jam, as my wife, Phyllis, loved this mixture of coconut, eggs and unrefined sugar. Tom and I would slip away to some other place to spend an hour or so in the Word and prayer, then he would go back to help his dad. Occasionally, Tom would come to my house and meet with the other men and youth and sometimes spend the night.

After a couple of years into this busy and happy schedule of teaching many discipleship classes and spending regular individual time with "Timothies" like Su-Kim, Tom and several others, something happened which changed the direction of my life and ministry.

I had committed to memory the first eight chapters of the Book of Romans, and taught this great letter with enthusiasm in some of my classes. Now Romans 1:14 continued to prick my heart, "I am a debtor both to the Greeks and to the Barbarians, both to the wise and to the unwise."

I pondered this verse and reasoned: *My assignment is mainly to win the educated, the cream of the crop. But what about the Chinese peasants who live in the villages? Do I have a responsibility to the common people? The Scriptures say—"both ... and"—both to the educated and to the uneducated.*

## "But I Think I Can Prove It"

At this point in time Singapore and the Federation of Malayan States had already been given their independence by the British to form a new nation called Malaysia. However, considerable friction existed between the Chinese and the Malay population due to vast differences in culture and religion. The communists had seized on these differences to infiltrate the Chinese peasants with their teachings and to urge them to disrupt the system of law and order handed down to the government of Malaysia by the British. Since most of the communist activities were carried out by the Chinese peasants, the British and the Malay soldiers erected a wall around every Chinese village and imposed a curfew after dark. Thus any Chinese who ventured out of his village at night would be shot or imprisoned. The measures were quite effective. The Chinese who live in these "fenced villages," however, felt threatened and humiliated by the Malay majority.

The China Inland Mission (CIM), now renamed the Overseas Missionary Fellowship (OMF), had transferred some of its best missionaries, who had evacuated from mainland China, to plant churches within the fenced villages of Malaysia. Since my first wife, Lois, was formerly a CIM missionary before we were married and the Lord had taken her home to heaven with an aneurysm, I still retained many close ties with my CIM/OMF friends from our Shanghai days.

When I was invited to lecture at the OMF headquarters on the principles of discipleship, I got carried away in the enthusiasm of my message and boldly proclaimed that any missionary should reproduce anywhere within six months once he learned the language.

I further boasted rather rashly that I could bring a gospel team into any Chinese fenced village in Malaysia and have conversions within a week. This had actually been my quick response to the news that some of the Chinese who lived in the fenced villages were so hardened to the Gospel that some of these churches had not had a single conversion in more than a year.

At lunchtime no one came up to congratulate me on my fiery preaching, but there was a buzzing of discussion going on at some of the other tables. Then one of my close friends came up to me and exclaimed, "Roy, you have split the mission right in half. Some argue that you are right; some argue that you are wrong!"

"But I think I can prove it," I answered more quietly.

And so "The Mission," as it is fondly called among insiders, chose the hardest area in Malaysia, a village called Buloh Kasap, and invited me to bring a team to preach the Gospel in that village.

So I first got hold of my spiritual "sons" Su-Kim and Tom.

"Hey, guys, the Word says we have an obligation to preach the Gospel both to the wise and the unwise—both the educated Singaporean students and the Chinese farmers in Malaysia," I began. "You are Chinese and you speak the local dialect of your mother tongue, so we are going together to preach the Gospel in the fenced village of Buloh Kasap."

*Or my name will be mud*, I thought.

The disciples I had trained replied, "We can do family talk and shopping in our native dialect, but all our formal education is in English. We can't even use the Bible in Chinese."

"Well, get busy and practice, for each of you will be preaching or giving a testimony in that Chinese dialect."

Su-Kim lived with me and he would go along to Malaysia, as well as a couple other men; but I particularly wanted Tom to go with us because he spoke the best colloquial Chinese. However, first we had to persuade his father, a staunch traditional Taoist Chinese.

So Su-Kim and I went to Tom's place to try to persuade his dad to let his son take off a week from the shop to go and preach the Gospel in a fenced village in Malaysia. We talked and talked, drank tea and ate snacks, then talked some more. Mr. Lee was not persuaded.

We talked past midnight and into the wee hours of the morning before his father finally consented to this rash project.

Then Tom, Su-Kim and I went back to my house for a few hours of sleep. The next day we crammed five people and our baggage into my two-cylinder, 700-horsepower Toyota (which could make up to 60 miles per hour downhill) to tackle our first gospel team preaching effort in the Chinese villages.

Buloh Kasap, a village with about 5,000 people, had a small struggling church with only six baptized members plus a few stragglers who attended the services. But the inhabitants soon learned that a foreigner with some Chinese friends from Singapore were in town, so we didn't need much advertising to fill the church with curious spectators. The opening night went well; the people stayed to listen and only a few walked out on us. But no one dared publicly to receive Jesus and come forward.

The next night, however, two did come forward to be counseled by our team members. These two stayed for a long time clarifying the issues of salvation. Then two more came forward on the following night till we had a total of six by the end of the week. I actually had expected more, but after all, six solid commitments doubled the size of the church.

The meetings were considered quite successful, and our young budding students-turned-evangelists returned to their friends in Singapore with glorious stories of their evangelistic exploits.

By the time the next school vacation rolled around, a bunch of other students were ready to try their hand at preaching to the Chinese in the villages. The OMF mission assigned us another target and we were well underway in this ministry, gradually upgrading our standards of communicating, singing, and preaching. Later we added classes for discipling Christians and motivating local leadership as the size of our gospel team grew in numbers.

Over the next few years we recruited some keen and gifted young people through their desire to be part of a program taking the Gospel to reach their own countrymen who had never heard a clear gospel message. Among these were two brothers, Seto Wing-Hong and Seto Wing-Luk, who sang duets and gave their testimonies. The former is now a well-known Christian doctor, lecturing at the medical university in Hong Kong. He was instrumental in spearheading a ministry to medical professionals—doctors, nurses and dentists—as well as to high level business people who in turn have been able to reach into mainland China with their witness. His brother is a prominent writer.

On one occasion I recruited John Rhoads, my evangelist friend from Shanghai days, to work with us in launching a citywide crusade. We rented a public hall in Kelang, the port that serves Kuala Lumpur, the capital of Malaysia. This crusade targeted the Tamil-speaking Indian people who worked at the port facilities. Three car loads of Singaporeans took off a week from work or school to join us in leading the various aspects of a crusade. They helped with passing out invitations, conducting prayer meetings, making auditorium arrangements, the musical program, testimonies, counseling and follow-up. Evangelist John Rhoads preached with power and conviction, and the largely Indian audience responded readily to the invitation. It was a great experience for our team and an encouragement to the local churches that cooperated.

## Mighty Men and Godly Girls

In 1967 I returned from a short furlough to begin a second term in Singapore. While keeping the regular ministries going through our national co-workers, I decided to experiment with a strict one-on-one project. In my Old Testament devotional reading, I had come across the section where David's "Mighty Men" are listed by name (1 Chronicles 11:10-47). Apparently each one of the 30 men had a personal and loyal relationship with David. Through these men David could fight great wars and win great victories for the Lord.

*Lord*, I prayed silently, *please give me 30 mighty men as the fruit of this ministry in Singapore.*

My desire was that they would be men who were mighty spiritually—each able to win someone else to Christ, then able to follow up and develop that person, until he in turn was able to reach and teach others also.

So I planned to call all our key men together and exhort them to reach and teach at least one other person on a regular weekly basis.

I shared this exciting dream with my wife, who calmly asked, "And what about the girls?"

"Of course," I replied, as if I had them in mind all along, "we will call them the 30 Godly Girls."

In studying further the record found in 1 Chronicles 11 and in 1 Samuel 23, I noted that David had a "first three" and a "second three." At this time I also had six key men, so I made each of them a group leader over five other men. The arithmetic of that meant that six times five would give 30, so I had my 30 mighty men. Phyllis also appointed leaders among the women and began praying for 30 "Godly Girls."

Then we called the leaders of the men and women together to explain the project.

The plan was to raise up 30 men and 30 women in one year each of whom would qualify as a "Mighty Man" or a "Godly Girl."

To qualify you had to meet these five requirements:

(1) Lead someone to Christ, or at least latch on to a new Christian who has recently made a profession of faith.

(2) Spend regular time once a week one-on-one with the new believer.

(3) Require the new believer to memorize two new verses and do a written Bible study each week.

(4) Make sure each new believer is linked to some local church.

(5) Help this new believer become mature enough, so that he in turn can reproduce spiritually and begin to disciple another person.

Therefore, a mighty man or a godly girl is someone who helps his "Timothy" or her "Timothia" to reproduce spiritually.

God answered our prayers for this vision and enabled us to follow it beyond our expectations. At the end of the year 34 males qualified as Mighty Men. The women did even better as 37 ladies earned the title of Godly Girls. (Phyllis kept careful records of her ministry, which are reproduced in modified form in Appendix D.)

The raising up of spiritual generations begun in our missionary days in Singapore continues to the present time. The Navigators Singapore has a publishing house following the pattern of NavPress in the United States and has reprinted my book *The Timothy Principle*,[1] which is based on the ministry we had developed during my years in Singapore; that press has also published my book on the doctrine of the Christian life, which I have called *Journey of a Lifetime*,[2] as well as publications relevant to the ministry in Asia by other Navigator staff.

*The Timothy Principle*, together with its practical study book, *Timothy Training Workbook*[3] (also printed in the original book), is a manual on how to disciple another Christian on a one-on-one basis. Many keen disciples in Singapore are still reproducing spiritual generations by training faithful men and women, who in turn bring forth spiritual sons and daughters, who then teach others also.

ENDNOTES:
1. Roy Robertson, *The Timothy Principle*, Singapore: The Navigators, 1992. (The address is The Navigators Singapore, 117 Lorong K Telok Kurau, Singapore 425758.)
2. Roy Robertson, *Journey of a Lifetime* [formerly *The Road to Discipleship*], Singapore: The Navigators, 1992.
3. Roy Robertson, *Timothy Training Workbook*, Denton, Texas: Training Evangelistic Leadership, n.d., Singapore NavPress, 1999. The workbooks and books (above) are also available from TEL, Post Drawer E, Denton, TX 76202.

# Chapter 18

## THE NAVIGATORS SPAWN OTHER WORKS

By the grace of God I had the great privilege personally to be challenged and influenced by the five missionary leaders who are the centerpiece of this book. To begin with, Daws Trotman individually trained me as a "Timothy" (or spiritual son) while I lived in his home through the formative years of maturing in my Christian life and ministry.

Then Daws sent me, a green, inexperienced missionary, to the other side of the world to work under Dick Hillis. Dick became my teacher, confidant and spiritual leader to guide me into a positive bonding experience with the culture and people to whom I had been called and sent.

In essence, through Daws I was trained in follow-up and discipleship, and through Dick I was taught how to lead gospel teams in public evangelism and how to survive on the mission field. I learned how to live in harmony and with understanding among a people of a different culture and value system from mine.

I learned much from the other three leaders as well, for they all worked together as a team in the early days of the Youth for Christ movement in Asia. I accompanied David Morken on many of his preaching missions, being responsible under him for the training of counselors and the follow-up work in China and Japan, as well as in Indonesia. David became my hero and model on how to preach with power that comes only from God.

Spending much time in the company of this gifted preacher greatly motivated me to study and to learn the art of evangelistic preaching with particular emphasis on giving a public invitation for people to receive Christ openly. Both David and Hube Mitchell, his brother-in-law, were evangelists who used the Word of God constantly and sometimes quoted from memory whole chapters of the Bible. Hube was also gifted in music and personal evangelism.

Bob Pierce, too, became a great model for me to follow. He had a heart for God and a heart of compassion toward both the spiritual and physical needs of people that went beyond any man I have ever met. His compassion was not idealistic, but took a very practical form: "What can we do now? How can we get the Gospel out now to China or Korea or Vietnam before the door of opportunity closes?" Bob was a missionary statesman who also showed concern about overall missionary strategy, timing and priorities. He shared his burden both publicly and privately.

"I look around to find out where the Holy Spirit is working, then I try to pour my time and money and resources into meeting those needs," he said. And, above all, Bob had the gift of giving. His heart, tears and faith enabled many national workers and missionaries to carry on their strategic work for God.

God used those five men greatly to influence the direction of my missionary activities even to the present day. Many other individuals and groups have followed in the footsteps of these men of faith. It is an undeniable fact that those missionary leaders have altered the course of modern missionary history, being used by God to influence many of the thousands of American ex-servicemen who went to the mission field.

Sometimes a personal conversation with Dick or Daws would help steer the direction of my life and ministry. I recall a conversation I had with Dick when he visited us in Japan shortly after I had moved there to develop a system of follow-up for the Japanese in 1951.

"Dick, I have a problem! All Asian people are not alike. These Japanese are very different from the Chinese. They are supposed to be polite, but sometimes I find them to be rude and proud. I am a missionary and I am supposed to love them, but it is harder for me to love the Japanese than the Chinese people among whom I have recently worked."

"Roy," Dick replies, "you are adjusting to some cultural problems. But the answer is not to struggle in your heart to love these people; in the flesh it is hard to love any foreign group of people. Pray for the love of God, for He loves the Japanese. It is the love of Christ within us that enables us to love any race of people. Christ died for them and the love of Christ constrains us to love them too."

"Of course," I acknowledge, "I know that passage of Scripture—2 Corinthians 5:14. It is a verse I have memorized; I think I will do a Bible study on that whole chapter."

As I study 2 Corinthians 5 over the next few days, I feel that God is doing a deeper work in my heart. Not only am I reminded of God's love for a lost people, but my attention is focused on a significant phrase in verse 11, "Knowing therefore the terror of the Lord, we persuade men."

*Oh,* I start thinking, *I am obligated to witness to the Japanese people not only because of the love of God, but also because of the terrible judgment of God upon them. All these nicely dressed and polite Japanese people are heading straight for hell without Jesus Christ.*

*Oh, yes,* I continue to ponder in my heart, *the Bible teaches this, but do I really believe it? I think it is harder to believe in hell than it is to believe in heaven. I know that Dick has written a tract called* "Are the Heathen Lost?" *that has caused many people to think more deeply on this issue. But Dick is absolutely right! The heathen are lost.*

So I start to pray, *"Lord, ninety-nine percent of these people do not believe in You, and as a result they are heading straight for hell! Are the heathen lost? Yes! I must therefore dedicate the rest of my life to warning them. Lord, by faith I believe all these Japanese without Christ are lost; by faith I appropriate the love of Christ to motivate me to do all I can to see these people saved."*

God did change my heart. Over the years I developed an intimate trust and understanding with many Japanese individuals who became dear to my heart. Moreover, God put within my heart a respect and admiration for the loyalty and dedication of the Japanese people who also retain a deep appreciation for beauty and blending of nature and the human spirit.

## The Gospel Green Berets

The next conversation takes place when I return to the States in 1955 to work under Daws at Glen Eyrie, the new international head-quarters of The Navigators, at the foot of Pike's Peak in the Rocky Mountains of Colorado.

"Roy, can you ride a horse?" Daws asks me one day.

"Of course, Daws. I grew up in Texas. Besides, I was trained at Texas A & M for the horse-drawn field artillery!" Then I burst into a song which our outfit sang in our college days when we rode army mules that transported the field cannon:

> Over hill, over dale, we will hit the dusty trail,
>   As the caissons go rolling along.
> Counter march, round about, hear the wagon soldiers shout,
>   As the caissons go rolling along.
> Then it's hi, hi, hee, in the field artillery . . .

Ignoring my musical outburst, Daws says, "Then let us ride together over the Saddle Back Ridge where we can have some fellow-ship and talk. I'll ride the filly and you can ride the roan."

After a 45-minute ride over the ridge, we dismount in a small canyon to rest and feed our horses. After chatting about a variety of things, Daws finally begins sharing with me what is uppermost on his heart at this time.

"Roy, it is on my heart that we should form an international evangelistic strike team to be ready at any time to go wherever there is a great opportunity for the Gospel. All kinds of openings are out there today for a big gospel outreach, but by the time we get ready much of the opportunity is lost. We need to be prepared in advance.

"For example," he continues, "today great openings exist in Kenya to work among the Mau Mau in detention camps, as well as in all kinds of places in Asia, in Africa, and even in Europe. We can form a team to include some of our close friends who are evangelists, then add some of our own gang to do counseling and follow-up, and finally bring on some people with musical talent. Who do you think should be on that team?"

So we begin discussing various individuals and their talents and gifts who might be key members of such an international group.

## Let The Navigators Do It

About six months later I flew with Daws from Japan to Taiwan. He had come to the Land of the Rising Sun to visit with our staff at a very difficult period in that ministry to give guidance and encouragement. This would be the last time I would have fellowship with Daws before his death a few months later, but of course I did not know that.

"Daws," I began, "the American evangelists with Youth for Christ are not coming to Asia these days; you know that the Americans are not as popular as before. Daws, I believe there is a great need to work with Asian evangelists like Greg Tingson [Filipino], Andrew Gih [Chinese] and others. Then we can train younger Asians to take their place. We have a large follow-up staff of a dozen trained workers in Japan, but not much public evangelism is being done right now. We can't just sit around and wait for others. Souls are perishing without hearing the gospel message.

"Daws, I believe we should launch out and do our own evangelism. In fact, we can even hold our own evangelistic crusades. Our follow-up staff people can travel with the team and help in these meetings. Daws, we should take the lead in public evangelism as well as in follow-up. Our people are trained and motivated. We can do it!"

I don't remember Daws' exact words well enough to quote him, but he encouraged me to do all that was on my heart with his full blessing.

This was my last meaningful conversation with my beloved leader and spiritual father. He took a plane from Taiwan back to the States and a few months later, he drowned at the Schroon Lake conference grounds in New York state while giving his life to save another person from drowning.

That same week in which Daws drowned, the first Navigator evangelistic strike team left Glen Eyrie on very short notice and arrived in Kenya, Africa to work among the Mau Mau in the British detention camps. Thus the idea that Daws shared with me on our horseback ride at Glen Eyrie the previous year became reality.

The Lord also began to bring to realization the burdens of my heart to form Asian gospel teams that blended together clear public preaching with thorough individual counseling and follow-up. Daws had taught me the principles of biblical follow-up, while Dick had been my mentor for the concept of sending out local gospel teams to evangelize a given geographical area. These two concepts must be kept together because evangelism without adequate follow-up will not produce much lasting fruit.

In 1958 The Navigators held eight citywide crusades in Japan. We conducted most of these in cities located on the southern island of Kyushu ("nine states") and the northern end of the main island of Honshu ("many states"). Our evangelists were Greg Tingson (Filipino), Andrew Gih (Chinese), David Morken (Asia Youth for Christ director) and John Rhoads (American missionary to Japan).

Asian young men who were in training for the ministry of evangelism and follow-up composed our set-up and follow-up team. These men included Kuruvilla Abraham and George Ninan (India), George Lee (Taiwan), Hiroshi Ogama (Japan) and later Samuel Chan (Hong Kong). I invited these Asians to join a training program based in my home in Japan. We lived together after the pattern that Jesus had used in training His disciples; then we traveled together as a team to do the work of evangelism, counselor training and follow-up.

By God's grace these crusades were very fruitful. We recorded 5,994 clear decisions for Christ through our public evangelistic meetings in 1958. This occurred at a time when many people were saying that the Japanese do not respond well to public evangelistic meetings. Our experience demonstrated the contrary. Our overall average of the percentage of decisions to total attendance was nine per cent (9%), higher than any other country in Asia outside of the Philippines.

The Billy Graham Tokyo Crusade in 1992 recorded the highest percentage of seeker to audience ratio of any time in memory. On the closing Sunday afternoon at the Tokyo "Dome" baseball stadium more than 9,000 out of an estimated crowd of 32,000 came forward to be counseled. The Japanese do indeed respond when the Gospel is preached with power and integrity!

## Hello and Goodbye

April 10, 1959

"Lois, Sweetheart, I am calling from the Tokyo station . . . I am home two days early. The crusade in Kure [a Japanese naval base near Hiroshima] is not quite over, but I decided to come home early. Maybe we can get together with the kids this afternoon and go out for a picnic. Will that work out? . . . Fine! . . . See you about four?"

[Today is an important day in Japan. Millions of people are crowding central Tokyo waiting for the wedding procession of Crown Prince Akihito and commoner Michiko Shoda.]

"Lois, I'll join the mob and watch the parade at noon. I should be home about four, OK ? . . . Love you . . . ! How did I get to Tokyo? Well, I caught the 'Tokyu' [special express] without having a ticket when it stopped in Hiroshima for about two minutes. Normally I don't do this and apologized profusely to the conductor, using only English, of course. He did find me a seat and sold me a ticket, and I thanked him profusely. I had a strong feeling—I can't even explain it fully—that I wanted to be with you and the kids on this special day when all the world is watching the marriage of the Crown Prince and Michiko. Since I am here, I'll watch the parade, then see you about four, . . . and we will go to the park. Love you! Bye."

I call back about 2:30 that same afternoon.

"Hello! Who is this? . . . Oh, Hugh . . . I want to speak with my wife. . . . What? . . . She can't come to the phone? . . . Why?"

The voice of Hugh Harris, a missionary with The Navigators in Japan, is shaking.

"About an hour ago," he answers, "she went to be with the Lord in heaven. You'd better grab a taxi and come home."

I am stunned by the news. But within seconds Job 1:21 comes to mind, "Naked came I out of my mother's womb, and naked shall I return thither: the Lord gave, and the Lord has taken away; blessed be the name of the Lord."

This was the very same verse the Lord had given me when I learned that Lois could not marry me because of her promise to God to stay in China to work among the tribes in the Yunnan Province. Later the Lord closed all the CIM fields in China as the new communist regime outlawed all missionaries. The mission leadership then told all their members that they were free to go to another field the CIM would open in Asia or to another mission.

When I heard this in Taiwan I sent Lois a cable proposing an immediate wedding in Hong Kong. She accepted, so we had a lovely ceremony at the historic St. Andrew's Church in that Crown Colony on March 7, 1951.

Again the verse that had spoken to my heart in the midst of a postponed courtship comes back to mind. Now for the second time she has been taken away from me. But again, "The LORD gave and the LORD hath taken away. Blessed be the name of the LORD!" As I hang up the receiver, my first thought is, *Thank you, Lord, for eight years of a wonderful marriage!*

As I arrive at our Japanese-style home with its tatami mat floors, Hugh meets me with the words, "We have wrapped her body in dry ice. She is in that room."

I slide open the paper door and walked into the room and in tears embrace the body of my wife. But the moment I touch her body the reality of eternity hits me. This is not Lois. She is in heaven! So I kneel by her body and renew my vow to the living God, "Oh God, You have taken her, a beautiful, wonderful wife and mother, and so holy and godly. You should have taken me, not her.

"But, O God, You died so that others might live and have eternal life. God, I don't understand why . . . why she should die and I should live. But I promise You, O Lord, for the rest of my life as I live on borrowed time, I promise that henceforth I will no longer live to myself but live to preach the Gospel to those who are lost.

"O God, five thousand souls came to Christ last year because she was willing to share and sacrifice and constrain me to do this work. Lord, may more people come to Christ because of her sudden death than have come to Christ through her life."

My family and I set up a memorial fund to carry out the work of public evangelism in Japan. We urged people to give money for this cause rather than for flowers and funeral expenses. She was buried in a Christian cemetery in Karuizawa, Japan, as the children and I along with missionary friends honored her faithfulness to the Lord. And yes, more money came in to carry out the work of evangelism in Japan than had ever been received before. And the work continued into the next generation as Janet and Susan, who were only 6 and 5 years of age at the time of their mother's passing, married men gifted in the work of evangelism. Both families became missionaries to Africa with The Navigators. They have been used by God to lead hundreds of people to Jesus Christ.

## The Hong Kong Gift from God

Both my wife, Lois, and my spiritual father, Daws, were now with the Lord. When I returned to the United States with my three children, Janet (6), Susan (5) and Keith (18 months), I was given the position of Overseas Missionary Coordinator with The Navigators, working under the new Director, Lorne C. Sanny, at our headquarters at Glen Eyrie in Colorado Springs, Colorado. Friends graciously assisted me and helped in my home as I tried to take care of the children and also fulfill the extensive duties of coordinating the Navigator missionary program for about a year.

On one occasion, traveling with Lorne Sanny on a worldwide tour I routed my return journey through Hong Kong. In that city I visited David Morken and missionary friends, including Navigator staff. While at the Youth for Christ office I again met Phyllis Hapke, David's secretary on loan from The Navigators, who had lived in the Trotman home at "509" during the years that I had trained there. She had been in charge of handling The Navigators "Topical Memory System" under Daws and had memorized several thousand verses of Scripture. She had also served as a missionary to Europe under The Navigators.

I had always been impressed with her godliness and commitment to the Word of God. During my time in Hong Kong we discussed the possibility of a future getting together. We became officially engaged a few months later and were married at Glen Eyrie castle in Colorado on August 13, 1960 at a ceremony officiated by Lorne Sanny. Eventually the Lord gave us three children, Len, Lila and Lee, giving me a total of six, four of whom became foreign missionaries.

## Singapore It Is!

I served as overseas coordinator for The Navigators for two years. Then as my marriage and children were stabilized, I asked to go overseas again to a new assignment. As I considered all of Asia, I chose Singapore as the best place to develop disciples to influence the entire region for Christ. Here are the seven reasons I submitted to the Navigators leadership for the developing of Singapore as a new Asian base:

1. Geographical location—Within a 2,000-mile radius of Singapore lives half the population of the world, including most of China and India.

2. Multi-racial—The Travel Bureau calls Singapore "Instant Asia," as its population includes many of Asia's peoples.

3. High educational and economic standards—Under the British these standards became part and parcel of this society.

4. Strong Christian churches and an evangelical base greatly influenced by the Youth for Christ movement and the relocation of the China Inland Mission (now the Overseas Missionary Fellowship) and other missions here.

5. A small, reachable and independent country with a stable government from which missionaries and discipleship concepts could be sent throughout Asia and around the world.

6. A strong bi-cultural base—Singapore's strong Chinese culture and English language give it a worldwide influence.

7.   Attitudes of its people—Singapore's mixed population makes for a rugged, adaptable, tough and innovative people who are excellent material from which to develop disciples and missionaries.

The Navigators leadership approved my request, so my family and I arrived in Singapore in the fall of 1962 (see Chapter 17) to begin a Navigator ministry and to plan a future TEL ministry from that strategic city. Toward the end of my second term in Singapore, I turned over the leadership of the ministry of The Navigators to a new missionary I had handpicked—David L. Dawson. He took the people who had been raised up and molded them into a highly successful ministry. Under Dave's capable leadership, Singapore became the first country of The Navigators in Asia to send forth fully supported missionaries to other places.

After eight fruitful years in Singapore I had felt the Lord laying on my heart a vision and a burden to launch out into a wider ministry of public evangelism. In the period of about ten years which immediately followed World War II, I had been involved in the follow-up of men and women who were coming to Christ in unprecedented numbers in China, Japan, Taiwan and other parts of Asia. That great movement of God was spearheaded largely by American evangelists in partnership with new missionaries who had served in the armed forces during the war and had come to Christ during their military service. That had been an exciting time, but now it was 1970.

As I thought about those past 25 years and reminisced over the great work God had done through the American evangelists, I cried out in my heart, *Lord, do this again, only this time do it through national evangelists.*

How do you raise up national evangelists? This is done by following the pattern set by Jesus Christ during His earthly ministry as He called numerous disciples to Himself, and then "He ordained twelve that they should be with Him and that he might send them forth to preach" (Mark 3:14). They were trained by actually living with Jesus, then later He would send them forth to preach throughout Galilee, Judea and Perea, the Jewish areas in Roman-held Palestine.

So I consulted with the leaders of The Navigators who were supportive and encouraged me to launch a program to train national evangelists. We called the project Training Evangelistic Leadership (TEL), and The Navigators financed and staffed it.

I asked my close friend, John Rhoads, a Navigator staff member in Japan who was a powerful and gifted evangelist with whom I had worked before in various crusades under Youth for Christ in Shanghai and Japan, to co-labor with me in this project. I would major on the training; John would major on teaching the men how to preach. I would show the men how to do the set-up and follow-up for evangelistic meetings; John would show them how to handle the platform, that is, the preaching and the invitation. So the three components of effective public evangelism would be passed on to new generations of Asians: preparation, preaching and preservation of the fruit.

Yet we needed a large home to house the trainees if we were to follow the pattern of Jesus and have them live with us. Trinity Theological Seminary in Singapore had inherited a piece of beach property with a luxurious home and attached quarters for servants located some eight miles out on Upper East Coast Road with the stipulation that it had to be used for religious purposes only. The property was a long way from the seminary, so the Dean, Dr. Olin C. Stockwell, who had heard about the training programs held in our home offered to rent this choice property to us for a nominal rate of only U.S. $135 a month. The moment I took a look at the house, I exclaimed to my wife, "This is it!"

Indeed, this property was it! The spacious living room of the home, which I thought might once have been used for dancing parties, was shaped like an L. As I paced it off, I found it to be 90 feet along the entire front of the house and 120 feet deep along the side. This was our living room. I estimated that we could easily accommodate 250 people for a meeting or seat 175 for dining. The backyard overlooked the ocean, and waves splashed over a low brick wall for it was high tide. I noticed six tall trees loaded with coconuts in the front yard and a beautiful flame-of-the-forest tree in the backyard. The grounds were large enough for many sports. Inside the main house were four bedrooms, enough for our family of six children. The attached building had space for six to eight trainees to live and study.

The main house stood on concrete pillars about six feet off the ground so the air could flow through underneath it. This typical British colonial style of building is called a bungalow. It had enough space to sleep about 70 men under the house if we wanted to hold a youth camp over the weekend. In the back yard overlooking the sea were benches and picnic tables.

The Lord Jesus trained His 12 men, who were to be His future leaders, as they lived and traveled "with him" (Mark 3:14). His actual training "program" lasted a little over two years. So I reasoned, *Maybe I can handle about half this much, about six to eight people for one year of training.*

For the first official Training Evangelistic Leadership (TEL) project, I invited seven men from six countries to come and live with me and my family for a year of intensive training. Two men came from Indonesia (one with his wife) and one each from India, the Philippines, Singapore, Japan and Malaysia.[1] In our living room the former owner had left behind a huge oval oak table around which could accommodate 16 people for our main meals—eight Robertson family members and eight Asians.

According to the custom of that period, we did have servants— an Indian cook and a Malay cleaning lady. But my wife supervised the buying and preparing of all meals plus the running of the home and monitoring the activities of our six children. It takes a very special wife, one who is highly dedicated, self-sacrificing and talented, to run a home where training goes on day and night. Without such a committed wife and mother, there would never have been a home training center.

Some observers across the years have criticized our living style, predicting that it would confuse and possibly harm our children. Instead, however, they benefited from this rich heritage. Our children, surrounded by kind uncles and aunts of different cultures and nationalities, grew up feeling very much at home in almost any cultural setting. All graduated with university degrees, four of the six became missionaries and the other two entered the nursing profession.

Our program included three kinds of training: classroom

instruction, character building and ministry skills. Every morning, Monday through Friday, we scheduled three classes. In the first period of two hours it was my privilege to take the trainees book by book through a close study of the entire New Testament. Each book highlights a particular emphasis and we concentrated on developing this teaching in the context of that particular book. For instance, Matthew stresses spiritual authority and the role of the church in the Great Commission. Mark emphasizes the role of the evangelist to preach the Gospel to every creature. Luke is the servant Gospel and stresses forsaking all to follow Jesus. John majors on faith for salvation and obedience in discipleship. Romans is the only book that systematically gives us the plan of salvation. First Corinthians handles every problem a local church will face. First Thessalonians gives us a pattern for effective follow-up.

A Singaporean staff worker taught the second period on discipleship and Christian character. The content of this segment included the emphases of *The Timothy Principle*, that is, Self-discipline, the Quiet Time, Prayer Lists, Bible Study, Scripture Memory, Bible Meditation. J. Oswald Sanders, the General Director at that time of the Overseas Missionary Fellowship (OMF), would come sometimes and teach on Christian character, a topic he had written about extensively.

The third hour primarily developed ministry skills using various instructors on how to do different kinds of evangelism and follow-up. And whenever John Rhoads came from Japan to teach, we would load him with special classes in theology and preaching clinics. In fact, I learned much from John on how to preach more effectively. On weekends we launched out into the city on various ministry assignments.

For longer periods of time we went as evangelistic teams to the fenced villages of the Chinese in Malaysia (see Chapter 17). We also participated in ministry with local churches, in a variety of ethnic contacts in Singapore, in the high school ministries, and working with YFC. The trainees traveled with me in ministry.

## EXPO 70 World Fair

As a part of this first official TEL training program, we planned a trip to Japan for several months in 1970 to join with John Rhoads on a Gospel distribution project at the Expo 70 World Fair held in Osaka. The Pocket Testament League had printed a special Expo 70 edition of 300,000 Gospels of John in Japanese to be distributed at the fair grounds. The Japanese authorities at the fair had granted permission for this special printing, but as we learned later the Japanese police were not favorable toward a large-scale public distribution.

So this provided a good training ground for our budding Asian gospel team. As in much evangelistic work in foreign countries, this ministry was not exactly legal nor was it illegal. The laws were often vague. But as I had learned through previous experience in getting out the Gospel in a hostile or semi-hostile environment, "It is easier to get forgiveness than permission."

When stopped by the police from distributing our bundles of Gospels, we all learned to say, "*Sumimasen* [I am sorry]."

If the policeman broke into a string of Japanese invectives, we would always smile and say, "*Wakarimasen* [I don't understand]," along with another bow and an apology while pointing to the official seal of EXPO 70 on the cover of the Gospel. Even in other instances, like driving a car, the veteran missionary tends to forget quickly his knowledge of Japanese when confronted by a *junsan* [policeman].

So began our little game of "cat and mouse." Expo 70 had four main gates, marked East, West, North and South. We would meet for prayer, then alternate gates and stagger the hours of our distribution.

"*Kore wa Yohanne no Fukuin Sho* [This is the Gospel of John]. *Dozo, yonde kudasai* [Please read it].

Most of the people who came to EXPO 70 received it with thanks. We learned to walk with the flow of the people and cause very little disturbance, thus not attracting the attention of the police. Printed in the back of the Gospel John were the plan of salvation and a decision slip to mail in to our follow-up office. Hundreds of people recorded their personal decisions for Christ and each was sent the Gospel of John follow-up Bible study.

When the project was finished and all the Gospels had been distributed, a couple of our Asian team members along with our Japanese trainee, Inoue-san, actually went to the police headquarters on the fairgrounds and thanked them for their leniency. Some of the police asked for copies for themselves.

EXPO 70 was an international fair with many countries erecting pavilions to display their own goods and services. The Pocket Testament League had already printed the Gospel of John in some 25 foreign languages. So our gospel team decided to distribute these Gospels in the appropriate language in many of the other international pavilions. We entered into the Dutch, German, French and Italian pavilions where we gave out the Gospels, and we lingered a bit longer in our favorite Italian restaurant. We also distributed Gospels in the pavilions of the Asian countries. Of course, our team members between them could speak most of the Asian languages.

Being an American, of special concern to me was the Russian Pavilion, the largest on the grounds, because it afforded opportunity to witness to people of a closed country during the Cold War.

## The Gospel Versus Marx

One day I enter the Russian Pavilion armed with a bag of Gospels in the Russian language. I carefully give out several. Then I notice a craftsman, who I think might be from Armenia, a Christian republic within the Soviet Union. He receives the Gospel with obvious joy and shakes my hand. While I am giving out a couple more, I feel a tap on my back. Turning I am confronted by an angry Russian official. He speaks to me roughly in Russian. I reply in English, so we get nowhere. Then he tries Japanese, which I understand, for we both have learned the language in order to work in Japan, he as a diplomat and I as a missionary.

I offer him a Russian Gospel of John, which he receives perhaps to gather evidence against me.

"You can't give these out here!"

"Why not, isn't there religious freedom in Russia?"

"Yes, but it is not allowed here."

I compliment him on his fluency in Japanese. Briefly we discuss the motivation each of us has to learn the Japanese language and I confess that I believe in Jesus Christ.

He claims there is no God. I am happy to argue the point but he cuts me off. *If you claim not to believe in God, then why are you afraid of this Gospel book?* I think.

He demands I give him all the Russian Gospels and I comply. He decides not to take me to his superior but warns me not to come again, and I depart with a prayer in my heart that he and others will read the Gospels.

While in Japan with our gospel team, I sometimes would slip away to a coffee house, where one can study or talk to a friend while listening to good music, often classical music. We came up with an idea to arrange with the owner of "Trio," one of the coffee shops, to attract additional customers by having our team members give a program in English one night a week. The idea worked extremely well. Our act drew many new people and we all bought coffee while presenting a program of folk music, followed by gospel music, then our testimonies. It offered excellent training for our team as they all took turns in singing, games, skits and presenting the Gospel.

Returning to Singapore we continued several more months of classes. Then we finished off the training program by taking the team to Indonesia, where we had one evangelistic crusade with John preaching and some smaller evangelistic meetings with our trainees preaching, singing, testifying and handling the follow-up.

In this first official TEL training program which began in 1970 we trained seven national evangelists from six countries. We held the second program in Karuizawa, Japan from 1972 to 1973, where we again trained in our home seven men from six countries. Then I moved my family to Surabaya, Indonesia, where we trained four men from four countries between 1974 and 1975. All four of these graduates later led their own training programs in various countries, patterned on the same model as ours. Parenthetically, about this time we incorporated Training Evangelistic Leadership (TEL) first in Indonesia in

1974, and then in Amercia in 1976 as a non-profit organization so as to generate more funds for supporting the evangelists we had trained. So this became the first of several other organizations generated by The Navigators as well, which I will describe in another chapter.

Over the years TEL has set up live-in home training programs in other Asian countries, namely, the Philippines, India, Hong Kong, Indonesia and China. In Manila my wife and I invited five Filipino young men to live in our home for a one-year training program. Two American TEL staff workers assisted in the ministry: Dave Craymer handled the discipleship and Christian character development, while Bill Bussard, a gifted evangelist, instructed the trainees in the art of public evangelism and preaching skills.

We concentrated on our studies for two or three months, then the men formed a gospel team and traveled extensively throughout the Philippines for public evangelistic outreach. The Filipino people, still very responsive to the Gospel, recorded more than 3,000 decisions for Christ during our evangelistic travels that year.

Public evangelism is a team effort requiring the development of various skills. One trainee might be gifted in operating electrical and sound equipment, another in leading the music, another in follow-up, another in teaching and directing the counseling of new believers, another in crowd control and yet others in preaching. But all were part of the team of evangelists bringing the Gospel to the villages, towns, and cities of their respective countries, for all were taught to give a testimony and to preach publicly.

We have sought across the years to train faithful men who are capable of training others within their own cultures. So some of the graduates from our multi-Asian training centers have started their own national training centers, while other graduates from our national programs have set up modified training programs in their own regions or dialects.

I am convinced that by God's grace and with His blessing on them, these works will reproduce themselves and filter down to provide training at various local levels. Our "with him" type of training, where the trainees live with their mentor, may be small by nature, but it is highly selective. More than 90% of the graduates of all the TEL

Asian and national training programs during the past two decades are still in Christian service today.

Phyllis and I estimate that through the years about 50 people have lived in our home and received intensive training. We look on them as our spiritual sons and daughters. Some even call us *Ibu* and *Bapa* [Mom and Dad].

Training people according to the biblical "with him" principle practiced by Jesus pays ongoing dividends both now and into eternity.

ENDNOTES:
1. The participants in the first TEL training program were: Erich Natan (wife Deborah) and Iman Santoso (Indonesia), Kaoru Inoue (Japan), Daniel Macwan (India), Godfrey Catanus (Philippines), David Loo (Malaysia), John Goh (Singapore) and the Robertson family (Singapore/U.S.).

# Chapter 19

## ONE-TO-ONE COUNSELING WITH 9,000 SEEKERS

In the 1977 Billy Graham Metro Manila Crusade I coordinated the training of about 4,000 qualified counselors in English, Tagalog (the official Filipino language), and Chinese. The five-day Crusade climaxed in Luneta Park on Sunday afternoon, November 27th. Its spacious grounds overlooked famous Manila Hotel, site of General Douglas MacArthur's headquarters during the liberation of the Philippines in World War II. The First Lady at that time, Imelda Marcos, had personally intervened over the objections of bureaucrats to grant permission to hold the final meeting in this strategic location.

We had already witnessed four nights of successful meetings, with about 3,000 people per night coming forward to the front of the platform. These were counseled one-to-one in an orderly fashion, according as I had been trained to do by Dawson Trotman. We had put into practice the same procedures over the years, particularly in Youth for Christ meetings throughout Asia. But that Sunday afternoon we anticipated an even greater harvest of souls.

Arriving two hours early, I was shocked to see our usual counseling area fenced off and inaccessible to seekers and counselors, so as to make room for VIPs. Many seats in this area beyond the fence were marked with the names of high-ranking government and military leaders. Also, in front of the platform a road was barricaded so that the Billy Graham team could leave immediately after the meeting to catch a flight to their next destination.

"The seekers are the VIPs," I grumbled to a policeman who remained impassive to my plea to remove the barrier that restricted access to the counseling area.

Every night prior to this the seekers came forward to the edge of the platform and were then ushered into a counseling area reserved for the true VIPs, the souls that were seeking Christ. At this point I recalled the words of Jesus, "Likewise, I say unto you, there is joy in the presence of the angels of God over one sinner that repenteth" (Luke 15:10).

We had stored 10,000 New Testaments (bearing the Metro Manila Billy Graham Crusade logo) and follow-up packets under that platform, for use that afternoon. We needed to move them to a place outside the barrier, readily accessible for our counselors to give to people coming forward to make decisions for Christ.

I picked up a box of materials and cleared a path to take it to a new location. I quickly reserved a rather large area to be used only for counseling and planted a big sign used each night for this purpose marked "ENGLISH".

Near a loudspeaker on the right side of the grounds, where an interpreter would give simultaneous translation into the Filipino language, we set up our "TAGALOG" base and sign. Then we moved the tables and Tagalog materials to this place.

On the other side of the field a smaller loudspeaker would broadcast the message in a Chinese dialect, and here we hoisted our "CHINESE" sign written in Chinese characters; we then moved the materials in that language to that new point.

As counselors began to arrive, they observed my frantic activities. Of course, they began to help move all these follow-up materials to their proper new locations. They secured and guarded the counseling areas so the crowd could not occupy those spaces. Otherwise we would have been unable to counsel one-to-one in an orderly manner. Since decision time is the most important part of a crusade, everything must be prepared carefully so that a seeker can make a clear, prayerful decision to receive Jesus Christ into his or her heart.

We transferred the basic follow-up materials fairly quickly, but transporting the 10,000 New Testaments proved to be quite a job. I soon shed my suit coat, then my tie. The grounds filled with people and the choir began to sing. But I still continued moving boxes of

New Testaments to the place where they would be available to the counselors. Some of the people sitting nearby watched me curiously, as they saw sweat rolling down the face and perspiration soaking the shirt of this foreigner who struggled to move all those boxes with the help of only a few other people. I did not realize it then, for I believed I was only doing my job; but apparently this small act of manual labor made a greater impression on my Filipino friends than all my teaching of classes and coordinating of the follow-up program during the previous few weeks. Much later, after the Crusade ended, people still commented on this American missionary who would work hard and sweat to help the Filipino people.

Then Billy Graham stood up to preach his usual clear and powerful message. The boxes of follow-up materials were now all in place under the control of counselor captains and section leaders. We specifically instructed counselors not to give a packet or special crusade edition of the New Testament to anyone until he or she had first heard the gospel explanation one-to-one and had prayed in his own words the prayer of believing in the Lord Jesus and receiving Christ as his own personal Savior.

If more people came than could be handled one-to-one, then each one must line up behind a counselor and wait his turn. I relayed these additional instructions to the counselors, "Don't rush. This is the most important time in a person's life. Spend about 15 to 20 minutes dealing with each individual."

At Dr. Graham's invitation, a flood of people came forward. But we had reserved adequate space to handle the counseling and kept strict control over all the materials. Our leaders relayed instructions to the many seekers, "Please wait in a prayerful manner . . . We have plenty of time . . . We will counsel each one individually and then give out the follow-up materials."

Filipinos are by nature a very patient people. An atmosphere of a reverent hush prevailed over the counseling area in the stadium as several thousand counselors spoke earnestly and quietly with some of the persons who had come forward, while still other thousands stood quietly in lines waiting their turn to be counseled individually.

*This is a sacred moment in the history of the nation*, I thought sometime in the midst of the business of supervising the counseling. *Surely the angels of God are rejoicing in heaven to witness this multitude of people turning to Christ.*

Then the Billy Graham team departed, the choir left for the members' homes, more of the security personnel left as well; but still the counseling continued for another two-and-a-half hours. My twins, Lila and Lee, were involved, each counseling two and three seekers, while my son Leonard counseled seven. A prominent business leader brought his grown daughter for me to counsel personally.

As the sun set over Manila Bay and over the city, a few of our counselors were still earnestly engaged in telling another person about receiving a Savior who would give them eternal life.

On the Day of Pentecost about 3,000 men and women made a public profession to receive The Lord Jesus as their personal Saviour (Acts 2:41) in Jerusalem, the ancient capital city of Israel. Some nineteen-and-a-half centuries later in Luneta Park in Manila, the modern capital of the Philippines, more than 9,000 (three times the number at Pentecost) men and women came forward that Sunday afternoon to receive Jesus Christ as their personal Savior. Most were not members of any evangelical church. This is only a work that God could have done! To God alone be all the glory!

But as Dawson Trotman taught me so many years ago, decision is 5 percent; follow-up is 95 percent!

### The Ongoing Follow-up Ministry

George and Corrine Cruz were in charge of the follow-up office. A veteran missionary couple, Gene and Helen Tabor, who led an intensive program in training disciples in a third world context, had trained this dedicated young couple. George and Corrine took the 9,000-plus decision slips into the follow-up office along with a few faithful co-workers, pots of coffee and many snacks. They worked around the clock for more than 27 hours processing the decision slips and designating them into church follow-up and nurture group classes. They grabbed a few hours of sleep at the office and were at it again, working feverishly with members of their follow-up core group for about a week until the job was completed. To faithful Filipino disciples like these should go most of the credit for a highly effective follow-up operation, which some Filipino Christian leaders said was the most extensive ever attempted in the Philippines.

Following the Metro Manila Billy Graham Crusade in 1977, Bishop George Castro, the executive director for the crusade, invited me to form a gospel team to help his denomination with outreach in the rural areas. Bishop Castro headed the independent Methodist churches in the Philippines (IEMELIF). Over the next couple of years our TEL gospel team held half a dozen or so "mini crusades" that included training of counselors, public preaching and testimonies by Filipino evangelists, and extensive follow-up on the new converts. The bishop expressed publicly that this training and evangelistic program produced results beyond his expectations and stimulated their local church groups.

In 1978 the TEL team linked with well-known Filipino evangelist Greg Tingson and some leading evangelists from other Asian countries to hold a week-long, citywide crusade in Davao City on the island of Mindanao. The open-air meetings held in Magsaysay Park on the waterfront resulted in 2,212 people receiving personal counseling as they made decisions to receive the Lord Jesus Christ as their personal Savior. After the main meetings in Davao City, smaller gospel teams scattered to other cities in the area, including Tagum and General Santos, where additional hundreds of people responded to the invitations. Also, in 1978 we trained three other Filipinos in public evangelism for another Christian organization—Lakas Angkan Ministries (see below).

In 1980-1981 TEL invited six Filipino young men for a one-year, full-time training program in public evangelism and follow-up. They lived in our home as they studied the Word, prayed and did evangelism together. As this team traveled extensively into various parts of the Philippines, they rejoiced to see more than 3,000 people make public commitments to Christ.

This process has been repeated over the past two decades with various national training programs and evangelistic projects. By the beginning of the third millennium we had fielded two full-time evangelistic teams in the Philippines operating under the TEL banner.

## The Navigators Spawn Additional Indigenous Works

The Youth for Christ movement gave birth to dozens of other organizations. The Billy Graham Crusade, O.C. Ministries and World Vision are among the most prominent. Even so, The Navigators is a discipleship movement which also spawned various groups particularly in an overseas setting. I consider Training Evangelistic Leadership to have roots both in YFC and The Navigators.

Two prominent disciplemaking groups were started by Navigator staff leaders in the Philippines, beginning with Gene Tabor. Gene and Helen Tabor not only trained people like George and Corrine Cruz to handle the Billy Graham follow-up office, but also had discipled scores of singles and couples throughout the Philippines.

While Gene served in the U.S. Navy during the Korean War he met The Navigators leadership in the Philippines and helped in their work. Upon his discharge and more missionary orientation, The Navigators sent Gene and family to the Philippines in 1962 to lead the ministry. Gene was appalled by the corruption of various officials when he tried to get his household goods through customs. He determined not to give bribes to speed up the process, so spent many long hours in customs offices waiting for things to happen. He later observed that the fabric of deceit and dishonesty extended into nearly every other area of Filipino life.

Gene reasoned that if we are to make disciples in a Filipino context, then we must raise up people with a biblical standard of morality, who in turn would benefit the whole nation morally, economically and spiritually. With computer technology donated by friends, he produced a set of indigenous Bible study and Scripture memory materials which were printed in several Filipino dialects as well as basic English. He studied the Filipino culture and how best to disciple people within it.

## REACH, Incorporated

Eventually, the group around Gene Tabor founded a Filipino discipleship ministry called REACH (Resources Employment And Community Horizons). Today REACH has some 18 disciplemaking entities located throughout the Philippines, from northern Luzon to southern Mindanao.

"REACH believes it must take broader responsibility not only for the logistic support of the ministry, but also for active disciple-making among the millions of poor Filipinos. Not only among the poor, but also among people from all walks of life—the small and the great—with a view of presenting whole, mature persons in Christ."[1]

Scores of other people that Gene trained as university students have now obtained positions in high places of civil and government departments, particularly in the fields of agriculture, fishing, forestry, education, medicine and developing national products. These Christian Filipinos have begun to change their own society and in turn are providing lay missionaries who go into other countries with the Gospel.

By 1983 REACH had come into prominence as one of only six groups in the nation singled out by a Filipino research institute as making significant and lasting changes in Filipino "worldview, attitudes, and value system to permeate it with real Christians." A 1987 report illustrates one woman's successful influence in her work place.

"When Simplicia Pasicolan went to work for the Philippine government's Forestry Research Institute (FORI) in 1975, she knew of only three Christians in FORI. Today there are 1,000 employees in 15 offices around the country—95% of the employees have heard the Gospel, 60% profess to know Christ as Savior. Bible studies thrive. Christians are occasionally ridiculed for their faith, but administrators value their work. They can be trusted, work hard, and get along well with their co-workers."[2]

This kind of story continues to be repeated in a number of other government agencies and businesses in the Philippines. Christians can witness, hold Bible studies, and even sponsor evangelistic services on government property. During coffee breaks, lunch hours and after work, opportunities abound for discipling younger believers. Because of this unique approach, REACH personnel have permeated the offices of FORI, the Central Bank, the Ports Authority and various universities with the Gospel and lead Bible studies with their colleagues.

Some years ago a number of these agencies were seedbeds of corruption and inefficiency. Because of the growing number of Christians in these agencies, even at the executive and administrator levels, they are changing for the good.

## Lakas Angkan Ministry, Inc. (LAMI)

Another indigenous Filipino outgrowth of The Navigators is the Lakas Angkan Ministry, Inc.(LAMI) led by Boni and Luming Arzadon. Lakas Angkan translates roughly from the Tagalog language to mean "the power of the clan [that is, the power to reproduce and become mighty]," and is based on the promise in Isaiah 60:22: "A little one shall become a thousand, and a small one a strong nation; I the Lord will hasten it in his time".

This disciplemaking ministry stresses not only making disciples, but strongly emphasizes evangelism of all kinds. In addition, the organization has ordained leaders, be they full time or bi-vocational, and in many of its ministry areas it also has worship centers for its members, for their families, and for interested others in its respective communities. It too is penetrating all strata of Philippine society in many ways.

Some of its members, for example, initiated a unique evangelistic outreach in high schools through the president's moral values program. They enter a high school and present the Gospel by wearing T-shirts which picture the Bridge Illustration, then explain it in classes or in an auditorium, and sell the T-shirts to students and faculty afterward.

LAMI ties in closely with TEL. Boni serves on the TEL Philippines Board, and its members participate in TEL training programs (three men in Tagaytay in 1998). TEL personnel taught in LAMI's leadership training institute for two months in 1999, and LAMI provides manpower and counseling personnel for TEL-sponsored public evangelistic meetings. Two TEL evangelistic teams presently operate in the Philippines, available to any evangelical church or organization for meetings in their areas.

The Philippines today is one of the most receptive countries to the Gospel in the world at the beginning of this new millennium.

ENDNOTES:
1. "REACH Communiqué," Volume I, Number 1, May-June, 1978, page 3.
2. "Reach Ministries International Newsletter," July 31, 1987.

# Chapter 20

## FULL CIRCLE — CHINA AGAIN

At the end of 1950 I prepared to leave a China occupied by a communist government that seemed intent on stamping out the influence of Christianity by closing the doors of all churches and replacing the Bible with the sayings of Chairman Mao Tse-Tung. Eventually, not only churches but nearly all kinds of businesses and private education were closed. The government even shut down the famous conservatory of music in Shanghai because they said it taught the decadent classical music of a bourgeois society.

However, before leaving the country I looked forward in faith and hope to the time that I could return to China again to renew my missionary activity. I claimed this promise from the Word of God: "And behold, I am with thee, and will keep thee in all places whither thou goest, and will bring thee again into this land; for I will not leave thee until I have done that which I have spoken to thee of" (Genesis 28:15).

Then I prayed in my heart, *Lord, bring me back to this land, and let me disciple people again, both students and military. Lord, I want to live to witness the Gospel proclaimed again in public places in the city of Shanghai.*

Many years went by, and from time to time I remembered this passage I had claimed through prayer. I told some of my friends, "Yes, China will open again in my generation and in my lifetime." I reasoned that since China is the largest country in the world, God would not close it to the gospel message for longer than one generation, so I continued reading my Chinese Bible with the hope of using the language again to teach the Word to the people of China.

## The Plan to Return

In 1984, nearly 35 years after having left China with the prayer and hope of returning again, I believed that the political and religious climates had changed sufficiently to allow me to enter China once again. But how? I certainly did not want to go on a guided tour or to hit the tourist trail that leads to the Great Wall of China or to the tombs of clay soldiers unearthed beneath the ancient imperial city of Xian.

At this time my son-in-law, David Rice, led The Navigators ministry at Texas Tech University. In August 1984 Phyllis and I invited him to bring his family, including our daughter Susan and our grandchildren, plus about 15 university students, to hold a short training program in our TEL home in Denton, Texas. I lectured to the students on missions, and afterwards we all ate together at three tables in our living room where I related some of my China missionary "adventures."

After the meal one of the students, Kurt Diederich, described his adventures in riding a bicycle from Texas to New York and spending nights in his sleeping bag at appropriate stops along the way. Kurt was a member of a biking sports club.

At that point I became excited, "Hey Kurt, what if we gather a group of college students and bike across China?"

"Wow, that would be great!" was Kurt's immediate response. Others at the table expressed an interest in joining such a trip.

"But can we get in?" Kurt asked.

"Leave the China part to me," I replied. "You show us how to get the bicycles and all the other gear together and we'll plan that trip."

As we talked further, I explained that this would be a unique summer training program. Our primary goal would be to witness, but we also could have the adventure of biking across parts of China that foreigners have seldom seen. Forming a biking club of university students would give us a legitimate reason to get beyond the surveillance of the bureaucrats who controlled tourism. We would hope to get out into the countryside and bike through villages where no American had been since the communists took over.

In my earlier ministry I had developed a gospel tract called "The Bridge," which explained the plan of salvation step by step. It had originally been printed in Chinese, but we also had copies in English. If we could make personal friendships with the Chinese we met on our trip, then we could legally explain the Gospel to them by using the Bridge tract and a bilingual New Testament.

So Kurt and I busily recruited a bicycle riding evangelistic team to enter China. I went to Texas A&M University, where I had attended college before being called up for World War II duty, and recruited five Aggies eager to go to China to share their faith. Others joined us from Dave Rice's ministry at Texas Tech. In Houston a veteran Navigator staff leader, Kay Crumbie, joined us with students from Rice University. So in June 1985 our bicycle team assembled in Hong Kong, composed of 13 university students plus two leaders. Now we were ready to cross into China.

Kurt would be our "biking expert," Kay our "drill sergeant" to keep everyone in line; I was the "old China hand" who would deal with language and culture. Everyone on the team was committed to a ministry of evangelism and discipleship. I had prepared gospel tracts and New Testaments to be given out carefully on an individual basis to people with whom we would first make friends before sharing the Gospel. Some team members brought a collection of souvenirs with them, such as coins, stamps and buttons to hand out to children and students. Our basic witnessing materials were the Salvation Bridge tracts and the Gospel of John in a Chinese and English parallel edition.

I taught our group their first Chinese lesson: *Hao Hsiao Hsi* ["the Good News"]. And some of the team had memorized certain Scripture verses in Chinese. Our bicycle experts visited various bicycle outlets in Hong Kong and decided on a three-gear, 15-speed mountain model made in Taiwan.

## The June/July 1985 China Trip

Below is a condensation from my diary of our bicycle trip through China during those two months of 1985.

Monday, June 24, 1985—A typhoon blew into the Hong Kong

area just after I arrived from India on Saturday, and I found that one of the men had already arrived. The airline lost my sleeping bag, so I used this as an excuse to get inside the baggage area today in order to meet the other 13 men still due to fly in from the States and give them instructions where to go for accommodations. But only eight of the men showed up; five did not, even though the trip has been planned for weeks in advance. As I checked around, I was told that the remaining five would arrive on various planes within the next few days. (They did!)

Friday, June 28—As a team project we prepared all the materials today; I was in charge of the Chinese materials. The Bridge tract was photocopied, cut, stapled and assembled by hand. Each team member received 30 Bridge tracts, two or three Gospels of John, and two bilingual New Testaments. These would be distributed within our clothing and packs so as not to attract undue attention when we would pass through customs in China. I also brought my personal Chinese Bible and some other witnessing materials.

We wrapped souvenir ball point pens and buttons, to be given away as well as assorted coins and stamps in pieces of bright shiny paper. Kay supervised these activities. Kurt demonstrated how we could pack our gear into a saddle bag, which lay across the back of the luggage carrier and hung over the two sides of the bike, or into a black camera bag that could be attached to the handle bars. We limited ourselves to 20 pounds each, which included necessary clothing, sleeping bags, a water bottle, as well as assorted toiletries, medicines, mosquito spray, bicycle repair kit, a Bible, a notebook and stationery.

Saturday, June 29—This is D-day! Today we invade China! The team did an excellent job of bargaining for the purchase of the 15 bicycles. We bought these mountain tourist bikes for only U.S. $98 each, whereas their list price had been about U.S. $150 per bike.

We purchased tickets to go on the overnight ferry from Hong Kong to Guangzhou (formerly better known as Canton), so we went with all our gear to the ferry pier about two hours before loading time. Quite a group of curious Hong Kong local people gathered to watch the 15 Americans (some, like me, were not very gifted in assembling mechanical things) and they giggled among themselves at our inept activities. But this led to some excellent opportunities to tell various ones about our mission to China; some team members explained the Gospel to interested individuals. Thus we began our witness to the Chinese people.

We left through Hong Kong customs and boarded the ferry. Hong Kong at night is one of the most beautiful sights in the world. We ate together in the excellent Chinese restaurant on the ferry while looking out over the water at multicolored lights and neon signs along the shore. It was an exciting time, for tomorrow I would be returning to China again after 35 years.

Sunday, June 30—This is my mother's birthday. We had no problems with customs as the officials were smiling and helpful. No one had to open his bag. (This was far easier than my recent unpleasant experience with customs in India.) Everyone was thankful for getting through so easily and excited as we saw God working in our midst. We gathered on the pier and spent a couple of hours equipping each bike with its carrier rack and getting all our gear in place. Our first team purchase in China was 15 bottles of Coca-Cola and they sure tasted great!

Imagine my excitement as I actually started biking in a city in mainland China with 14 men behind me. I led the way across the city of Guangzhou northward toward the Lien Hua Hotel near a park by the lake. About halfway there I looked back and found that some of our students were missing. We sent a couple of men back to look for the stragglers, while the rest of us waited by the side of the road at a noodle shop. Meanwhile, two of the trainees, Doug and Peter, bought a bowl of noodles and began to talk with some of the other customers.

"The response here is incredible," Doug reported later as he came back to my table. He and Peter had explained in English the pictures in the Chinese bridge tract while pointing to Chinese characters that told how God had sent Jesus to give us eternal life. People had smiled and had responded to the invitation to receive Christ. The proprietor had responded by giving the team a present of a packet of ginseng leaf tea.

After about an hour our two scouts returned with the missing team members, who had trouble with their equipment, and we got settled in our modest hotel accommodations.

That afternoon I took several team members into the park to give them another Chinese lesson on key words to explain the Gospel. Everyone could now point to the Chinese characters in the tract and say in Mandarin such key words as "Good News, sin, death, Jesus, cross, eternal life." Several team members have had courses in Mandarin already and are somewhat fluent in the language.

Then we scattered across the park and looked for witnessing opportunities. I presented the Gospel for an hour to two men from the province of Hunan who were keenly interested. Willie Williams, a Texas Aggie, spoke with a woman of about 40 who professed to believe in Jesus. She gave us her address so that we could visit her home sometime in the future in the Szechuan Province. Then we met a young man about 20 years of age named Fan. He was a cook who went on duty about 4:00 A.M. each day. He knew something about the Christian faith and told us the location of a church although he had never attended there. He handed us his address and invited us to visit him when we could.

We talked with many people during the afternoon and were amazed at how open and friendly they were. Most of our team members had opportunities to share the Gospel with someone, and two or three people professed to believe in Christ.

Monday, July 1—We moved out of the Lien Hua Hotel into a less expensive one that caters to the Chinese people who are called *hua chiao* ["Chinese who live overseas"]. This day we also bought our train tickets for the next stage of our journey to visit the famous scenic mountain area of Guilin [25° North, 110° East], which former President Nixon on his visit to China had proclaimed to be the most beautiful place in all the earth.

Summary: The team members have scattered into small groups over the past few days and have aggressively visited various parks, historic buildings and restaurants with many opportunities to share the Gospel both in English and by using the Chinese gospel pictures of the steps needed to cross the bridge into eternal life. Everyone has collected some names and addresses of those who are keenly interested or even have professed to believe.

My good friend, the Reverend Samuel Chan, formerly my co-worker with The Navigators in Hong Kong and now the pastor of the Presbyterian Mandarin-speaking church in Hong Kong, will handle the follow-up. His young people will address envelopes by hand in Chinese writing so the mail will flow smoothly to its destination. Inside will be follow-up materials and a personal letter written in English to this new Chinese friend who is interested in Christianity.

Our three days in the city of Guangzhou have been productive beyond all expectations. Now we will travel for twenty hours by train into the heart of China.

Tuesday, July 2—Trying to get our bicycles onto the baggage car of our train bound for Guilin proved to be quite a hassle. At first we were turned down flat. Clerks told us to send the bicycles by freight which might take days or weeks to arrive. I intervened personally, and with the help of a sympathetic policeman managed to talk with someone who had more authority. When I was a green young missionary in Shanghai, my senior missionary and tutor, Dick Hillis, had taught me many valuable lessons about Chinese culture. For one thing, "It can't be done" is probably just an excuse. If you have patience and skill, *i ko fa tsu* [there is always a way]. So we finally worked out a way: Each student filled out four forms for his bike and attached it to his railway ticket. Each man would work his way to the baggage counter with his bike and pay the cashier 42 yuan (about 16 dollars). That was the theory; in practice, however, after we got the first bike through, everything was collected together.

Actually we traveled third class with assigned seat numbers but no berths, and the entire 20-hour ride cost less than US $10 per person. Later we found out why the tickets were so cheap.

Total bedlam reigned in the train station. With the help of a friendly train police officer we squeezed our way into the proper coach, but people already occupied our seats and most of them refused to move. Other friendlier passengers moved over to share a part of their seats. The general rule of thumb seemed to be that three people occupied two narrow bench seats, while across the aisle four people occupied three tiny seats. The seats had no dividers between them, providing a very cozy arrangement. Some people sat on the floor or on top of their luggage. The train was so crowded that only part of the luggage could be placed on overhead racks.

Well, at least we were not on the tourist trail; we could see no other foreigners in our part of the train. At one end of each coach was a boiler that prepared *kaisui* [boiled drinking water]. Everyone used his own private drinking cup. I put some dry tea leaves in the bottom of my cup and turned on the faucet to fill my cup with scalding hot water. For many years now I had appreciated hot boiled water as a very refreshing drink as did most of the Chinese passengers who lined up with their cups in front of the faucet. The Chinese believe that a piping hot drink is more cooling to the body on a hot sultry day than ice drinks; furthermore, no ice drinks were available. The bottled coke or orange drinks were not refrigerated, yet most of our team bought them anyway.

The team was in high spirits till about midnight as we were able to share Christ with other passengers. They found it difficult to sleep on a hard straight back bench-type seat with three people on the bench and three people facing you so closely that your knees touched constantly. Some of the men tried sleeping on the luggage on the floor or crawling into tight spaces under their benches. After 16 hours, however, it became an endurance contest. There were yet four more hours before the train reached Guilin that Wednesday at midday. The team was now experiencing a taste of what it was really like to live in the interior of an undeveloped country.

Wednesday, July 3—We settled into a Chinese-style hotel and the team displayed a great attitude here in interior China. We assembled our bikes and started out on our first gospel team excursion into the countryside. The scenery was fabulous. Throughout the legendary days of various Chinese dynasties, some of their famous poets and artists had come to Guilin to gain inspiration for their work. Even today, if you look at a typical Chinese scroll, you will see a picturesque painting of jagged mountains, a stream of water, rocks, trees, and misty clouds. The scenery is intended to produce a feeling of harmony, intrigue and romanticism in the mind of the beholder.

About 20 kilometers outside the city we reached a village of tribal people. They were very curious, friendly, and appreciative of the souvenirs that we gave them. We then began talking to three young men who were keenly interested in our gospel presentation. One had attended a church in Guilin city, and he began explaining the Good News to the other two. This attracted others and the audience soon grew to about 20 people with whom we were able to speak for about 20 minutes.

In the meantime two of our team members spoke with a man who said he wanted to believe, and subsequently he confirmed his decision as we talked and prayed together in Chinese. Rabih's seeker had studied English previously and was now studying for his Ph.D. He prayed in English to receive Christ. One of the women also told us that she had believed. That was quite a harvest in this village! The Spirit of God had done His preparatory work in hearts so that many were ready to trust in Jesus. Apparently we were the first foreign witnesses who had come to their village in their lifetime.

Thursday, July 4—One team member, Peter Van Vliet, who had come from the Netherlands to study in Texas, had never been baptized. He wanted me to baptize him in a river in China. So our team took our bikes and followed a stream looking for a place where the water flowed fast and clear. After biking many kilometers uphill we found such a place where the water was deep and refreshing. Hardly anyone was in sight as we began our baptismal service, but soon people appeared as if out of nowhere to watch this curious sight. Peter had commissioned me to speak in Chinese, thus the baptismal rites were understood by the onlookers. They stood by respectfully as I explained the meaning of baptism, then prayed to the eternal God in heaven as I baptized Peter in the name of the Triune God. After the ceremony ended we distributed tracts to our Chinese audience.

Suddenly I heard a splash as one of our students dived into the pool of refreshing water; then with another splash a second team member dived in and swam about in his underwear. Some Chinese boys then dived in to join in the fun, but they swam without their underwear. Soon nearly everyone had taken a quick swim on this hot summer day at the "old swimming hole." The American and Chinese cultures do indeed have some similarities.

It was a good thing that we had gotten wet while swimming, for on the way back to the village we rode through a severe thunderstorm with heavy rain and got thoroughly soaked.

Friday, July 5—This was a day to rest for us as we caught up on correspondence and any personal matters. In the afternoon I gave a nearly 2-hour lecture to the team on Chinese phrases and how to present the Gospel in a Chinese setting. I pointed out some of the positive things about the Chinese people; they are industrious, curious, loyal to their families, and able to endure incredible hardship by bending yet not breaking. But on the negative side they are very critical and quick to accuse, and, of course, engage in the ordinary sins of unsaved people. The Chinese culture highly respects *tien* [heavenly authority] and does have a keen sense of justice and fairness. The people are strong in the importance of relationships and the necessity of a *baojen* [a go-between] for all important affairs of life such as marriage and business. Thus Jesus can be presented as the go-between that brings a person to God in order for him or her to obtain eternal life. The concept of presenting the Gospel through the Bridge illustration, with the cross of Jesus Christ as the Bridge to salvation, was originally developed within the Chinese culture on the island of Taiwan.

Saturday, July 6—We leave about 11 A.M. on another bike excursion into a different area. About twelve kilometers out the road dead ends at a certain village. I talk to two young men, one of whom volunteers in Mandarin, "My friend here is a Christian but I am not."

So one fellow believes but does not speak Mandarin, the other fellow speaks Mandarin but does not believe. But all Chinese read from the same Bible. So we read together from my Chinese Bible and the Christian explains the Gospel verses into the local dialect which they both understand. After a long chat the seeker seems to understand the Gospel and I give him a New Testament which he appreciates greatly and promises to read. Then we take photos and exchange addresses. Some of the other team members also have good witnessing opportunities this day.

Sunday, July 7—Today we attended the official local church of Guilin. It is the only one for a population of over one million people. Church services in present-day China start at noon and are officially endorsed by the government. If you are a Muslim, you can get off work to attend a mosque on Friday at noon; if you are a Christian, you may get off work to attend a local church on Sunday at noon.

I walked over to the Guilin church around ten o'clock this Sunday morning. The front doors were still locked, so I went into a side alley and found the door open there. Behind the main sanctuary was a small area for chapel and family services, while the pastor and his wife lived upstairs. The main sanctuary, a solid stone structure built by former missionaries, held about 300 people downstairs plus a balcony that could seat another 100 worshipers.

I appeared at the door and introduced myself to the pastor who was very gracious. I asked his honorable age and he apologized for having only attained 65 years, so I assured him that he was more honorable than I who was a mere 64. Knowing that I was certainly a missionary, he asked me for my denomination. I replied that my spiritual roots were *Chin Hsin Huei* [Southern Baptist]. He was delighted and immediately switched to English, "This church was formerly Southern Baptist, but now all denominations in the city worship here."

As we talked further I discovered that he had attended a Baptist church in Shanghai during the same time period that I had taught a weekly Bible class at the Baptist Seminary on Pao Shan Road in 1949. We had mutual friends among the faculty of that long-gone era.

Then we had a long professional talk for perhaps an hour as he answered rather intimate questions about the condition of the churches throughout China and we speculated about the future direction of the government regarding church affairs. In turn I told him about religious conditions in Hong Kong and in America. I showed him our gospel tracts and memory verses, then gave him one of my foreign-printed Chinese New Testaments and a beautifully decorated children's storybook printed in Taiwan. He hugged me with tears in his eyes as he clutched this precious material in his hands.

The church service was to start at 12:30, so the pastor invited the whole team to attend. "We want to help in the local offering," I volunteered. "Can we use *jen min pi* [tourist certificate money]?" I asked.

"You can bring any kind of money," he replied smiling.

So I gathered the team together and we parked our 15 bicycles in front of the church. The service proceeded according to typical Chinese style with which I was familiar from my early days in Shanghai; it is the pattern that is still used in many Chinese churches in Taiwan and Hong Kong. The first verse of a hymn is sung over and over again until the audience becomes familiar with the simple western tune. Then the other verses are added. Thus the people practice singing the songs that are on the program before the official worship service begins. The preaching is highly biblical and fundamental.

This Sunday a 70-year-old woman preacher retold the story of the rich man and Lazarus from Luke 16. Then she elaborated from James 5 on the judgment awaiting the rich who are wicked and from Revelation 20:11-15 on the great white throne judgment of God's wrath poured out upon all sinners who do not repent and believe in Jesus during their lifetimes. (Those western critics who infer that the pastors who preach in official churches in China are soft on sin perhaps have never attended a typical modern-day Chinese service.)

Yet there were some problems. The invitation hymn was "Just As I Am," but the pastor did not invite anyone to make a public commitment. The preacher spoke in Mandarin, but most of the people spoke only their local dialect. The message seemed heavy and abstract, as well as lacking in illustrations. Some people listened well, but several girls put their heads on the back of the seats and slept unashamedly. About 200 attended that morning, of which about half are baptized believers out of a city of one million people.

I discovered that only a few Christians met in private homes. The city had no visible sign of any significant underground church or witnessing group. Yes, the church survived under Communism and many stood valiantly for Christ in the midst of severe persecutions, but the claim that a great revival is sweeping across China and tens of millions have embraced Christianity would be an exaggeration. As in Japan or Northern India, the total Christian population of Mainland China of all kinds and categories would not exceed 1%.

My heart bleeds for the desperate Chinese church, for there is no Sunday school, no training program, and only a handful gather for the prayer meetings. In most rural churches there is no choir, no leadership training, no discipleship. The leaders are mainly elderly and the seminaries are graduating very few students, most of whom do not want to accept the sacrificial job of a pastor but are looking for opportunities abroad or in the business world.

The Chinese church desperately needs help from the outside. It needs encouragement, teaching, materials, methodology, funds to build new churches and our loving prayers. Jesus prayed that his church might become as one by loving and helping one another (John 17:21-23).

Monday, July 8—Biking from Guilin to Yang Shua. We departed about 8:00 A.M. and bicycled along the beautiful Li [Plum] River toward Yang Shua some 30 kilometers away. Around noon we stopped at a village to buy some watermelon. I talked to a man who spoke good Mandarin. Keith Kline shared the Bridge Illustration in English and called me over to share the Gospel more clearly in Chinese. I was right in the middle of eating juicy watermelon with my hands. Dripping watermelon from my left hand I explained the Bridge with my right hand while Keith flipped through the pages. Then Keith rescued the watermelon out of my left hand as I got more involved in explaining the tract and the Bible.

The man was very interested. After we had presented the Bridge Illustration, I explained chapter three of the Gospel of John (the story of Jesus and Nicodemus). I had no more Gospels of John left, so I gave him Keith's copy which the man promised to read. He was about 35 and well educated. To the best of his knowledge there were no Christians in that area. He had never met a Christian before, but he had heard vaguely about some of their teachings. He promised that he would read the Gospel of John and invited us to come with him to see his village.

We arrived there about 2:30 P.M., then all of us crowded into a restaurant for a hearty meal of ten Chinese dishes with rice, soup, and tea, which cost less than 25 cents per person (American money).

Later this day as we entered Yang Shua, we were greeted by many firecrackers announcing the opening of a new hotel. The owner showed us the bright new rooms upstairs all ready to be occupied for less than a dollar per person. Then we all went down to his restaurant to drink tea and eat peanuts while they got the rooms ready.

However, after a while the owner returned with sincere apologies, "Sorry, but the local authorities will not give permission for us to lodge foreigners."

Most of our team remained at the restaurant while Kay Crumbie and I went out to look for a hotel. We checked out several locations and settled on one that was both clean and economical. When we returned to the restaurant, we found that our team had a very fruitful time in witnessing. Four people had prayed to receive Christ, including the hotel owner, a school teacher, a waitress, and a salesgirl from a nearby shop.

Then a young man came up to me and told us to stop talking about religion. I apologized *tui pu chi* ["sorry!"] and started to walk away. He followed me and told me that there are three religions in China and we should not propagate a foreign one. I wanted to inform him that Christianity had come to the capital of ancient China more than 1,000 years ago, in the days of the Nestorians; but I doubted if he knew much older Chinese history, so I held my tongue and walked away.

That night ten members of our team went back to the restaurant to do follow-up. All four who had made professions of faith acknowledged that they currently believed in Jesus Christ as their personal Savior, so we gave out follow-up materials to each one of them.

Tuesday, July 9—This morning I met with the 22-year-old school teacher for more instruction and prayer, then we took a round-trip boat voyage down the Li River through some magnificent scenery. We snapped many pictures of places that looked like the scenery painted on many Chinese scrolls. The tour guide on the boat also took us to a commune. This form of living was out of vogue now, but in the days of the Cultural Revolution (1965-1975) many educated people, including Christians and businessmen from the cities were banished to communes to do forced manual labor. Inside the commune I spoke with an elderly man whom I discovered to be about my age. I quoted some Scripture verses in Chinese and explained the Gospel to him. This man was familiar with the gospel story but had never been to a church. We sat down together and talked about many things; he was open to the teaching, but there is no church in this area. We must find a way to join with our Chinese Christian brethren to send laborers into this wide open harvest.

On the return boat ride we witnessed to an Australian. Then a retired 70-year-old Chinese professor told us about some of the humiliating experiences he had suffered at the hands of the "Red Guards" during the Cultural Revolution. He now had a daughter in America and would like to visit her. Kay later tried to witness to this man but he was full of humanistic philosophy. He claimed that the older Chinese leaders had been corrupt but the present ones were good for the country.

It was already dark when the boat returned to Yang Shua. The elderly professor could not see too well at night but wanted to visit some of his foreign friends. I accompanied him to the place where they were supposed to be, but no one answered the door. So I walked him back to the hotel. I never knew whether he was spying on us or was merely disoriented, but he certainly was vocal in expressing the communist party line.

This evening I returned to the restaurant and met again with three of the keen new believers—the hotel owner, the waitress and the salesgirl. I had met in the morning with the 22-year-old teacher named Tung. These were the four who had prayed last night and now earnestly wanted to be nurtured in the faith. What a pity that there was no church, nor pastor, nor missionary in Yang Shua, a city of about 100,000 people. As a team we prayed to the Lord of the harvest to send out laborers into His Chinese harvest. We took some more pictures and I promised to send copies to the four when I got back to Hong Kong. I also made some additional contacts in the restaurant through these new believers.

Wednesday, July 10—One of our team members went to an art shop early in the morning to buy some souvenirs and the owner identified himself as a Christian. Thus we now had located a Christian family in Yang Shua, so we paid them a visit. The husband was an artist who had heard the Gospel from an American many years ago and had believed. His wife was from a Christian family and her uncle was a pastor. They operated a small shop that sold his paintings and other Chinese art objects. The artist told us that there was one other Christian in town and occasionally they got together but not on a regular basis. No other Christian group of any kind in the area was known to him. The closest church was in Guilin about 30 kilometers away. I told him about the four new believers and suggested that they meet together periodically for mutual encouragement.

Our whole team then visited his art shop and we bought some paintings to send to our American friends. I also promised to send him some discipleship materials from Hong Kong. Tomorrow we will be leaving Yang Shua. Our visit to this city has indeed been a remarkable experience.

Thursday, July 11—A little after midnight some workers had unloaded a huge boiler for purifying water, weighing several tons, in the back of our hotel right near my room. They had attached a bright light outside the building and were working at night trying to roll the boiler along some logs to its designated location. It was impossible to sleep, so I visited with some Chinese guests across the hall.

Two of these guests were from Nanning, which is in Guangxi Province, where they ran a chopsticks factory. One of them was a believer who attended the local church in Nanning, where there were about 25 Christians; but his knowledge of the Scriptures was very limited. I gave him one of my last New Testaments and encouraged him in the faith.

In the meantime the workmen rolled the huge boiler in place and finally about 1:45 A.M. turned off the bright light outside. At last I was able to crawl under my mosquito net to get some sleep, but at 5:15 A.M. Keith threw a rock into the room hoping to wake up my roommate, but woke me instead. We ate breakfast at 6:30 and prepared to ride our bikes to another city called Ping Lo.

Ping Lo lay 83 kilometers to the southwest. With only a short stop for drinks and snacks, we rode into Ping Lo hot and tired in the late afternoon and headed for the main hotel in the middle of the town. When we arrived the proprietor informed us that Ping Lo is off limits to all foreigners, so we could not spend the night there. The city is an out-of-the-way place with no railway or even regular bus service, and the closest major city to it was Yang Shua, many biking hours away behind us.

"Can we eat in your restaurant?" I asked. So we ordered a full rice meal, ate it gladly, and waited for further instructions. Before dark the officials came to interrogate us about why we had come illegally to Ping Lo; they also spoke English. (I expected to come back to China as a professional Christian worker, but Kay was just a tourist from Texas. So he took over giving all the explanations and taking responsibility for the team. I posed as an elderly man who was a kind of chaperone for the students on this bicycle trip.)

Kay explained in English that the town of Ping Lo had been recommended to us by the government hotel officials in Yang Shua, so we merely had followed their advice. After the proper amount of arguing and discussing the issues among themselves, the officials of Ping Lo allowed our team to spend the night at the hotel in their city.

Friday, July 12—Ping Lo. I gave instructions to our team not to be aggressive in witnessing in this place and to be very polite to the authorities.

But the team was not sensitive to the intense surroundings and began distributing many Bridge tracts to people in the town. On top of that, Kay, our American leader, who had been an officer in the U.S. military, lectured the communist officials on the values of our democratic system and our rights as American citizens in their country. I tried to disappear and went off alone into a park to pray and meditate.

Saturday morning, July 13—About 2:00 A.M. while I was sleeping in my underwear a flashlight shone in my face. Three people in uniform, two men and a woman, were in my room; she was the interpreter. They asked me all kinds of questions. They flashed one of the Bridge tracts in my face and I answered their questions in English.

"Are you connected with your government?" they asked.

"No, we have no connection with the U.S. government," I replied.

"Are you Christians?"

"Yes, we are Christians. Nearly every one in America is a Christian."

"What do all these younger men do?"

"These are all university students. They all attend one of the universities in our state of Texas."

"What do they study?"

"Goodness, everything: engineering, business, computer, arts." More questions came at me; then . . .

"Why did you come to Ping Lo?"

"We are seeing your beautiful country on bicycles. Your people have treated us wonderfully. China is a wonderful place to visit." And so on.

All my answers were truthful. The one question they did not ask was, "Who are you?" Then they switched to Chinese and the leader asked me not to give out any more of the white pamphlets (Bridge tracts); he also told me that we would be sent back to Yang Shua on a hired truck, but we must pay the expenses. We negotiated a price to which I agreed. I volunteered that our leader, Kay, would take care of the bill. The truck would be ready Sunday morning.

Several of our team had some minor medical problems, so we were allowed to visit the government clinic staffed by two young doctors from out of town. The doctors, who spoke fairly good English, not only treated our team members without charge but offered all kinds of general advice and information. Our men explained the Gospel to them and the doctors asked many questions about Christianity in private.

Then, still in private, they expressed their opinion to us whom they now trusted, "Our government is very corrupt, but you people are good."

We exchanged various gifts with one another. The doctors gave us food and medicine, while we gave them some English books and various souvenirs. One of the doctors professed to believe in Jesus.

Sunday, July 14—Early this morning we heard a police siren. A decorated police officer rode in the sidecar of a motor vehicle that had a flag mounted on a pole, and the contraption stopped in front of our hotel. It looked just like a German motorcycle sidecar one would see in a vintage World War II film. The officer climbed out stiffly and appeared to be very self-important. It was a hilarious sight, but we didn't dare reveal our thoughts publicly.

Kay gathered all the team members with their bicycles and equipment in the downstairs hotel lobby as the police came in to escort us out of their city. Outside several hundred curious bystanders formed a circle around us and the police as they watched the spectacle. This was a big event in the drab lives of these ordinary people. The crowd was definitely on our side and some showed their support by their smiles and body language. The two doctors and other acquaintances waved goodbye. We rode in a special bus while our bicycles followed us in a truck; we were being sent to another province to the city of Wu Dzou, located where the Kuei River and Pearl River met together. The road meandered along the Kuei River through absolutely magnificent scenery.

As I reflected on the events of the past few days in Ping Lo, I gave thanks to the Lord for His protection and guidance. In spite of my cautioning the team had witnessed boldly and effectively for Jesus and I was proud of them. Though we were being escorted out of the province, their spirits were high. As Jesus' disciples, we could rejoice in the privilege of being somewhat "mistreated" while lifting up the name of the Lord. Yet we were treated with respect and courtesy by the authorities, perhaps because of our quiet compliance to their demands and perhaps also because they sensed that we had the support of the people.

My friend Kay was more aggressive in defending the correctness of our position and our rights as American citizens than I would have been; yet even so he argued so firmly and boldly that I believe the authorities became somewhat confused and cautious, though perhaps a bit angry. Anyway, I let Kay do the talking through the woman interpreter because he doesn't intend to do future work in China. They did raise the price for hiring their trucks above what we had originally agreed on and Kay argued the point but lost that battle.

A jolly plump fellow in a white sport shirt accompanied us in the bus. He spoke good English and told us he was our friend and would find us a good hotel in the next province. The authorities obviously sent him and behind his back we called him our "tail."

When we reached Wu Dzou that evening another jolly plump fellow, also in a white sports shirt, took us to our hotel. There were no rooms available that Sunday, but they told us we could sleep on cots in the hall and get our own rooms the next day. Our new "tail" was extremely friendly and loved to practice his English. It would have been easy to shake him, for all we had to do was get on our bicycles and ride out into the countryside.

Monday, July 15—We moved into nice rooms on the seventh floor of our hotel this morning. We occupied five rooms with three people to a room. Soap, towels and hot water were provided, so we enjoyed our first hot bath in more than a week. This to us was luxury.

Wu Dzou is located on the Pearl River which flows all the way to Guangzhou several hundred miles away. Actually the main part of the city of Wu Dzou is an island, and the Pearl River divides and flows by it on either side. We took an exploratory bike trip in the afternoon to look over the area.

Tuesday, July 16—We scheduled a team bike ride traveling along the Pearl River for ten kilometers, then turned into a dirt road to ride into the countryside.

Around noon we stopped at a village to eat noodles and chat with the people. The Chinese in the rural areas are much easier to meet and have time on their hands to chat. They would listen to our stories about Jesus for as long as we were willing to talk. We still had some gospel tracts with us, so we distributed them sparingly to those most interested.

Wednesday, July 17—Today we biked further out into the countryside. We stopped in front of a school and ordered *chi sui* [bottled drinks]. At first the village looked almost deserted, but soon a crowd appeared to get a look at these strange foreigners. The different team members did their thing to make friends among the villagers. Kurt performed rope tricks and sleight of hand feats. Doug got a shy young girl of about five years of age to sit on his lap while he showed her a children's picture book. Rabih gave the Bridge Illustration of salvation through Jesus Christ. One village girl practiced the English phrases she had learned at school. I did my pantomime tricks for the children.

Soon one family invited us into their house for lunch and treated our whole team to a great full rice meal with many vegetable dishes. We stayed for two hours talking with the people and sharing the Gospel. The villagers here had vaguely heard about Christianity but no church or Christian group existed anywhere near them. We had the great privilege of being able to sow the seed of the Word of God among those who have not yet heard the Good News of Jesus.

In the evening our team ate in a nice restaurant along the Pearl River, and after our meal we strolled across the Kuei River bridge adorned with multicolored lights on a lovely moonlight evening.

Thursday, July 18—Our "guide" in the white sport shirt helped us purchase our tickets to go by ferry boat on an overnight trip down the Pearl River to Guangzhou. He insisted that we buy our tickets through him rather than going to the local ticket office. We complied and this made him happy as he received a small financial award, so he accompanied us to the ferry and got our bikes properly stored as well. Later on I decided that each province had its own local authorities and special agents to keep tab on tourists. This was not necessarily bad because these agents would try to protect the tourist from being robbed or cheated or from suffering embarrassment; they are curious but seldom interfere with normal activities if one operates within the law. Their jurisdiction seems to be confined within the province where they work. Their pay seems to come as much from selling favors to the tourists as from the government. After we said goodbye to this man we never picked up another "tail" in a white sport shirt on this trip.

In Chinese history this system dates back to the days of the Mandarin officials of the imperial dynasties who were the overseers of local affairs. The present government merely revised the system somewhat by replacing the Mandarin official with a communist cadre official. He has limited power to handle local affairs at his discretion as long as he stays loyal to Beijing and follows the generally accepted party line.

The overnight ferry ride down the Pearl River from Wu Dzou to Guangzhou was picturesque. Returning to Guangzhou is like entering the modern world with its five star hotels and department stores. We stayed for several days visiting the local churches and making new friends among the unsaved. We also took more bike trips out into the rural areas with lots of interesting contacts with students, factory workers and farmers.

Summary—In the four weeks we have been in China, we have made about 70 contacts with individuals who have prayed to receive Christ or at least professed a deep interest in studying the Bible. When we reached Hong Kong, we felt like we had entered a modern American city. Each team member gathered the names of contacts he had made in China and wrote each one a personal letter in English. Then the Chinese young people of the Presbyterian Mandarin-speaking church addressed all the envelopes in Chinese handwriting, enclosing appropriate follow-up materials.

This has been an historic trip on which TEL would build its future ministry in China. Two of the team members, Keith Kline and Mike Harrison, would become part of our TEL missionary staff.

## The 1987 China Trip

In 1987 I gathered another team of several college students and took a second trip into China. This time my son Len went with us.[2] We traveled by train to Shanghai to revisit this largest city of China where I had begun my missionary service in January 1949.

During the month of May the victorious communist army had marched down Nanking Road in front of my apartment and overran Shanghai. At first the newly installed communist government put on a show of being fair to the Christians, but as time went on many of the Christian leaders were sent off into the countryside for forced indoctrination. My Chinese co-worker, evangelist John Goo, was put in prison and died a martyr for the faith.

The worst time of harassment for Christians occurred in the ten-year period of 1965 to 1975, commonly known as the Cultural Revolution. During this time every church was closed and many Bibles and hymn books confiscated. Chairman Mao Tse Tung boasted that after his death the Bible would become obsolete and his own "red book" containing his famous sayings would be found everywhere in China.

Mao died in 1976. Since then a miraculous thing has taken place. The Chinese people, embarrassed by the injustices and corruption of the Mao era, have largely repudiated his theories. In fact, 20 years after Mao's death one would have to search diligently to find even one copy of Mao's "little red book" of sayings. However, every Sunday many earnest Chinese believers in every larger city of China flock into local churches that have reopened their doors, so now these Christians can listen to the wonderful Word of God and sing hymns of praise to the Lord God whom they worship.

When I returned to Shanghai with my son Len and several other college students, I worshipped at Moore Memorial Methodist Church where I had taught my first follow-up classes for the converts of the David Morken and Andrew Gih YFC Shanghai Crusade. I learned that this church, now renamed Moore Grace Church, had been the first church to reopen after Mao's death. While participating in the service by singing the hymns and reciting the responses in proper Chinese Mandarin, I attracted the attention of some local church members. They insisted on introducing me to their senior pastor who had led the first services for the reopening of the Chinese churches on Palm Sunday 1979.

"It was marvelous," he recounted to me over a cup of tea while showing some photos of that momentous occasion.

At that first service people pressed into every available space, not only occupying all the seats and aisle spaces but even standing on the platform and peering in through the open windows. The pastor could hardly find room to preach. Loudspeakers placed in adjacent rooms and outside enabled the audience to hear. He estimated more than 2,500 people attended that first service on Palm Sunday morning. Then they held another service and yet another and still another. They continued all that day holding five services, all of which were filled and overflowing. The pastor estimated that more than 12,000 people worshiped at his church on that first Sunday. Oh what joy, what tears, what excitement as the people were once more allowed to worship God in a public service in China!

So now I have gone full circle. I have come back to Shanghai, China and into the very church where I first began my missionary career some 28 years before. The Chinese church loves and admires the missionary who will understand the language and blend into the culture.

But as the missionary comes back, he should come to be a servant not to be in charge or to control. And he does not come to set up a new group, but builds on the one foundation of Jesus Christ that was laid by the early missionaries through their sacrificial work.

In a nation of a billion people there is a small but genuine church enduring persecution in the midst of a hostile environment with a minimum of resources and trained leadership.

Who will volunteer to go as a servant-missionary?

ENDNOTES:
1. Team members who went on the 1985 trip were: Jim Briscoe, Kay Crumby, Kurt Diederich, Jackie Giddens, Mike Harrison, Keith Kline, Bruce Moore, Lee Pardue, Sam Pyeatte, Roy Robertson, Rabih Sabra, Peter Van Vliet, Doug Wendel, William Williams, Doug Wilson.
2. Team members who went on the 1987 trip were: Brian Hutt, Barry Moore, Len Robertson, Roy Robertson.

# CHALLENGE FOR
# THE FUTURE

*(2000 A.D. until the Rapture)*

International Servant-Missionary Pattern

# BACKGROUND

Part V is the climax of the book, the point toward which all the historical and personal data has been moving. It is the "passing of the torch" to the next generation, those who by God's grace will possibly complete the task of God's world mission in their generation. It is still God's mission, not ours; we must still use God's strategy, not ours; we have the mandate and the strategy still laid out in Scripture and the history of the past two millennia to show us what to do and what not to do.

This book has been written to emphasize positive action. Here is a workable strategy to evangelize the world, which when followed by committed men and women does indeed work! The past 50 years give clear testimony of how the job can be done effectively. So the torch is being passed on. The completion of the task begun by those who labored faithfully now becomes a real challenge to the new generation. Now it's your turn! Go to it for God's glory!

# Chapter 21

## A NEW KIND OF MISSIONARY

Often I hear the statement made that such and such a country is now closed to missionaries. For instance, someone will point out that the government of India or the government of China is no longer inviting missionaries. My immediate response, though not always vocalized, is this: "Are you ignorant of missionary history or of the clear commands of the Scriptures? When were missionaries ever invited? Missionaries are not invited; they are sent!"

Carey was not invited to India; not only did the Hindu leaders oppose him, but the British East India commercial interests would not allow him to settle in Calcutta. So Carey took refuge in the nearby Danish protectorate of Serampore.

In the days of Hudson Taylor the British Parliament debated at one point whether to order Taylor and the China Inland Mission out of China. Some argued that missionaries interfered with the commercial interests of England such as tea and the profitable opium trade. Other critics argued that missionaries were responsible for local riots in the interior of China. In the days of the apostle Paul the Roman government certainly did not invite Paul to evangelize within their domain. Yes, throughout history the principalities and powers of this world and spiritual wickedness in high places oppose the advance of the Gospel (Ephesians 6:12). The missionary is not invited; he is sent.

I have heard others say, "But now that an indigenous national church has been established, missionaries are no longer needed." Immediately I argue that this premise is faulty in logic and contrary to the Scriptures.

My first argument is based on a major tenet of the New Testament which teaches that the church is one body of which Christ is the head (Ephesians 1:22,23; Colossians 1:18). Jesus prayed in the garden of Gethsemane that the future believers from all nations might be one in unity with the Father and the Son. "I in them, and Thou in me, that they may be made perfect in one; and that the world may know that Thou hast sent me, and hast loved them, as Thou hast loved me" (John 17:23).

The world will try to turn the Christians against one another so it is very important that true believers stand together against all the attacks of the enemy, especially in times of fiery trials and persecutions. The Communist government in the terrible days of the Cultural Revolution (1965-1975) set out to destroy the Word of God and the church of Jesus Christ. The basic strategy was to divide and conquer, first by turning the local Christians against the missionary. The Communists aimed their deceitful devices to attack the historical roots of the local church denominations so as to isolate the Chinese Christians from the worldwide fellowship of believers. The next attack was to turn Christian groups within China one against another by sowing seeds of mistrust and fear. The body of Christ worldwide must stand together.

Even with a greatly improved situation in China the presence of foreigners, especially the missionary who understands the language and culture, is a deterrent against harsh and unfair treatment. Generally speaking, the more foreigners, the more freedom, because China is particularly sensitive to world opinion. It is also true that although the official policy of almost any non-Christian government will be to try to discourage any missionary activity, most of the Chinese Christians love and revere the missionary and long for fellowship with those who come to them from other lands. So, the argument that the Chinese church is indigenous and therefore needs no outside help or influences plays into the hands of those who oppose the advance of the Gospel.

My second argument is that any church or culture which isolates itself from all outside forces will become self-centered and stagnant. Every individual or group has certain "blind spots;" this is true even of nationalities. The American church is greatly enriched by those who come from all nations to live among us. The hundreds of thousands of international students in our universities increase our insight and world vision. So the missionary can open windows to broaden the horizon and give encouragement to local Chinese Christians. It is even significant that the missionary be a foreigner, a non-Chinese, one from an outside culture who thinks from a different perspective, and also one who is not obligated to any particular side. All countries have factions and prejudices. The godly missionary can be a peacemaker from his neutral or non-aligned position, particularly to bring reconciliation and understanding between the official church and house church groups. Some of the TEL missionaries in China have done just that. For example, when a certain young man was courting an attractive lady from the other church group, the non-aligned foreigner was called upon to help prepare the marriage.

The third reason lies in the fact that the body is one, but the gifts are many. Each divinely called missionary is sent out with his gift to add to the local body. The American church has rich heritage and talents and resources. So has the church of Singapore and Korea. The American church has developed concepts and methods of ministry that can increase the effectiveness and expand the outreach of churches in other lands. So we must continue to send missionaries as the Bible instructs in order to fulfill the Great Commission.

Yet today's missionary should be very sensitive to the feelings and culture of the country to which he is sent. The church has already been established. The leadership is in place. He must not control or criticize or tear down the existing structures. He does not go to take command, but rather to serve. His role is delicate—not primarily a leader who serves those who work under him, but rather a servant where leadership is displayed by setting a godly example.

## The International Servant-Missionary

Millions of dollars and thousands of lives have been sacrificed to lay the foundations. A national church has now been formed and with its own leadership. But the task is far from complete. Multitudes have not yet heard the gospel message. In many interior areas there is not yet a church or even a gospel witness. The missionary and local church leaders should cooperate in tackling the great problems which remain. We must serve sacrificially with great sensitivity to local cultural feelings.

## High Priority

WANTED: The humble, sensitive servant-missionary who will serve alongside the local Christian leadership while sacrificing himself for the people to whom God sends him. A new kind of missionary—the International Servant-Missionary.

Here are some recent examples how a missionary can return to help a church which was founded by missionaries with great sacrifice and difficulties in troubled times but is now established and led by the nationals. We can help and bless one another.

*Scene 1: Ho Chi Minh City, Vietnam*

Weng K., a young missionary sent out from Singapore to Vietnam, and I are crossing the street at dusk near the central market of downtown Ho Chi Minh City, formerly called Saigon. As we start to cross the main thoroughfare, a big truck approaches and Weng K. grabs my arm and pulls me back. He does not want his elderly friend (that's me) to take a chance on not being able to make it across in time. Closely following this truck are several other trucks and so we wait for all of them to pass. Just as we resume the crossing, a motorcycle with its license plate covered and carrying two helmeted riders zooms in front of us. The rider in front hits against my arm and the rider in back snatches my briefcase. Weng K. lets out a yell and begins to chase the motorbike on foot but has no chance to catch up with them.

As he returns in frustration, Weng K. asks me the obvious question, "What was in your briefcase?"

"No money, of course," I reply. "But my passport was in the briefcase because we are heading to the money changers and they require it for identification. Wah, this is the only time I have ever carried my passport with me since I arrived in Vietnam. It also contained a Vietnamese language book and my glasses, but I have an extra pair."

"It is my fault," Weng K. says dejectedly. "I should not have insisted you change your money tonight instead of tomorrow morning, as you suggested. And I should have let you continue on across the street."

"No," I assert, "the circumstances are too strange. This is the only time I have carried my passport out on the street. And the timing of the caravan of trucks is not just an ordinary thing."

I assure him, "It is not your fault; it is not my fault. I have enough missionary experience to know that this has been arranged by God. Although it appears to be an attack from the enemy, God has allowed this to happen. Weng K., at this point I cannot understand why this has happened, but in a few days God will show us the reason."

After discussing the matter further while eating in a Chinese restaurant, we then go to the local police station to report the theft. The next day Weng K. contacts the American Embassy and reports to me this distressing news.

"There is no American Embassy in Ho Chi Minh City. We must fly to Hanoi, over 1,000 kilometers away, and it usually takes five working days to obtain a new American passport. This Friday, Saturday, and Sunday are big Vietnamese national holidays and Monday is an American holiday. The American Embassy will be closed all four days."

"Wow, I must fly out on Tuesday morning. Our whole Filipino staff is traveling from various parts of the Philippines to attend our annual staff conference at which I will speak. Usually, I have a flexible schedule, but this time everything is tightly booked."

We are still in Ho Chi Minh City. Somehow we must get airplane tickets to Hanoi, then go through all the procedures to obtain a new passport at the American Embassy within the next 48 hours. So Weng K., a sharp young Asian, springs into action. He calls the American Embassy in Hanoi and talks to the woman in charge of issuing passports. He faxes her all passport information and the local police verification of the theft. He gets her to talk to me personally, so I can explain my predicament.

"It normally takes five working days," she explains to me patiently. "If a passport is stolen we must contact Washington. And this weekend, Friday through Monday, are not working days. They are all holidays."

"But I must be in Manila for an important conference where I am the main speaker. I live in Hong Kong. I have my Hong Kong residency card."

"Well, come in on Thursday morning and I will see what I can do."

Weng K. and I go to the airline's office to book a flight to Hanoi on Wednesday. Of course all the flights are fully booked. But booking airline flights is my personal expertise. I calmly switch over to the International department, and with my American Express Gold card and other credentials obtain two seats on the "fully booked" flight.

So Weng K. and I fly up to Hanoi on Wednesday and he gets us into an Asian guest house that is much cheaper than the tourist hotels. On Thursday morning we report to the American Embassy passport office and are sent to a designated photo shop to get the right kind of passport photo. Even though it is a hot day, I am dressed in my best suit. I want to appear to be an important person.

It takes two hours to develop the color passport photograph. By the time we return to the American Embassy and fill in all of the forms it is already 11:00 A.M., and the office will close at noon for the rest of the day. The local clerk accepts all the documents and instructs us, "Come back on Tuesday morning."

Weng K. explains in the local dialect that the department head has promised personally to handle our application. After considerable persuasion she concedes, "Wait. I'll see."

Fifteen minutes later I hear my name called, and the American department head appears at the window and says these wonderful words, "Raise your right hand. . . sign here . . . here is your new passport!"

We return to the guest house rejoicing that the Lord has wonderfully paved the way to enable us to obtain the passport in just a few hours, not the five days to a week normally required. But has the Lord sent us to Hanoi for other reasons also?

On Thursday afternoon we set out to explore Hanoi and to locate the only Protestant church in this city, the capital of Vietnam. We find it—a stone structure that can seat about 250 people on the main floor and more in the balcony. It is located near a market in the heart of the old part of the city. This church had been founded by missionaries of the Christian and Missionary Alliance; nearly all the non-Catholic churches in Vietnam have been founded by this mission. Though under severe harassment by the communist officials, this church continued to hold Sunday services through all the years of the terrible war.

Entering into these church grounds is a deep, emotional experience. This is God's lighthouse planted in the heart of the city of Hanoi, the headquarters of the Vietcong, the enemy against whom we fought for so many years. My thoughts drifted back to Saigon where I had spent three months in 1966 during the height of the Vietnamese War. I was not a soldier, but rather a missionary who came to Saigon to train counselors and set up a citywide crusade so that national evangelists from five Asian countries could preach in the football stadium to bring the Gospel to the people. It was the only citywide crusade ever held in Vietnam. During that time in Saigon I had the privilege to encourage both American and South Vietnamese servicemen to do the Navigators Bible study courses and to memorize Scripture consistently through a workable program.

But this is Hanoi and these are the grounds where a persecuted church has continued to bear witness that is founded on the Rock, Christ Jesus. Maybe the Lord also will give us some opportunity to encourage the believers in Hanoi.

Weng K. is a Singaporean of Cantonese background. He not only looks like a Vietnamese but can also speak quite a bit of the language which has some similarities to his own Chinese dialect. Since an American attracts attention, Weng K. calls on the pastor privately to assess the situation.

Actually there is not just one pastor but three. The old pastor who ministered in this church for many years has passed away. But before moving on to his reward in heaven, he had trained three men to carry on the work. This was done privately because all the Bible schools and seminaries were closed after the victorious Vietcong armies occupied the whole country.

The three young pastors, who are all about thirty years of age, live in separate apartments on the church grounds with their families, except for the one who is not yet married.

"Would you like to meet an American missionary who has worked many years in China which is another country controlled by a communist style government?" asks Weng K..

"Yes, please bring him; we would like to meet him."

So late Thursday afternoon we visit the church compound again and meet all the pastors in one of their small apartments. When Weng K. introduces me, one of the pastors reaches over to his book case and pulls out a copy of *The Timothy Principle*[1] printed in Vietnamese with my picture on the back cover.

"Are you the author of this book?" he asks.

"Yes, I am."

The pastor explains in Vietnamese that he has just received 30 copies of this book from the church leaders in Ho Chi Minh City for distribution among the churches in North Vietnam. He has been blessed in reading it. He marvels at the timing that brings the author right into their home on the same week that the books arrive.

Now Weng K. describes our adventures resulting from the theft of the passport that led us to Hanoi even though we had no previous intention of coming to this city.

The pastors understand some English, but mainly through Weng K.'s interpretation we discuss many things for about an hour. The pastors are interested to know about the church in China. I explain how the Timothy Principle discipleship course in Chinese has been taught in one of the seminaries and in some of the local churches. We discuss the problem of how to train leadership in Vietnam where all the seminaries have been closed. One answer, I suggest, is to conduct training programs.

Weng K. tells the pastor how we have just held all-day training courses on discipleship for the lay leaders in four different areas of Ho Chi Minh City. The pastor who is in charge of the tribal work in the north asks permission to translate *The Timothy Principle* into the tribal languages. Of course, we are happy to do this.

Then one of the pastors makes this proposal. "We usually do not have outside speakers because we need to be careful. But since the Lord has brought Mr. Robertson to Hanoi in such an unusual way, I think we can arrange for him to speak to the young adults fellowship on Saturday night, if we can find a good interpreter."

"I will find an interpreter," volunteers the unmarried pastor.

On Saturday night Weng K. and I arrive early to meet with the young man selected to interpret for me. To my surprise I find out that he had been converted while restricted to a detention camp in Hong Kong where the Vietnamese "boat people" had been detained.

"Why, I live in Hong Kong," I reply excitedly. "I coordinated the counseling and follow-up for the Billy Graham Hong Kong Crusade in 1990. I made arrangements to bring boat people on special buses from the detention camps to the crusade stadium."

"Yes, I came to that crusade," said my interpreter. "Some of my friends received Christ at those meetings. However, I received the Lord through the instruction times that followed."

Then he introduces me to his fiancée who was also at the Hong Kong crusade and made a commitment to receive Christ. In fact, many of the present young leaders in the Hanoi church are those who received Christ while staying in the Vietnamese detention camps in Hong Kong. While under the teaching of missionaries, they learned about the Gospel; they also learned English and other skills, and they learned about democracy and the outside world. After their return to Hanoi many have quickly risen to places of leadership, both in the business world and also in the church. God's ways of spreading the Gospel are marvelous to behold.

That evening I teach a chapter from *The Timothy Principle*, emphasizing the need for each Christian to know Christ through His Word and then begin to disciple others. I show them that the basic illustrations are already translated into Vietnamese. About 60 young adults, many of them college graduates or career people, attend the fellowship. I am told that they number about 200 and some meet together in other places.

After the meeting a group of the leaders get together with Weng K. and me to map out a strategy for Christian outreach. We distribute to them our remaining discipleship materials both in English and Vietnamese.

The next day we attend the regular Sunday morning service. The church is nearly full for the regular service, but after that the crowd increases until every available seat is taken and others stand outside. Two of the young people are being married.

I am amazed at the pastor's topic for the Sunday service. The pastor preaches on Timothy training, which he just learned the night before from two servant-missionaries.

After church I remark to my co-worker, "Weng K., now we know why my passport was stolen!" And yes, I did arrive in Manila on time.


*Scene 2: Hyderabad, Andhra Pradesh, India*

"The bishop will see you now."

So Jacob Prabhu, the Indian leader of the Training Evangelistic Leadership (TEL) mission, the Rev. Elia Pradeep, who is pastor of the large Centenary Methodist Church, and my son-in-law David Rice, go with me into the bishop's office.

After tea and social comments, Bishop Nimrod Christian, the bishop of the Methodist churches in the Telegu-speaking province of Andhra Pradesh gets quite serious. "I have over a hundred pastors in my diocese who work among the 65 million people in this province. We have many problems, but our main problems are not financial; they are spiritual.

"You and Reverend Prabhu have done a wonderful job of teaching our lay leaders in the churches of Hyderabad. Now I propose a conference to teach all our pastors, particularly those who are struggling as they lead small churches in the countryside."

As we continue to discuss the basic format for such a conference, the bishop turns directly to me again and says, "Many of our pastors feel no personal call from God to do the ministry. Some are probably not truly born again. I am deeply concerned about the spiritual welfare of the pastors and their families in my diocese."

So in 1995 we proceed to hold a three-day conference for all the Methodist pastors in the Andhra Pradesh province. The bishop arranges to set up dormitory and eating facilities in one of the Methodist schools during a semester break. The teaching sessions are held in a chapel nearby, and another missionary assists me in the program. I prepare four sessions with workshops and discussion questions centered around these vital topics for pastors:

The Pastor and his Calling

The Pastor and his Cottage (wife and children)

The Pastor and his Commitment (to the Word of God and prayer life)

The Pastor and his Commission (evangelize through his people)

After the conference the bishop makes this statement, "It is 25 years since we have had a conference like this that has addressed the spiritual needs of our leaders. World Vision used to hold such conferences many years ago."

The bishop writes a letter asking us to come again and hold conferences to upgrade the ministry. He says he knows of other bishops who would like to have us come to serve them also.

Here is an open door, a plea, to serve the existing churches in India at many levels. There is room for scores of servant-missionaries in India.

*Scene 3: Mong Kok, Hong Kong*

"We have been attending the Mandarin-speaking church in Mong Kok for a whole year, and they don't seem to be overly friendly," Phyllis, my wife, complains to me one day.

"It just takes time for the Hong Kong people to accept you," I try to explain. "Most foreigners just come and go. We have to take the time to convince them we really want to serve them."

That very week the pastor and his wife asked to meet with us. They would like for us to teach a Sunday school class in English for the high school age group. Phyllis and I teach the class together and get deeply involved with the young people. They come to visit our home on Peng Chau island, which is a 50-minute ferry ride from the central Hong Kong ferry pier. Then we are invited into the homes of some of their parents. Before long a flock of people of all ages surround my wife after every service. It is difficult to get away.

After this I have the opportunity to teach a discipleship class in Mandarin on a week night. Finally the pastor invites me to speak in Mandarin at a regular Sunday morning worship service.

The roots of this church *Chung Hua Chi Tu Chiao Hui* [Church of Christ in China] were laid by the Southern Presbyterian Mission. This is the same mission that Dr. Graham Bell, Billy Graham's father-in-law, served under for many years in China. It is the largest denomination in Hong Kong, but all their missionaries have gone back to their home countries.

I am the only missionary who preaches in Chinese in one of their local churches, and I am not even Presbyterian. However, I am a link to the American missionaries who served them in the past. I generally preach on every fifth Sunday of the month, about once a quarter. The Hong Kong Church and the other churches in China want to link with the servant-missionary who will reach out to be a faithful friend. You need not be ordained; any Christian lay servant can provide this link.

*Scene 4: Guangzhou (Canton), China*

"Everyone in Guangzhou knows your son Len," concluded a TEL staff member reporting on our China work among pastors, university students, professors and businessmen. "He has a knack of getting involved in the lives of people in many stratas of society, including students and workers and people in need.

One day in 1999 while exiting Sun Yat Sen University after his Mandarin class, Len asks the gatekeeper about an old lady crawling down the street. "Oh, she comes here every day to beg at our bus stop."

Len approached the woman. "What happened to you, Ma'am?" he asks in fluent Cantonese, the local dialect. However, she speaks only Mandarin which he is just learning, but he pieces together her story.

"Six weeks ago I fell and broke my hip. My husband is missing. My family lives far away in the north. I have no money to see a doctor."

As the Good Samaritan love of Christ flows through Len's 6' 2" frame, he scoops her frail body into his arms. Momentarily he considers taking her to a hospital by bus because of limited funds, but heads instead for a taxi.

Walking through the hospital entrance with the limp woman in his arms, the first person Len sees is one of two doctors he teaches in a weekly "Timothy Training" Bible class. They had recently put their faith in Christ as Savior at a church evangelistic meeting and the woman pastor had assigned them to Len for follow-up.

The doctor beckons him into the emergency room where Len pays for an x-ray. After his examination the doctor announces, "We will put her in a charity home, and after recovery will return her by train to her family up north." Happy ending.

In 1986, I had taken Len on a short term mission trip to Shanghai. And after graduating from a Texas university Len spent his first two years in China teaching English and helping in two of Guangzhou's eight registered Chinese churches. As time went on Len studied Cantonese and Mandarin in various schools. His life became a kaleidoscope of witnessing, good works and servanthood to others; and all the pastors came to know him by his Chinese name, Lo Lam. In one university he led a Chinese roommate to Christ and took him to church. Edward is still zealous for the Lord and is actively growing in his church. Len subsequently led other students to Christ.

Monday nights he practices singing in Mandarin with an award-winning community choir made up of Chinese businessmen, doctors, professionals and homemakers at the Y.W.C.A. The Y's director, Helen Sun, encourages community involvement and service. Her father who founded the Y, died in a labor camp during the war.

One night, rushing by bicycle from a public choir performance back to school to beat the 11: 00 P.M. curfew, Len notices a little boy lying on the sidewalk near his school. *"He's another beggar,"* Len thinks. *"His mother will soon be back to take care of him."*

However, as he hurriedly cycles home after another choir performance the next night, he again sees the boy lying on the cold sidewalk. This time the bottle beside him is overturned. Bread and pineapple donations remain uneaten. Money sticks out of his pockets.

While looking at the boy, Len recalled the time when he had arrived after curfew and spent the night locked outside on the gate guardhouse porch. A huge rat had raced by and scared him half to death. Now he thinks, *"This little boy needs my help."* He stops to see if he is dead, but the lad opens his eyes and looks up at him. He makes a motion with his twisted hand toward his mouth. *Obviously he can't talk, walk or feed himself,* thinks Len.

Just then a man behind him on a bicycle also stops and says, "He is motioning for water, and his parents have abandoned him." When Len states his plan to take the boy home with him, the man offers to help by giving him 10 Yuan, which is about 1% of his monthly salary. "You should take him instead to the nearby tuberculosis sanitarium," he advises.

Together they look at the boy's blistered lips and sunburned face. His couple layers of clothes are much too big for him—but enough to keep him warm—for underneath he is very skinny and his head seems too big for his body. He appears to be about five years old. His eyes seem to stick out of his eye sockets from deprivation, with lots of white showing around his black eyes.

This scares Len a bit, but he picks up the boy in one arm, disregarding a scab on his head or possible fleas or disease he might catch from him. Straddling his bicycle Len carries the lad on his lap which soils his tuxedo pants. Weak from hunger the boy keeps slipping off, unable to hang on as they ride together. He can scarcely hold up his head, so lets it hang back and looks up with his big eyes at Len in the moonlight.

Surprisingly, the university guard allows them to enter the gate, and Len carries him to the school clinic. There he washes him and can tell that he had soiled his pants for days. The doctors kindly allow them to stay for the night on the examining beds at the clinic. Len feeds him leftover rolls and cakes from the choir performance, and the boy eats so much Len thinks he will burst!

The next morning sympathetic school authorities forbid him to keep the boy, but offer the school car and chauffeur to drive them to the welfare department downtown, where Len feeds him a bowl of rice porridge. Soon the lad is making contented sounds and seems to understand Len's Cantonese. The authorities put him in a state care facility outside of town with others like him who need total care. Later Len, who has helped in several orphanages, hears that the boy is still alive and well, so his gift of mercy and service to others again pays off.

### Scene 5: Sukohardjo, Central Java, Indonesia

"Please come to our home for dinner," Mrs. Sarbini urges me and my son Lee after I have preached at the Sunday worship service in Indonesian at the local Baptist church. My Indonesian is not all that fluent, but I have *berani* [courage] and the local people are very patient with the missionary's valiant efforts to communicate.

We drive in our gospel van to the home of Mrs. Sarbini. Her husband helped start the Baptist church in their home town, Sukoharjo, but he passed away many years ago. Mrs. Sarbini has three daughters and one son.

While I carry on a conversation with Mrs. Sarbini, Lee seems engrossed in talking with one of her daughters—Anna. In fact they begin a correspondence, and Lee frequently finds excuses to visit the Sarbini home, as well as excuses to do business at the Baptist seminary where Anna attends.

After two years I am invited back to their home for an official *melamar* [engagement party]. As the father of my son I ask permission through an interpreter to the mother of the bride-to-be for my son to marry her daughter. This elaborate ceremony is conducted in the Javanese dialect through an interpreter so as not to embarrass anyone with the possibility of a direct refusal.

A year later when the wedding takes place more than 700 guests—nearly the whole village—turn up. The wedding lasts for three hours with three changes of costume for the bride and groom amid eating, folk dancing and pageantry. Anna is a descendant of the royalty of the ancient Javanese kingdom but is also from a Christian family. The ceremony combines local customs with Christian prayers and sermons. I bless the bride and groom who kneel at my knees.

So another way to serve in foreign missions is to blend into the culture and language. You don't have to marry there; but you can make it your home. The Indonesian people are kind, hospitable and open to foreigners. After his marriage Lee preached the Gospel with expertise in cities and villages all over the country. Opportunities abound to come and serve in many cultures of the world today. Where are the servant-missionaries of tomorrow?

## Conclusion

Although many missionary opportunities still exist in church planting and preaching missions, the greatest challenge across the board worldwide, as we have entered into the third millennium (A.D. 2000 and beyond), is to become a servant-missionary.

The world will never be evangelized unless we as national and missionary bond together in a common cause. Great obstacles face the advance of the Gospel, especially in those countries where the church operates under a hostile government, such as Communism or an aggressive persecuting religion such as Hinduism or Islam. If the foreign missionary, who has the benefits of a Christian heritage and worldwide support, will not stand openly for the name of Jesus Christ under such difficulties, how can he expect the exposed, isolated national to make such a sacrifice? Perhaps he can survive but hardly make aggressive headway. One part of the Body of Christ is not meant to stand by itself while other parts suffer. Jesus pronounced that the whole body was one, and if one part suffers, the whole body suffers with it.

The strategy of the enemy is to divide the church, the one church with one Lord, one calling, one hope; it is one body. Satan will try to create friction and mistrust between the missionary and the national, between one nationality or group of people and another. Satan's strategy is to divide and conquer the people of God.

Jesus clearly laid out His strategy while pouring out His heart before God the Father in the Garden of Gethsemane, "Neither pray I for them alone, but for them also which shall believe on Me through their word; that they all may be one; as Thou, Father, art in Me, and I in Thee, that they also may be one in Us: That the world may believe that Thou hast sent Me" (John 17:20-21).

When we who are from various nations and backgrounds become as one in our love for God and for one another, then the world will believe that the Savior Jesus has been sent by the Father.

Kenneth Scott Latourette (1884-1968), the church historian, called the nineteenth century (the 1800s) "The Great Century" for missions.[2] Foundations for church planting and church growth were laid in nearly every major country in the world. In the 1900s, the 20th century, this focus was continued until every nation under heaven had at least a form of the church. The presence of the church was extended into nearly every nation. In addition to presence, there must also be proclamation, for we must work together to proclaim the Gospel to a lost world.

In all of Asia there are few countries besides Korea, Singapore and the Philippines where the Protestant Christian population (even nominal Christianity) will reach 5%; most are at 3% or below.

So what is the greatest need in missions today? Let us begin with India. William Carey baptized the first Hindu convert at the turn of the century (1800). Some 200 years later the church is established, but the nation is far from being evangelized. India gained her independence in 1947, yet the Indian church has been struggling within its newfound freedoms for the past 50 years with little increase in the percentage of Christian believers.

What is needed? Laborers! The harvest in India is great, but the laborers are still too few. India needs more faithful laborers—committed and trained men and women—nationals and missionaries. What kind of missionaries? Servant-missionaries who will come not to plant copies of American churches or start new groups, but work under the existing church . . . to witness, to teach, to disciple, to train, or just to encourage. This kind of missionary is welcome in any culture in the world.

TODAY'S GREATEST NEED: The International Servant-Missionary!

ENDNOTES:
1. *The Timothy Principle* (U.S. $6.00), the accompanying *Timothy Training Workbook* (U.S. $2.50), and *Journey of a Lifetime* [formerly *The Road to Discipleship*] (U.S. $5.00) are three critical publications for the ministry of training Christian disciples to reproduce their lives spiritually in the lives of others. They may be purchased from Training Evangelistic Leadership (TEL), Post Drawer E, Denton, TX 76202, or from The Navigators, 117 Lorong K Telok Kurau, Singapore 425758.
2. Kenneth Scott Latourette, *A History of Christianity.*, New York: Harper & Row, Publishers, 1953, page 1061.

# WANTED: A NEW GENERATION OF MISSIONARIES

In this book we have traced the three great advances in modern missionary history (1790-2000) and added one projection. Overwhelming needs still exist for new missionaries who will forsake their homes and cultures to follow in the footsteps of the heroes of the faith who went before us. The first three advances represent three basic approaches to missions that are still applicable. A new projection is to return to a field that already has a church and be an international servant-missionary to enhance its development.

Many opportunities are available in each category. It is a "Mission Impossible" humanly speaking, but for the grace of God which makes His mission achievable. The words of the apostle Paul still apply today, "For a great and effectual is opened unto me, and there are many adversaries" (1 Corinthians 16:9).

### The Great Commission

The Great Commission is not contained in just one passage of Scripture but is found in a slightly different form and emphasis in each of the Gospels and Acts. These passages are all related and in this chapter each missionary advance will be linked to a particular passage that is part of what we have commonly called in Christendom "The Great Commission."

### The First Advance:  In the Footsteps of William Carey

Plant a church, baptize the converts, teach all the Scriptures in every nation! The key passage for this great missionary mandate is:

Matthew 28:18-20—"All power is given unto Me in heaven and in earth. "

"Go ye therefore and teach all nations, baptizing them in the name of the Father and of the Son and of the Holy Spirit:"

"Teaching them to observe all things whatsoever I have commanded you; and lo, I am with you alway, even unto the end of the world. Amen."

The first advance followed in the footsteps of William Carey (1792) who formed a missionary agency to plant a church in India. Other denominational church groups followed this pattern to plant churches in countries around the world. To teach all things that Jesus commanded also puts a priority on translating and publishing the Scriptures so each group of people can worship in their own language. Carey and his colleagues translated and published portions of the Scriptures in some 40 different languages. But the job is not finished. Wycliffe Bible Translators, New Tribes Mission, various Bible societies and many other missionary agencies are pleading for laborers who will join in the task of translating and publishing the Scriptures into the languages of the earth that do not yet have Bibles available.

The first wave of missionaries who entered the heathen environments and into lands of pagan practices can be credited with introducing many social reforms that benefited the welfare of the local people. For instance, the presence of Carey brought pressure on the predominantly Hindu society to forbid the horrible custom of burning widows alive on the funeral pyres of their dead husbands, as well as the terrible practice of female infanticide—drowning baby girls in an endeavor to ease the financial burdens on impoverished families.

David Livingstone is remembered and honored for his sacrificial efforts to eliminate the slave trade in Africa. The early China missionaries also helped eliminate other cruel practices, such as the painful binding of women's feet in childhood. Besides this, the missionaries also introduced a system of education for all, including women, as well as modern medical facilities.

The cry for morality and justice that arose within a society because of the godly example and biblical teaching of the foreign missionary continues on to the present time. Even in Communist controlled and Islamic dominated countries, the presence today of a missionary witness who lives within a foreign culture is a deterrent against the abuse of human rights and the persecution of the Christian minority.

The continuing relevancy of the church-planting missionary must always be kept before us. My son Lee, a missionary to Indonesia, has already planted one Baptist church in a predominately Islamic village and is in the process of planting another. Nearly all the major denominations are seeking to recruit missionaries who will devote the rest of their lives to work within a particular country or culture. Although the task of the new missionary may take various forms to include evangelism, education, and social work, the focal point still remains to plant new churches.

## The Second Advance: In the Footsteps of Hudson Taylor

Plant an indigenous church in every area where there is no gospel witness. The key statement for this era was:

Romans 15:20—"Yea, so have I strived to preach the Gospel, not where Christ was named, lest I should build upon another man's foundation."

Hudson Taylor was burdened with the fact that in his day there were 300,000,000 people in the twelve provinces of inland China where there was no gospel witness. He shared his burden in a letter to a relative quoting these words:

"If Thou forbear to deliver them that are drawn unto death, and those that are ready to be slain; if Thou sayest, 'Behold we knew it not; doth not He that pondereth the heart consider it? And He that keepeth thy soul, doth not He know it? And shall not He render to every man according to his works?'" (Proverbs 24:11-12).

He asked God to give him 24 willing, skillful laborers, two for each province, to plant a witness in every province of inland China.

The second advance followed in the footsteps of Hudson Taylor (1865) with the goal to plant a witness, then an indigenous church in every area where the Gospel had not penetrated. It is not enough to build a church in the major cities where people are somewhat familiar with international standards, but the church must be planted in the interior areas in a setting that is compatible with the local language and culture.

Taylor called his enterprise the China Inland Mission and his ideas called forth a new effort to reach into various languages and cultures within a given nation.

Other groups, such as the African Inland Mission (AIM) and the Sudan Interior Mission (SIM) followed that pattern closely. Yet other societies adopted certain parts of Taylor's philosophy. The emphasis was an "indigenous" style of church that would not depend on foreign aid for its growth but would become self-governing, self-supporting and self-propagating as soon as possible. The focal point of the second advance was to plant a Chinese-style church in every province of China and the pattern to be extended to every major country of the world.

Today the clarion call is to plant an ethnic church in every people group on this earth. Much study and analysis has been made so that the people groups not yet penetrated can get top priority. Many new missionaries are needed to fulfill this goal. Also there is a recent awareness that some educated Americans, whose original roots are in some ethnic culture that does not have a virile witnessing church, should consider going back as missionaries to their own original people.

By any standards, the harvest is great and the laborers are few. Christians everywhere should be praying for more laborers to be thrust out into the harvest fields of the world (again see Matthew 9:36-10:5).

### The Third Advance: In the Footsteps of the Veterans of World War II

Mass public evangelism and follow-up still characterize this era. The key words for this advance were and are:

Mark 16:15—"And He said unto them, 'Go ye into all the world, and preach the Gospel to every creature.'"

Matthew 24:14 —"And this Gospel of the kingdom shall be preached in all the world for a witness unto all the nations; and then shall the end come."

The Third Advance grew out of the great missionary mandate to preach the Gospel to every person in the world (Mark 16:15). In 1945, following World War II, the battle cry within evangelical Christendom rang out loudly, "Let us preach the Gospel to every person in our generation." Even though churches had been planted in most countries, both in the major cities and in the interior regions, the gospel message had not reached the ears and hearts of most of the people. "How then shall they call on Him in whom they have not believed? And how shall they believe in Him of whom they have not heard? And how shall they hear without a preacher?" (Romans 10:14).

What we needed was the evangelist, the gifted preacher who would proclaim the Good News to the multitudes so that everyone would have the opportunity to hear the Gospel preached at least once in his or her lifetime. This was the compelling goal passed on to me by Dick Hillis who indoctrinated me into the world of missions.

God did a sovereign work in the hearts of thousands of American servicemen during World War II, centered not in the local churches but through a sodality (a term coined by Dr. Ralph Winter), which is a fellowship among believers who have a common goal, a movement of God sometimes called "the parachurch." The Youth for Christ movement along with The Navigators and many other such organizations propelled thousands of servicemen into Bible schools, Christian colleges and seminaries to prepare to become missionaries to carry the Gospel into all the world.

The new focal point of this movement was the evangelist who would proclaim the Gospel publicly to the multitudes. In the days of John Wesley and George Whitefield, the evangelist struggled to communicate to large audiences without the aid of a sound system. Following World War II new advances in sound projection equipment plus the introduction of gospel films greatly extended the potential to preach to multitudes of people. The aim was not to diminish in any way the importance of the local church but rather to mobilize the believers of all local churches into a crusade for Christ. From the roots of the Youth for Christ movement came the Billy Graham Crusades, and in Asia this movement became known as Orient Crusades, now called O.C. Ministries.

The influence of The Navigators within this movement took the form of training counselors with the goal of matching up every inquirer with a local believer who would clarify the issues of salvation and pray with the seeker as he or she received the Lord Jesus Christ into his or her heart. Then would begin the process of individual follow-up. Particular effort was made to link every new believer into some existing local church fellowship.

This book has traced some of the trials and victories attached to this third great missionary advance with particular attention to our five prayer warriors and pioneers, David Morken, Hube Mitchell, Dick Hillis, Dawson Trotman and Bob Pierce.

The third advance majored in the public preaching of the Gospel, accompanied by personal follow-up. At first the evangelists were mainly Americans. As nationalism and prejudices against America increased, an obvious need arose to train nationals of many countries to preach the Gospel effectively to their own people. Among other groups, Training Evangelistic Leadership (TEL) came into being to fulfill this need. This organization is seeking to enlist full-time missionaries who will help train national workers who will be sent out in gospel teams that will use creative means to reach the people of a given area with the Good News of salvation.

Subsequently, some of my friends who are national evangelists have formed their own organizations. They have told me consistently that they want American missionaries to assist them in the kinds of things that Americans do particularly well—the training of counselors, the follow-up, the business of coordinating a cooperative evangelistic outreach. Let us send out missionaries to labor together with the national evangelist for the advance of the Kingdom.

## A New Projection: To be a Servant-Missionary to the Existing Church

Genuine servanthood and a willingness to work under leaders of other cultures is the key as we see it for world evangelization in the next generation, portrayed in the following crucial Acts passages:

Acts 1:8—"But ye shall receive power after that the Holy Spirit is come upon you; and ye shall be witnesses unto Me both in Jerusalem, and in all Judea and in Samaria, and unto the uttermost part of the earth."

These words were spoken by Jesus to many of His disciples, probably about 120 people, men and women, who then went into an upper room in Jerusalem as a united body to pray and to wait for the coming of the Holy Spirit. The Acts record would then show that the Gospel was spread early in the church mainly through the witness of individual committed Christians. This witness of these individual members of the many churches went hand in hand with the public preaching of the Gospel.

Peter gave the church a "jump start" at Pentecost in Jerusalem when 3,000 Jewish people were converted under his public preaching. The follow-up was done by the apostles and Jesus' other disciples. Through the united witness of these new converts the church grew steadily.

When persecution arose, it was the new believers who carried the Gospel to Samaria and everywhere else in that Roman world and eventually beyond its boundaries.

"And at that time there was a great persecution against the church which was at Jerusalem; and they were all scattered abroad throughout the regions of Judea and Samaria, except the apostles" (Acts 8:1).

"Therefore they that who were scattered abroad went everywhere preaching the word. Then Philip went down to the city of Samaria and preached Christ unto them" (Acts 8:4-5).

"Now they which who were scattered abroad after the persecution that arose about Stephen traveled as far as Phoenicia, and Cyprus and Antioch, preaching the word to none but unto the Jews only. And some . . . spoke unto the Grecians, preaching the Lord Jesus. And the hand of the Lord was with them, and a great number believed and turned unto the Lord" (Acts 11:19-21).

Today the work of spreading the Gospel through so-called "lay" Christians (the non-professional, non-ordained, not seminary or Bible college trained) has tremendous potential. But converts must be trained to become disciples. The foreign servant-missionary can be the catalyst for a disciple-producing explosion. But it is important that this missionary serve alongside the existing national church and under its leaders, and not try to build his own group, especially if he works in a country that is sensitive and hostile to foreign influences.

So here is that tremendous opportunity of tomorrow. May the Lord raise up many new servant-missionaries for the task of finishing world evangelization in the next generation.


## Does China Still Need Missionaries?

Let us consider China, the largest country in the world, with an ethnic Chinese population of more than one billion people. The first missionary, Robert Morrison, entered Macau in 1807 and translated the Bible into Chinese. Against great odds, thousands of missionaries over the next 142 years pushed into all provinces and major sections of China establishing churches, schools, hospitals, and exalting the name of Jesus Christ so that the term *Chi Tui Chiao* [Christianity] became a household word whether one accepted the Christian faith or not. A true foundation was laid and it does not need to be replaced, "For other foundation can no man lay than that is laid, which is Jesus Christ" (1 Corinthians 3:11).

This foundation, laid by those missionaries, produced Chinese believers who took hold of the faith and withstood the fires of persecution. I am a witness to this truth for some of my Chinese co-workers died as martyrs for the faith. Not everyone stood the test of fire, for some of the materials were "wood, hay, and straw." But true believers, who were "gold, silver, and precious stones" endured to the end (1 Corinthians 3:12-13). These include many local pastors and lay leaders of all groups and denominations who were sent by the

Communists into rural communes for political indoctrination under severe hardship. Yes, they survived, but many would retain deep emotional scars that are hard to erase.

Today there exists in China a virile but struggling Chinese national church. At this point, particularly in the major cities, it is relatively free from governmental interference. Prior to 1990 the government program to control Protestant churches exercised a rather heavy hand on local church affairs. This form of control dates back to 1979 when the first Protestant churches were allowed to reopen after having been plundered and closed down by the excesses of the Cultural Revolution (1965-1975). Much earlier the government had instituted what was called the Three-Self Patriotic Movement (TSPM) to "encourage" Christians to cooperate with the new Communist regime, but from 1979 till 1990 it was designed to provide a peaceful transition to open church life activities.

The three-self concept (self-governing, self-supporting, self-propagating) had been enthusiastically advocated by some of the former China missionaries themselves as an ideal goal for missions, and the Chinese government found it useful to bend this concept to fit their own purposes. Originally the TSPM was made up of delegates (not necessarily Christian believers) appointed by the government to monitor the religious affairs of the nation; a section exists for every major religion in the country—Protestant, Catholic, Muslim and Buddhist.

This system is not much different from that under which we must do our ministering in most of the non-Christian countries of Asia. For instance, in Indonesia, the Departamen Agama [Department of Religion] is the government arm that monitors all religious activities. In Indonesia, and most other countries of Asia, the church must register with the government or it will not be allowed to hold services. Even in the United States the churches must register with and be accountable to the not-so-accommodating agency known as the Internal Revenue Service (IRS), America's taxing branch of the Department of the Treasury.

The Communist government in China did indeed become infamous for its role in threatening and harassing Christians, particularly in rural areas, during the Cultural Revolution and some years thereafter. But around 1990 the Chinese Christian churches had enough testimony and respectability to form their own church council made up of the pastors and leaders of the local churches. Usually today these pastors are not members of the TSPM bureaucracy and are now enjoying about the same amount of freedom as local pastors would have under a non-Christian country like Indonesia. Moreover, those who are official delegates to this government rarely attend a local church service, for they are bureaucrats and would not feel at home in a genuine worship setting.

At the present time in China it is illegal for the foreigner to establish his own church to reach ethnic Chinese people with the Gospel. However, foreigners have a wide open door to attend any registered local church and great freedom to evangelize and disciple among the people attending church as long as they can cultivate open and friendly relationships with their respective local pastors. Of course, this also holds true for almost any other country or culture; nearly any pastor would be delighted if a lay Christian came to him with an offer to serve.

"Pastor, I would like to serve in your church; I am willing to do anything you would like me to do! How can I be of assistance?"

Today in the city of Guangzhou you will find a dozen registered churches and a couple of house churches; in addition, the foreign community (expatriates) has two or three locations where they meet for worship. Most of the TEL staff missionaries have visited all three kinds of churches on occasion, but we recommend that each one attach himself to one local church, attend regularly, and get to know its leaders.

At the present time we (TEL) have excellent *kuang hsi* [personal relationships] in several of the largest Chinese churches in Guangzhou. In an informal manner we find various ways to serve the believers here. Nearly every one of our TEL staff participates in a young people's fellowship that generally meets on Sunday afternoons at one of the churches; we also meet with small groups for tea or a meal to encourage one another and pray. Some of our more fluent Chinese-speaking staff have actually taught classes in Chinese to the whole group; others have led in singing or teaching new games or skits that enliven the program. After a time of such involvement we are accepted as part of the fellowship, similar to the way some international students who come to our country can work their way into being accepted as part of our respective fellowships.

After a year or so our influence can grow. Perhaps the pastor or other church leaders might invite us for tea; at a later date we might be invited to one of their homes for a family dinner. Perhaps the pastor's son or daughter will be traveling abroad and we would be asked for advice or contacts. Eventually the pastor might come to us with some major problem in the congregation, some decisions facing his church members, or even a difficulty in his personal life.

The pastor thus seeks advice from someone he believes is objective and one whom he can trust. In the communist environment he will rarely trust any other church official with delicate matters, but the true servant-missionary, because he knows God and is not intimidated by local pressures, can be a source of spiritual encouragement and guidance to any fellow Chinese believer. This ministry, moreover, is a "two-way street." If one truly serves, he will receive honor and protection; if one of our missionaries has a problem, the local church leaders often find ways to be of help.

The local government officials will seldom move against a foreigner on religious affairs if he has good *kuang hsi* with the local church leaders. So the servant-missionary has an important role. When the national and the missionary become as one, they will have much more effectiveness in reaching into a hostile, pagan world.

## The Missionary Mandate to Every Christian

Every generation has the mandate from our Lord Jesus Christ to carry the Gospel into every tribe and tongue and people and nation so as to reach all people in every area of society and every walk of life. The apostle Paul cried out from the depths of his soul, "I am debtor both to the Greeks and to the barbarians, both to the wise and to the unwise" (Romans 1:14). He felt intensely his obligation to reach all peoples everywhere. Now to whom was Paul in debt?

Paul most certainly was not in debt to pay God back for the precious gift of salvation, for that is freely given to every unworthy sinner who comes to God through faith. Our works cannot obtain salvation, nor can our works repay God for this salvation. So Paul is not in debt to God, but to people. To what people? To all people, for Jesus died for the world of people.

The Gospel is intended for the ears of people who are scattered abroad under all kinds of oppressive governments and harsh economic conditions. The light of Jesus must be brought to a people who walk in darkness, to a land where the inhabitants dwelling in spiritual bondage walk in the shadow of death (Isaiah 9:2).

Jesus came into this sin-cursed world to deliver the captives out of bondage, to lift up the downtrodden, to comfort the broken-hearted, to give sight to the blind and ignorant, and to rescue souls out of the pit of death and hell into the hands of a loving Father God (Luke 4:18; Psalm 40:2). God sent his beloved Son into such a world.

Jesus warned His disciples then and now, "If ye were of the world, the world would love his own: but because ye are not of the world, but I have chosen you out of the world, therefore the world hateth you" (John 15:19).

Later the resurrected Lord appeared to His disciples and commissioned them with these significant words, "As My Father hath sent Me, even so send I you" (John 20:21).

Are you His disciple? Are you a true follower of Jesus Christ? Regardless of your nationality or heritage or church affiliation, you have been chosen and ordained by the Lord Jesus Christ to go into the world and bring forth fruit (see John 15:16). You are commissioned to sow the precious seed of the Gospel, the Word of God, into the hearts of people; some of them will believe and in turn will bring forth even more fruit to his glory (Mark 4:14-20). This is God's basic pattern for church growth—that every Christian will become fruitful in bringing others to Christ.

So every Christian is called on to reproduce spiritually. In fact this is one of the basic reasons for our existence. We are created in God's own image so that we can fellowship with the eternal God, and we are commanded to reproduce, "Be fruitful and multiply; replenish the earth and subdue it" (Genesis 1:26-28). As parents we are commanded to produce children, "Be fruitful and multiply, and replenish the earth" (Genesis 9:1). As Christians we are to reproduce spiritually so that through our union with the Lord Jesus Christ we bring forth sons and daughters of the faith with fruit that remains (John 15:16).

Someone once asked Dwight L. Moody while he was still working as a salesman in the shoe business, "What is your occupation?"

"My occupation is saving souls," replied Moody.

"Why I thought you were in the shoe business."

"My business is saving souls; I sell shoes to pay expenses."

The apostle Paul said that the vocation or calling of every Christian was to walk worthy of our Lord Jesus Christ so that he or she would be a testimony to the world in which we all live (Ephesians 4:1 with Colossians 1:10). So in this sense, every Christian is sent into the world to be a missionary.

But is there a special calling for some men and women to be in "full time" service or to be a foreign missionary? Yes, there is! When Jesus called the fishermen Peter and Andrew and James and John, He required that they leave their nets (or occupation) and follow Him (Matthew 4:19-22).

Today as through all of Christian history the Lord is calling some to leave their homes and cultures and go to foreign lands as missionaries.

"So Jesus answered and said, 'Verily I say unto you, There is no man that hath left house or brethren or sisters or father or mother or wife or children or lands, for My sake and the Gospel's, but he shall receive a hundredfold now in this time—houses and brethen and sisters and mothers and children and lands, with persecutions—and in the world to come, eternal life'" (Mark 10:29-30).

So there are two kinds of missionaries—one is called to remain in his or her own culture to be as salt and light to that world, whereas another as a foreign missionary is sent out by the Lord to go and live within another culture for the sake of the Gospel.

## The Foreign Missionary is Biblical and Irreplaceable

The highest calling of God is to be a full time missionary sent forth into a hostile world under the domination and power of Satan (see Acts 26:18 with 2 Corinthians 4:4). The root meaning of the word missionary is "one sent forth on a mission," which is similar to the term "apostle," which comes from the verb *apostello*, "to send forth." Thus in today's time a missionary and an apostle are really synonyms.

Jesus called twelve of His disciples, whom He named apostles, out of their own occupations and culture (Jewish Palestine) to follow Him wherever He would lead or send (see Luke 6:13). So some of His disciples ("followers, learners") were now commissioned to be apostles ("sent ones"). At that time their calling was more to an itinerant ministry rather than a fixed location, for Jesus Himself traveled constantly. But after Jesus' resurrection the calling became more geographical as the apostles were now sent out to the ends of the earth (see again John 20:21 and Acts 1:8).

Biblical data finds Paul penetrating much of the Roman Empire around the Mediterranean Basin, Peter active in northern Asia Minor, and John ending up in Ephesus. Early church history records various traditions of the original apostles heading out in all directions from Palestine.[1] Peter was supposed to have gone on to Sardinia, Corsica, and eventually to his death in Rome; Andrew is believed by some to have gone to what is now southern Russia, by others to the Celts in Scotland. James, the son of Zebedee, died early in the church's history (Acts 12:2), while his brother John was still alive in his 90s in the Book of The Revelation. Philip was said to have followed Peter to northern Asia Minor and Bartholomew was believed to have gone to eastern Arabia and Persia. Thomas ended up in India, said to be the father of the Mar-Thoma Church in the south, while Matthew is believed to have gone to Mesopotamia. James, the son of Alphaeus, traveled across Northern Africa, perhaps to Spain, while Simon the Zealot went in the other direction through northern Persia to Afghanistan. Judas, the son of James (not Iscariot, but also known as Thaddeus), went to southern Arabia; tradition places John Mark in Egypt and the Sudan.

The Book of Acts records the three great missionary journeys of the apostle Paul, as well as his long voyage to Rome as a "prisoner" who had made an appeal to Caesar. He would also record for us that the Lord had given to His body, the church, such leadership gifts as apostles and evangelists for a mobile ministry and prophets and pastor-teachers for a one-location ministry (see Ephesians 4:11-16). Although the original apostles were those who were eyewitnesses of the life, death, and resurrection of the Lord Jesus, the office or function of the apostle or missionary is certainly current at this time.

Missionary activities should be supported by God's people, as Paul was so faithfully by the church in Philippi. Biblical parallels may be seen in the Levites of the Old Testament (see Numbers 3:12; Joshua 13:33) and the evangelists in the New Testament (see 1 Corinthians 9:9-11, 14) depending on the offerings of God's people for their livelihood. Hudson Taylor trusted God to supply the needs of a thousand missionaries sent forth into inland China with the confidence that "God's work done in God's way will never lack God's supply."[2]

Today we find in many circles a strong trend to replace the full-time missionary with "the tentmaker" missionary who is self-supporting. This position has some attractive advantages in that it does reduce the missionary budget of a church or denomination considerably. The Lord certainly uses every faithful witness and He will surely use these and many other efforts for Jesus; but in the eyes of most church leaders and Christians on any given mission field the foreigner who has come to their country for business purposes, and is probably not very fluent in the local language or comfortable in that culture, cannot take the place of their beloved missionary who sacrificed his or her own security and comforts to bring them spiritual blessings.

We are sent into the harvest by the Lord (Luke 10:2; Matthew 28:18-20; John 20:21), yet in this age the Holy Spirit and a missionary agency work together in accomplishing this task (Acts 13:3-4; Matthew 18:19-20). From my observations few missionaries can survive alone. Missionary agencies provide direction, training, encouragement, accountability, protection and a sense of belonging.

Nor can a local church, which is by its very nature local and circumscribed in its primary focus, take the place of a missionary agency. God calls pastor-teachers to minister to their respective flocks; He calls prophets to declare the Word of God to their congregations;

He calls evangelists to carry the Good News of the Gospel into every nation of the world; and He calls missionaries to carry the message into foreign and different cultures. They each have a special calling, but all must work together in the economy of God.

So the Lord calls some of His choice disciples to leave their families and their cultures for the sake of the Gospel, but He promises to give manifold spiritual children and blessings in the land of their adoption although that ministry may be accompanied by some stress and persecution (Mark 10:28-30).

It takes years to learn a language and more years to be at home in a foreign culture. However, the true servant-missionary has a lifelong calling, and for the following good reasons is irreplaceable:

1. Forsaking one's own conveniences and culture to go into a foreign environment for the sake of the Gospel produces an "anointing" and spiritual quality that cannot be replaced by a person who has not made such a sacrifice.

2. The true servant-missionary through his "Roman citizenship" and his world Christian viewpoint can help set a people free from fear and intimidation by an oppressive government not favorable to Christianity. Also the missionary can set an example by not being conformed through local peer pressure to the standards of the world but by living the transformed life as a true disciple of Jesus within a hostile environment.

3. Cross-cultural influences enrich a society, and the true servant-missionary expands the horizons of a parochial ministry. To this can be added the indisputable fact that the missionary brings a variety of heritage and gifting to the culture to which he has been sent.

## "The Harvest Is Great . . . the Laborers Are Few"

These words of our Lord Jesus Christ (Luke 10:2) are still valid. The call of the Lord rings out afresh in every generation: Laborers are urgently needed to go into the ripened harvest. If this is true even in America, then multiply this need many times when applied to the world's mission fields. So whatever spiritual gifts you possess, they will be that much more valuable on the mission field to which the Lord sends you.

One survey on laborers worldwide, conducted by the West Indies Mission, showed the following statistics:

- 93% of all Christian workers labor in the English-speaking western world.

- 97% of all finances are spent in the English-speaking western world.

Sometimes financial gifts come to a missionary organization marked "Where Needed Most." But a greater gift would be a Christian's life given to the Lord for His use where needed most! Thus the call today is for a new generation of missionaries, men and women willing to go where God wants them to go. What about your life, O Reader? Are you ready to join God's mission in this generation? Will you help where needed most? To pray? To give? To go?

May God send forth from among the best and finest in our land a new group of harvest workers, men and women who will forsake their own culture and go out in obedience and faith. This has the highest priority in the heart of God and will help fulfill that which is most on His heart—the evangelization of the world!

END NOTES:
1. Ruth A. Tucker, *From Jerusalem to Irian Jaya*, Grand Rapids, Michigan: Zondervan Publishing House, 1983, map on page 26.
2. Dr. & Mrs. Howard Taylor, *Hudson Taylor in Early Years, The Growth of a Soul*, Singapore: An OMF Book, 1988.

## STUDY NOTES

### Chapter 1

A. A Missionary Principle:
   We do not labor alone in the harvest; it is God's work and we co-labor with Him.

B. Basic Biblical References:
   1. God sends His servants into the harvest.
      *John 20:21*

      *Matthew 9:38*

   2. We are co-workers in His harvest.
      *1 Corinthians 3:7*

      *1 Corinthians 3:9*

C. Crucial Personal Applications (These may be applied personally, whether you are serving as a foreign missionary or under some group or church in any kind of ministry).

   1. What is my present ministry assignment?

   2. Has God sent me here?

   3. What are the problems?

   4. What should be my response?

D.  Group Discussion : Yes, it is God's work, but ...
   1. As a missionary, what about my church leaders or mission leaders? What are my responsibilities to them?

   2. As a group that sends out missionaries, what is the extent of our control?

   3. How do we work together under God to carry out His will for us?

# Chapter 2

A.  A Missionary Principle:
    When the Lord sends us out to fulfill His Great Commission, He promises that His presence will go with us to deliver us from our adversaries.

B.  Basic Biblical References:
   1. The promise of His Presence
      *Matthew 28:20*

      *Exodus 33:14*

   2. His guidance
      *Exodus 13:21*

   3. His deliverance from enemies of the truth
      *Exodus 33:2*

      *II Timothy 4:17*

C.  Crucial Personal Applications:
   1. God does not always deliver me instantly out of all my troubles. Note in this chapter the various ways and means by which God protected His missionaries as they fled from the Japanese military.

2. Do I expect God to deliver me instantly and completely out of all my troubles? Why does God sometimes keep me under prolonged stress and difficulty?

3. Can you recall an instance in which God delivered you out of great danger?

D. Group Discussion:
1. Talk about some Old Testament stories in which God delivered His people out of physical danger. Yet sometimes they died for the faith (Hebrews 11:35).

2. Discuss some New Testament accounts of God's deliverance of His own?

3. Recall true stories of deliverance you have read or heard concerning modern missionaries.

4. Share with one another personal experiences of deliverance from the attacks of the enemies of God.

## Chapter 3

A. A Missionary Principle:
Not only should we preach the right message, but we should follow the pattern of Jesus in training others through our example to communicate this message to a lost world.

B. Basic Biblical References:
1. Jesus' method: The "with Him" principle. Recruit, train and send laborers into the harvest.
*Mark 3:14*

2. Paul's method: The workers traveled "with him."
*Acts 20:4*

C.  Crucial Personal Applications:
   1. Are you available to be trained by someone?

   2. Whom are you training?

   3. How are you doing this?

   4. How much time do you spend with that person?

D. Group Discussion:
   1. Discuss the steps Dick Hillis took to train the farmers in Honan in how to evangelize their own people.

   2. Should our churches and missionaries spend more time taking workers out to co-labor with them rather than only lecturing in the classroom? How can this be done? Give examples.


## Chapter 4

A.  A Missionary Principle:
   Great missionary projects can begin with just a few committed people who earnestly lay hold on God in prayer and claim promises from the Word of God.

B.  Basic Biblical References:
   1. *Jeremiah 33:3* —"Call unto Me and I will answer thee, and show thee great and mighty things, which thou knoweth not."

   2. *Mark 11:22-24*—Have faith in God ...

   3. *Matthew 18:19-20*—Where two or three agree on earth concerning their requests, the Lord Himself is there to answer their prayer.

C. Crucial Personal Applications:
  1. Does my ministry have enough prayer roots to make it fruitful? (John 15:7-8) How can I improve them?

  2. Who is my prayer partner? (Matthew 18:19-20)

  3. How effective is my personal prayer life? (James 5:16) What should I do about this?

  4. Is my life founded deeply enough in the Word and prayer that I can respond to greater ministry opportunities?

D. Group Discussion:
  1. What led to the rebuilding of the walls of Jerusalem? (Nehemiah 1:4)

  2. History traces the birth of the modern missionary movement to the time when a small group of concerned people led by William Carey claimed Isaiah 54:1-3 and agreed to form a society and use "means" to carry the Gospel to the heathen. Discuss the implications of this verse.

  3. The foundation of the China Inland Mission was laid when Hudson Taylor pleaded with God for 24 "willing and skillful" (1 Chronicles 28:21) workmen to reach the 12 inland provinces of China where 300 million people had never heard about Jesus Christ. Taylor also claimed Isaiah 28:16 that God would lay unshakeable foundations that could not be destroyed. Is this perhaps one reason why 35 years of persecution under Communism could not destroy the Chinese church?

  4. The Navigators as a service ministry was built on the promises of God claimed by Daws and his prayer partner Walt as they met with God every morning for 40 days. (Jeremiah 33:3; Isaiah 58:12; and many other verses). What are some other verses with promises that can be claimed?

5. Wycliffe Bible Translators came into being following an all night prayer meeting at the Keswick conference grounds when Cameron Townsend, Addison Raws, and others agreed to launch this mission to translate the Bible and make it available for every tribe, tongue, people, and nation (Revelation 5:9). Is the job finished yet?

6. The famous "haystack prayer meeting" launched a great missionary movement that sent many college graduates out to the mission field. InterVarsity Christian Fellowship's Urbana Missionary Conference held every third year is still a great launching pad for missions today. Discuss this further.

7. Give other examples of how prayer has launched an important ministry.

## Chapter 5

A. A Missionary Principle:
Going out by faith. "God's work done in God's way will never lack God's supplies."—J. Hudson Taylor

B. Basic Biblical References:
1. *Matthew 6:33*—"But seek ye first the kingdom of God and His righteousness; and all these things shall be added unto you."

2. *Luke 10:4* —"Carry neither purse, nor scrip, nor shoes: and salute no man by the way."

3. *Philippians 4:19*—"But my God shall supply all your need according to His riches in glory by Christ Jesus."

4. *Philippians 4:11*—"Not that I speak in respect of want: for I have learned, in whatsoever state I am, therewith to be content."

    5. *1 Timothy 6:8*—"And having food and raiment let us be therewith content."

C. Crucial Personal Applications
    1. If I obey the call of God, to what extent can I trust Him to provide my material needs? (There is a difference between needs and wants.)

    2. Can God also provide for the needs for my spouse and children?

    3. Do I trust Him to supply all my needs...
      a. always?
      b. sometimes?
      c. seldom?

D. Group Discussion:
    1. Missionary fund raising:
      a. How can it be done in a way that is a good testimony to God's faithfulness?
      b. What are some cautions toward excessive pleading for money?

    2. To what extent should the faith principles of Hudson Taylor apply to missionaries today?

## Chapter 6

A. A Missionary Principle:
The Lord commissions us to go forth into all the nations of the world and plant his church by baptizing disciples and teaching them to obey all of the Scriptures.

B.  Basic Biblical References:
    1.  *Isaiah 54:1-3*
        The promise claimed by Carey that those nations which were barren and desolate (like India and elsewhere) would produce much spiritual seed.

    2.  *Matthew 28:18-20*

C.  Crucial Personal Applications:
    1.  Am I available to go to a foreign field if God opens up a way for me to go?

    2.  What is my part in the Great Commission given to His church by Jesus Christ?

    3.  How am I helping those who are called to be missionaries to a foreign field ("ropeholding")?

    4.  To what extent do I pray regularly for people I know who are missionaries to a foreign field?

D.  Group Discussion:
    1.  Who is called to go to a foreign mission field? ... and how are we called?

    2.  What is the calling for every true believer in the carrying out of the Great Commission Jesus gave to all of us?

    3.  How can we prepare a new generation of missionaries?

## Chapter 7

A.  A Missionary Principle:
    "The Inland Concept" in modern terms—Not only should a witnessing church be planted in every nation, but the Gospel message should penetrate into every tribe and dialect and people group in the world.

B.  Basic Biblical References:
    1.  *Romans 15:20* —Preach to the ends of the earth.

    2.  *Revelation 5:9*—Redeemed out of every tribe, and tongue and people and nation.

C.  Crucial Personal Applications:
    1.  Is there an ethnic group in your area that has not been reached with the Gospel? What can be done to reach these people?

    2.  Is there a people group somewhere in the world that you would be interested in taking on as a prayer project for the Gospel to come to them?

D.  Group Discussion:
    1.  How can we best reach minority people, such as the Native Americans, Asians, Hispanics and African Americans, within our own country with the Gospel?

    2.  How can we reach a minority people living in communist countries or in countries where the governments favor the Hindu or Islamic religion? Discuss some specific strategies for reaching minorities under these conditions.


## Chapter 8

A.  A Missionary Principle:
    The Lord Jesus Christ promises great spiritual rewards to anyone who will leave his home environment and go to a foreign field for the sake of the Gospel.

B.  Basic Biblical References:
    1.  *Mark 10:28-30*

    2.  *Luke 14:33*

    3.  *John 20:20,21*

C.  Crucial Personal Applications:
1.  Are you willing to consider the possibility that the Lord may call you to leave your present position and go to a mission field?

2.  Have you ever attended a missionary conference? Will you make plans to attend such a conference?

3.  What is the benefit of being in direct relationship through gifts or prayer with someone on the mission field? Are you gleaning those benefits? If not, what plans will you make to begin such a relationship?

4.  What does Jesus mean to you personally when he says, "So send I you"?

D.  Group Discussion:
1.  Discuss how your church or society can be more involved in the worldwide missionary outreach.

2.  Discuss some ways we could open our respective homes to more missionary involvement.

## Chapter 9

A.  A Missionary Principle:
The work of the evangelist is to explain publicly the message of salvation so that each person in the audience can make a clear decision to believe on the Lord Jesus Christ as his personal Savior.

B.  Basic Biblical References: The Invitation
1.  *Deuteronomy 30:19* —Make a choice.

2.  *2 Corinthians 6:26; Acts 24:25; James 4:14* —Come to Jesus now!

3. *Acts 28:23* —Persuade. On one occasion Paul sought to persuade his countrymen from morning until evening—a 12-hour altar call!

4. *Matthew 10:32 - 33* —Profess publicly.

5. *Acts 28:24* —Reaping ... drawing the net. Whenever Paul preached there was a cleavage—some believed and some did not believe.

6. *Psalm 126:5,6*—Reaping is strenuous spiritual warfare. I heard Billy Graham testify in 1983 at the conference for itinerant evangelists in Amsterdam, "When I preach without giving an invitation, it is not so emotionally draining; but when I preach and press for people to come forward to be saved, I feel like I have been digging ditches and I come away completely exhausted.

C. Crucial Personal Applications:
1. What is your group doing to reach out and contact the lost?

2. In what way are you personally involved?

3. Have you ever publicly preached the Gospel and asked for decisions?

4. When was the last time you asked a person to believe in Jesus now?

D. Group Discussion:
Discuss some innovative ways and new strategies of how your church or group can reach the lost in your community and in your city.

## Chapter 10

A. A Missionary Principle:
God calls all believers to be a witness, and some He calls to go to other parts of the world.

B. Basic Biblical References:
1. *Ephesians 4:1* — Everyone is called to be a witness for the Lord right now, wherever he or she might be.

2. *Acts13:2-4*—God calls certain individuals to leave their fellowship and go out. The missionary is sent forth both by a fellowship of believers and by the Holy Spirit.

3. *John 20:21*—The missionary is sent by Jesus Himself.

C. Crucial Personal Applications:
1. Am I listening to the voice of God as to where I should minister?

2. Am I willing to go wherever He sends me?

3. Am I available to His leading?

4. How can I be more faithful in witnessing for Jesus in the place where I live and work or go to school?

D. Discussion Questions:
1. If you believe that you are called of God to be a foreign missionary, what steps should you take to be obedient to that call?

2. How can we prepare the young people to whom we might be ministering or those who are in our churches to respond to the missionary call?

# Chapter 11

A. A Missionary Principle: The Work Ethic.
The ability to labor faithfully in the role of a servant until the task is completed is a major test of the character of a missionary or a missionary organization.

B. Basic Biblical References:
1. *1 Corinthians 15:10*—Work abundantly. William Carey, the father of modern missions, is a fine example of dedicated, persistent labor in the missionary endeavor. Carey, in speaking of himself modestly, wrote that he was not always eloquent or clever, "but I can plod." And plod he did! He and his colleagues translated and printed portions of the Bible into some 40 languages during his lifetime.

2. *Acts 20:34-35*—Work with your own hands. Missionary work is not always glamorous. Often the day is full of tedious, monotonous tasks plus the grind of language study. Simple tasks can become a major chore in a foreign culture. Daily chores, such as, cooking, boiling water, washing dishes and clothes can become very time consuming. Shopping for something that can be bought in a few minutes at an American supermarket might take up to half a day. Often the electricity cuts off and the water pipes have no pressure. Filth—dirt—noise—all can be so irritating. These are some of the reasons why many missionaries do not return for a second term. Satan's tool is discouragement. It is easy to become discouraged. It takes grace, patience, and love to stick it out.

3. *John 9:4*—Work while there is opportunity.

4. *Romans 1:1*—"Paul, a servant of Jesus Christ..."

C. Personal Bible Study (Read the references below, then answer the questions).
1. What was the attack of the enemy? (Nehemiah 4:9)

2. Why was the bottom half of the wall completed so quickly? (Nehemiah 4:6)

3. What is God's promise to me? (Galatians 6:9)

4. How long did Eleazar, one of David's mighty men, continue to fight with his sword? (2 Samuel 23:10)

D. Group Discussion:
  1. Are we sending the same quality of missionaries out today as we did in the days of Carey, Taylor and Livingstone?

  2. How can we recruit more missionaries who will become proficient in the language and culture adjustment so as to stay out on the field for several decades?

  3. To what extent can short-timers who basically operate from an American base take the place of the traditional missionary?

  4. Can "tent-making" missionaries (those who have a regular job and do their missionary work on the side) do as effective a job as those who are full-time missionaries?


## Chapter 12

A. A Missionary Principle:
  "Follow-up is the process of bringing a babe in Christ into spiritual maturity"

B. Basic Biblical References:
  1. *1 Thessalonians 3:10*—"Night and day praying exceedingly that we may see your face and perfect what is lacking in your faith."

  2. *1 Thessalonians 2:7*—"But we were gentle among you, just as a nursing mother cherishes her own children"

3. *1 Thessalonians 2:11*—"As you know how we exhorted, and comforted, and charged every one of you, as a father does his own children."

4. *Acts 20:28*—"Therefore take heed to yourselves and to all the flock, among which the Holy Spirit has made you overseers, to shepherd the church of God, which He purchased with His own blood.

5. *Philippians 4:9*—"The things which you learned and received and heard and saw in me, do these, and the God of peace will be with you."

6. *2 Timothy 2:2*—"And the things that you have heard from me among many witnesses, commit these to faithful men who will be able to teach others also."

C. Crucial Personal Applications:
   1. Who has been the person who helped you grow in your spiritual life?

   2. To whom are you accountable now spiritually?

   3. Whom are you helping to grow spiritually at this time?

D. Discussion in Groups:
   1. Note these four basic methods of follow-up in Paul's first letter to the Thessalonians and discuss the content of these passages in context: (See *The Timothy Principle* - Chapter 9 - NavPress)
   *1 Thessalonians 3:10*—Prayer
   *1 Thessalonians 2:8-9; 3:10*—Personal contacts
   *1 Thessalonians 3:5*—Proxy, call for Timothy and others to help
   The whole Book of 1 Thessalonians is Paul's Personal Follow-up Letter to the church then and now.

   2. Discuss how these methods can be applied practically in developing a better follow-up ministry in your church, group, mission, or school.

## Chapter 13

A. A Missionary Principle:
   Persecution tests the church. If the believers are willing to give their lives for the faith, it will purify the church. If the believers are weak, they will be scattered and run away.

B. Basic Biblical References:
   1. *Matthew 5:10*—The key phrase here is "for righteousness' sake;" the world is full of persecution, injustice, and abuse; the down-trodden generally become more bitter and more filled with hatred. Rulers are ordained of God to punish criminals for their wicked deeds. But blessed is the righteous person when he is persecuted.

   **2.** *Mark 14:27; Zechariah 13:7*—At first the disciples were not ready to witness openly; they fled and hid. Later they would testify boldly before the Jewish leaders (Acts 4:12,13).

C. Crucial Personal Bible Study:
   1. What should be my attitude when I go through seasons of trouble and persecution because I am identifying with Jesus? (1 Peter 1:6; Romans 5:3)

   2. What good things happen when we endure persecution with the proper conduct and attitude? (1 Peter 1:7; Romans 5:3-5)

   3. What reward is given to the church or individual that is willing to die for his faith? (Revelation 3:10; James 1:12)

   4. Yet, what warning does Peter give? (1 Peter 4:15)
      Warning: "Crisis does not make a man; it reveals a man"—Dawson Trotman. Persecution can punish or destroy a society or group that is not true to its faith.

      Some examples are:
      a. The French Revolution and the destruction of the church.

b. Christendom of northern Africa overrun by the Moors (Islam).
c. Roman persecution of Jesus did not turn the Jewish leaders to the Messiah.
d. The judgment of God, as in the case of Israel at various times in the Old Testament.

Charles Dickens, in the opening words of his famous novel on the French Revolution, *A Tale of Two Cities*, said, "It was the best of times, it was the worst of times."

So what does the apostle Peter advise us to do? (1 Peter 3:15-17)

D. Discussion in Groups:
1. Is the concept of the church going "underground" really a Biblical concept? (II Tmothy 1:7)

2. What does Jesus say following His remarks in Matthew 5:10-12 about persecution? (Matthew 5:14-15)

3. How can we become the "salt of the earth"? (Matthew 5:13)

4. What is the purpose of our open witness before the world? (Matthew 5:16)

## Chapter 14

A. A Missionary Principle:
We are under obligation as Christians to proclaim the Gospel publicly. In this chapter Dick Hillis takes advantage of an unprecedented harvest opportunity to send out gospel teams, so that everyone has the opportunity to hear the Gospel at least once. He argued, "No one has the right to hear the Gospel twice till everyone has heard the Gospel once."

B. Basic Biblical References:
   1. *Mark 16:15* —Jesus told His disciples to go into all the world and proclaim the gospel to every person.

   2. *Mark 13:10* —Before the end of this age the gospel must first be published among all nations.

   3. *Matthew 9:36-38*—Jesus had compassion on the multitudes that were lost as sheep without a shepherd. He told His disciples that the harvest is great but the laborers few, so pray that the Lord would send forth laborers into the harvest.

   4. *John 4:34-38*—Jesus said, Don't say the harvest is not ripe until four months later, for the harvest of souls is ripe now. He that reaps in this harvest gathers fruit unto life eternal. Those laborers who do the sowing of the Gospel are those who reap decisions for Christ rejoice together in the fruit.

C. Critical Personal Bible Study:
   1. Have you ever shared the Gospel or given your personal testimony in a public meeting? What was the result?

   2. Have you ever considered planning an evangelistic outreach in your home, school, or neighborhood?

   3. Answer these questions from the following Scripture—Mark 13:10.
      a. Have you ever been part of a gospel team?
      b. Have you personally proclaimed or shared the Gospel and invited people to be saved?
      c. Should your church or group endeavor to send forth a gospel team to reach the unsaved in your community?
      d. Are you willing to become involved in some effort to proclaim the Gospel to the lost?

D. Discussion in Groups:
   1. In nearly all of the "Awakenings" in English and American church history God raised up some prominent evangelist to

reach the hearts of the masses with the Good News of salvation. As you are able, discuss the roles of John Wesley, George Whitefield, Charles G. Finney, Dwight L. Moody, Billy Graham, and others in reaching the lost in their respective generations. (If you are able to obtain it, the following book deals with all five of the above: William G. McLaughlin, *Revivals, Awakenings, and Reform*, Chicago: The University of Chicago Press, 1978; otherwise the Evangelical Awakenings writings of J. Edwin Orr would have data on these men.)

2. What is the continuing role of the evangelist today ...
   a. ... in places where many churches may be seen everywhere, such as in America or a developed Asian Christian base like Singapore?
   b. ... in countries where Christians are a tiny minority?

3. We hear much talk in missionary circles today about concentrating our energies so as to reach only a certain segment of people—sometimes called "the hidden people." What was the apostle Paul's burden? (Romans 1:14-16)

4. Of course we should reach every tribe and language and people, but the Bible certainly consistently speaks in "both"/ "and" not "either"/"or" terms. Discuss how we/you can have a balanced missionary strategy with both ...
   a. ... villages and cities.
   b. ... college students and peasants.
   c. ... individuals and multitudes.
   d. ... preaching the Gospel and nurturing the saints.

# Chapter 15

A. Missionary Principle:
The vision to reach a lost world should be linked with a plan that begins in a certain place but reaches out unto the whole world.

B. Basic Biblical References:
   1. *Acts 26:19*—Paul: "Therefore, King Agrippa, I was not disobedient to the heavenly vision."

   2. *Acts 1:8*—Jesus: "But ye shall be witnesses unto Me both in Jerusalem, and in all Judea and in Samaria, and unto the uttermost parts of the earth."

   3. *1 Thessalonians 1:8*—Beginning in Thessalonica, the converts of Paul proclaimed the Word of the Lord throughout the province of Macedonia, then on into Achaia, and finally everywhere they could.

   4. *Romans 1:8*—The Apostle Paul rejoices that the faith of the Christians in Rome had spread throughout the whole [Roman] world.

C. Crucial Personal Applications:
   1. What is your vision or dream for your life?

   2. What are your plans for accomplishing this vision?

   3. Have you considered volunteering your life for God's highest calling—that of being a missionary?

D. Discussion in Groups:
   1. Share your vision, hopes, and dreams with one another.

   2. What are the needs of your community that you and your church should have a vision to reach?

   3. What can we expect from God to help us fulfill our vision?

   4. How can we participate in actually meeting those needs?

# Chapter 16

A. A Missionary Principle:
Rewards are not handed out to the early sprinters but to those who finish the course in triumph.

B. Basic Biblical References:
1. *1 Corinthians 9:24-25*
Note : We are urged to finish the race of life, so as to receive an incorruptible crown.

2. *2 Timothy 4:7-8*
The apostle Paul says, I have faught a good fight, I have finished my course, I have kept the faith. Henceforth I shall receive a crown of righteousness, which will be given to me and all others who live looking to Jesus.

3. *Matthew 25:21* - The ultimate reward is a "Well done, good and faithful servant!" from the mouth of our Lord Jesus Christ. These are the finest words we can ever hear as His disciples.

*"Only one life, 'twill soon be past;*
*Only what's done for Christ will last."*
*—Anonymous*

C. Crucial Personal Applications:
1. For what are you giving your life? (John 6:27)

2. These are the five missionary statesmen in this book—David, Hube, Dick, Bob, Daws. Select a character trait or quality in each of these men that is a challenge to your own life today.
3. With which of these men can you identify the most?

4. What kind of ministry gift has God given you? Find something from these 22 chapters that is most helpful to you personally in discovering, developing, and using your gift or gifts.

D. Discussion in a Group
   1. To what extent can we reach the world in our generation, as we enter the 21st century?

   2. What kind of leaders does the church need today?

   3. How can all of us become more involved in the Great Commission in our generation?

## Chapter 17

A. A Missionary Principle:
The Timothy Principle. Paul trained Timothy, who in turn trained faithful people, who then reached out to others also (2 Timothy 2:2). The fastest and deepest method for church growth is by spiritual reproduction—the multiplication process of each one reproducing his or her life in the life of another.

B. Basic Biblical References:
   1. *2 Timothy 2:2*—Every Christian should be training another to be a spiritual reproducer.

   2. *Genesis 1:28*—As parents we are to bear fruit physically, which holistically means spiritually as well.

   3. *John 15:16*—Jesus specifically notes here that we as Christians are to bear fruit spiritually.

   4. *Isaiah 58:12*—This is the text on which Dawson Trotman based his great message "Born to Reproduce."

C. Crucial Personal Applications:
   1. Are you a parent of the reproduction process? Have you "produced" a spiritual son or daughter?

2. The term disciple means "student, follower, learner." Disciples must have teachers. Do you have anyone to whom you are accountable that is teaching you spiritual things?

3. What individual are you helping in his or her spiritual growth?

4. If you are not currently involved in this reproducing ministry, are you willing to become part of the process?

D. Discussion for Groups:
1. Discuss the difference between teaching a class and helping or teaching an individual on a one-to-one basis.

2. What is the difference between teaching (what we need to know) and training (how we are to perform)?

3. Give specific examples of how this principle is working in your life and in the life of your church.

# Chapter 18

A. A Missionary Principle:
The most effective way to train laborers is demonstrated by the Lord Jesus Christ through the "with him" principle. He asked His early disciples to leave their fishing nets and come live with Him.

B. Basic Biblical References:
1. *Mark 3:14*—The "with him" principle is based on this verse: "Then He [Jesus] appointed twelve, that they might be with Him and that He might send them out to preach."

2. *Matthew 4:19-20*—Jesus told His diciples, "Follow Me, and I will make you fishers of men." They immediately left their nets and followed Him.

3. *Romans 10:13-15a*—Here is God's divine reasoning: "For whoever calls the name of the LORD shall be saved. How then shall they call on Him in whom they have not heard? And how shall they hear without a preacher? And how shall they preach unless they are sent?" And we add, "How can they be sent unless they are trained?"

C. Crucial Personal Applications:
1. What is your goal in your Christian life? What training do you need to equip yourself to do this?

2. What do you think of inviting international students or members of your Sunday School class to your home for instruction and fellowship?

3. Do you use your own home for discipling and training other Christians? Why or why not?

4. Have you ever lived in the home of a Christian leader? Would that be helpful to you in your growth to maturity?

D. Discussion in Groups:
Three elements of an effective training program are the selection, the training, and the sending.
1. What is the need for training in your local church or group?

2. How can this be carried out? Who will do it?

3. Discuss the process of selection, training, and sending of future laborers as you envision them in your church going out into your community.

# Chapter 19

A.  A Missionary Principle:
   The missionary should develop sensitivity to the culture in which he works. Many things are not either right or wrong, but are simply different; they are not black or white but multicolored. Learn to be sensitive to the other viewpoint and appreciate the value system of a different society.

B.  Basic Biblical References:
   1.  *Philemon 14a*—Don't force your own opinions on another person (or culture); try to influence him so that he will do what you suggest willingly; don't act too quickly and be patient.
      Note : In working with another culture we must exercise Christian diplomacy or Christian sensitivity. It is not simply a matter of right or wrong, but the right thing must be done in the right way at the right time with the right attitude. God provides us with the right time (Ecclesiastes 3:1-8), a proper way so as not to offend another brother (1 Corinthians 8:13) and a proper spirit of heart (2 Chronicles 25:2).

   2.  *Acts 6:1-4*—The problem between the Jewish Diaspora ("Hellenists") and Palestinian ("Hebrews") widows was a clash of cultures and nationalities. Even the apostles did not try to settle this difficulty by direct command, but rather enlisted culturally sensitive people (the deacons) to help them act wisely.

C.  Crucial Personal Applications:
   1.  What about foreign students who are studying in our own community? How can I help them bridge the culture gap they face while living in our country?

   2.  Do I avoid the foreigners or people of another sub-culture or ethnic group who visit our church? How should I go about making friends with them?

D.  Discussion in Groups:
    1.  How can our church or group reach internationals with the
        Gospel in our community?
    2.  List some cultural things that we know would offend other
        ethnic groups and nationalities. Are there some things in our
        own culture that cause us to overact to foreigners?

    3.  The Golden Rule, "Do unto others as you would have others
        do unto you," bridges almost any culture. Discuss how this
        applies to your own situation.

## Chapter 20

A.  A Missionary Principle:
    God has prepared people from all nations, all languages, and all
    cultures to receive the Gospel.

B.  Basic Biblical References:
    1.  *Acts 10:34-35*—In every nation there are those who will fear
        God and desire His righteousness.

    2.  *Romans 1:19*—Every person knows in his or her heart some-
        thing about God; we have been created in the image of God
        with the capacity to know Him.

    3.  *Genesis 1:27*—God created man in his own image. Man is
        created for the purpose of having fellowship with the living God.

    4.  *John 4:24*—People of all nations can come to God and worship
        Him in spirit and truth.

    5.  *Romans 1:20*—Creation points to God, so there are no excuses
        to reject Him.

    6.  *Romans 1:25*—Man worshipped God before he rebelled and
        turned to idols.

Therefore: The Gospel speaks to every heart in every nation and every culture. Let us clearly teach this truth and trust God to open blinded hearts to his salvation.

C.  Crucial Personal Applications:
1.  What keeps me from witnessing clearly and boldly to my lost relatives and friends?

2.  Am I fully persuaded that the Gospel is indeed the power of God unto salvation?

3.  Why am I so reluctant to share my faith with others?

D.  Discussion in Groups:
1.  To what degree do you believe the Gospel should be accommodated to reach another culture?

2.  Can a group of young people or senior citizens be effective in going to a foreign country on a witnessing project? What are some key factors to their effectiveness?

# Chapter 21

A.  A Missionary Principle:
Even after a church has been planted in a given area, the whole body of Christ must continue the ministry of assisting other parts of the body. The servant-missionary should work alongside the local believers of that culture and together with the national workers he can have an important role in penetrating a given society with the Gospel message and biblical teachings.

B.  Basic Biblical References:
1.  *John 17:21*—"That they all may be one, as Thou, Father, art in Me, and I in Thee, that they also may be one in Us: that the world may believe that Thou hast sent Me".

2. *John 13:14-15* — "If I then, your Lord and Master, have washed your feet, ye also ought to wash one another's feet. For I have given you an example, that ye should do as I have done to you" (KJV).

3. *Ephesians 4:1-6* — In meekness and love we should strive to maintain unity in the body of believing Christians, for we are all one in Christ.

4. *2 Corinthians 4:4* — Our adversaries are not other Christian groups, which may have a different philosophy of ministry, but our adversary is Satan who blinds the minds of people to keep them from coming to Christ.

C. Crucial Personal Applications:
1. Am I willing to become a servant-missionary?

2. How can I assist in serving my local church here?

3. Can I assist or participate in sending a group from my local church to some missionary project on a foreign field?

D. Discussion in Groups:
1. Discuss how missionaries from our local church can serve national churches.

2. Discuss the difference between starting a new work and serving an existing work on a foreign field.

3. Are the people of our church willing to be servants in another culture?

4. Are the people of our church willing to be servants in our community? Or in a minority group in our city?

## Chapter 22

A.  A Missionary Principle:
    The evangelization of the world is on the heart of God—that men
    and women might come to know Him, Whom to know is life
    eternal.

B.  Basic Biblical References:
    1.  *Genesis 1:26-28*—God's desire in the creation of man as male
        and female was that through them He would exercise loving
        dominion over the whole creation, including all future
        generations of humanity.

    2.  *John 3:16*—God's love for humanity was so great that He made
        the ultimate sacrifice to achieve man's redemption.

    3.  *John 17:3*—"And this is eternal life, that they may know You,
        the only true God, and Jesus Christ whom You have sent."

C.  Crucial Personal Applications:
    1.  Does my heart line up with what is on God's heart?

    2.  How great is my concern for the lost? In my own country? In
        foreign lands?

    3.  Am I really open and available to God's call to be used by Him
        anyway—anytime—anywhere?

D.  Discussion in Groups:
    1.  Is my church or group giving enough priority to those things
        which are most on the heart of God?

    2.  What can we do to give greater priority to missions—both
        domestic and foreign?

# APPENDIX A

## Phyllis Robertson's "Godly Girls Tree" (SINGAPORE)

During the latter part of the Robertson's ministry in Singapore, Roy was impressed by the 30 "Mighty Men" that David had prior to assuming the kingship of Israel. So he claimed God's promises for 30 "Mighty Men" in Singapore, based on 1 Samuel 23 and 1 Chronicles 11. He concentrated on one-to-one spiritual reproduction to strengthen the ministry in this strategic city (see chapter 17), particularly since he was gone on frequent trips laying foundations for opening a Navigator ministry in Indonesia.

Whenever he was in town, he met with six key men individually for instruction and check-up. Some of their Timothies eventually met the qualifications to become "Mighty Men." He gathered other key people together who were meeting with others one-on-one and challenged them to encourage their contacts to reproduce. Phyllis likewise prayed for 30 "Godly Girls" and followed the same procedure with the women.

The principle of a spiritual "tree" is that which was taught by the apostle Paul to his companion Timothy: "And the things that you (the disciple) have heard from me (the disciplemaker) among many witnesses, commit these to faithful men who will be able to teach others also" (2 Timothy 2:2). So the disciplemaker who teaches the disciple who teaches faithful men, who in turn teaches others also, reaches into four spiritual generations. This principle of disciplemaking or spiritual reproduction comprises the very heart of the message of this book. The illustration which follows shows the "Godly Girls Tree."

# The "Godly Girls Tree"
## PHYLLIS ROBERTSON and SELENE CHEW

| Lois Ward | Teo Yew Lian | Khor Siew Ngoh | Ang Kin Hwee | Florence Tan |
|---|---|---|---|---|
| Lee Shuit Kuin<br>*Chan Nang Fong*<br>*Rosalind Koh*<br><br>Ho So Cheng<br>*Sally Goh*<br>*Lena Goh*<br><br>Margaret Lim<br>*Lily Chua*<br>*Pee Poh Yan*<br>*Pang Lee Leng*<br><br>Belinda Lim<br>*Molly Chua*<br>*Pang Li Kin*<br>*Lim Lea Keow*<br>*Lim Kuck Heng*<br><br>Nancy Lim<br>*Cynthia Tan*<br>*Jenny Lim*<br><br>Jane<br>*Annie Soh*<br>*Janet Wong* | Peck Hong<br>*Lye Hong*<br>*Miew Kim*<br><br>Florence Lim<br>*Maureen*<br>*Gek Suan*<br><br>Lucy Tan<br>*Chek Kim*<br>*Susie Tan*<br>*Quee Eng*<br><br>Kim Tan<br>*Lily Toh*<br>*Hui Hua*<br><br>Rosalind Tan<br>*Rosalind Goh*<br><br>Tan Geok Neo<br>*Saramah*<br>*Tio Siok* | Lim Kwee Hong<br>*Chan Choy Wan*<br><br>Wong Mei Ying<br>*Ho Peck Foon*<br><br>Wong Lai Yin<br>*Chia Kwee Tin*<br>*Chia Kwee Cheng*<br>*Chew Chai Bee*<br><br>Chew Wan Nee | Choo Siok Hoe<br>*Loong Ah Lek*<br><br>Millie Tay<br>*Shanti Annamalang*<br>*Seet Pek Hoon*<br>*Tam Siew Kim*<br><br>Sita Shanmugan<br>*Yeo Cheh Hoon* | Tan Khee Boon<br>*Giam Kim Koon*<br><br>Tan Ching Eng<br>*Yap Wah Choo* |

# APPENDIX B

## The Bridge Illustration

One of the most effective gospel presentations has been a synthesis between Dawson Trotman's sequence of verses for explaining the Gospel (the old Topical Memory System of The Navigators) and a China Inland Mission poster showing people traveling down a broad road that ended abruptly at a cliff.

Daws's Bible verses transitioned from a ministry to junior high boys to sailors in the U.S. Navy. They were:

1.  Romans 3:23

2.  Romans 6:23

3.  Hebrews 9:27

4.  Romans 5:8

5.  Ephesians 2:8-9

6.  John 1:12

The CIM's pictorial presentation showed the people, as they came to the edge of the cliff, "their hands reached frantically upward trying to escape the burning abyss at the foot of the cliff into which they were tumbling. "However, a Cross stood at the beginning of a turn that led up a hill. A few people turned toward the Cross to take the upward path that led to heaven.

During my ministry on Taiwan (see Chapter 15), I combined the logical sequence of Daws's verses on the play of salvation with the Chinese vivid picture of hell, heaven, and salvation. This illustration has subsequently been used as an effective means of presenting the Gospel in many parts of the world.

The presentation of The Bridge Illustration comes in a sequence of four sections, the details of each being drawn on a piece of paper for the individual or in some visual form for a group.[1] This illustration called "crossing the bridge" is given in Chapter 7 of *The Timothy Principle* by the author. It is reproduced below:[2]

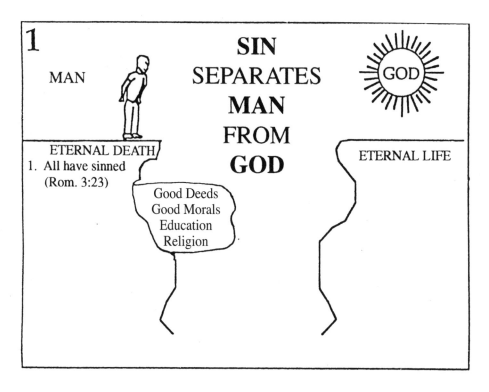

In the beginning man and God had fellowship with each other. God and Adam walked together in the Garden of Eden. Then Adam and Eve both sinned and were separated from God's presence. The Bible teaches (Romans Chap. 1, 2 & 3) that all men, whether born in a heathen family or Christian family, have sinned.
**"For all have sinned and come short of the glory of God"** (Romans 3 :23).

Man desperately tries to build his own bridges to heaven. The most common way that man tries to get to heaven is through his own good works. But **"our good deeds are as filthy rags in the sight of a holy God"** (Isa.64:6).

Others try ethics or good morals to reach God, but generally man does not live up to his own standard of values, much less God's standard of righteousness. He can't even keep the " Ten Commandments" which are only the elementary laws of God. The problem lies in **man's deceitful heart** (Jer. 17:9).

Nor is education the answer. Knowledge increases our feeling of guilt. God does not excuse our sin merely because we have been taught the truth. **"For not the hearers of the law are just before God, but the doers of the law shall be justified"** (Rom.2:13).

"But surely religion will save us" some will say. No, not even religion will bring us back into fellowship with the living God. Religion is good ... it offers good advice and tells us what we should and should not do. But religion, whether Hindu, Islam, Jewish, Catholic or Protestant cannot forgive our sins and save our souls. Only God can do that. Sinful man does not need more religion, he needs a Savior.

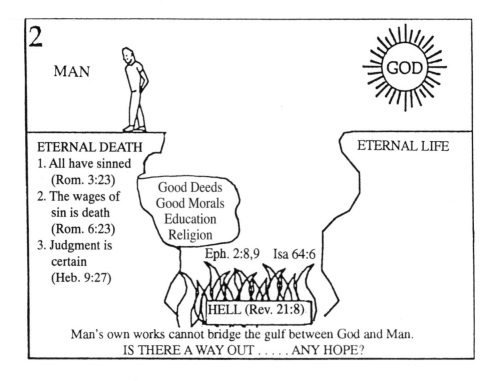

Not only have all men sinned, but the result of sin is death. **"For the wages of sin is death"** (Rom.6:23). Man was not created to die but to live in fellowship with God. Yet because of Adam's sin man inherits death.

And that is not all. The Bible tells us that **"it is appointed unto men once to die, but after this the judgment"** (Heb.9:27).

Judgment is certain . . . it is inevitable. Every person is judged by the Almighty God, and those whose sins are not forgiven are sent to **hell, a place that was originally prepared for Satan and his demons** (Matt.25:41).

It is a terrible picture. Man cannot bridge the gap to heaven. Left to his own devices man is helpless.

Man is cut off from God and condemned by his own sins. **Sin . . . death . . . judgment . . . hell. Man's condition is hopeless** (Eph.2: 12).

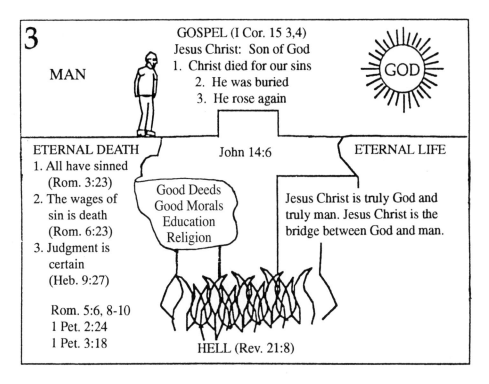

**3**

MAN

GOSPEL (I Cor. 15 3,4)
Jesus Christ: Son of God
1. Christ died for our sins
2. He was buried
3. He rose again

GOD

ETERNAL DEATH
1. All have sinned
(Rom. 3:23)
2. The wages of
sin is death
(Rom. 6:23)
3. Judgment is
certain
(Heb. 9:27)

Rom. 5:6, 8-10
1 Pet. 2:24
1 Pet. 3:18

John 14:6

Good Deeds
Good Morals
Education
Religion

ETERNAL LIFE

Jesus Christ is truly God and
truly man. Jesus Christ is the
bridge between God and man.

HELL (Rev. 21:8)

God in His great love provided a way of deliverance. Before the world began, God had a wonderful plan to bring men back to live with Him forever. Only man could bridge the gap that separated man from God. That man must be both man and God. If he is not man he cannot represent us; if he is not God, he cannot save us.

So, God sent His only Son, Jesus Christ to be born as a man. Jesus is the Son of Man born of Mary, and the Son of God conceived through the Holy Spirit. He is not part man and part God but 100% man and 100% God. In theology he is called "Very God" and "Very Man." There is but one qualfied to become our Savior, the Lord Jesus Christ.

This man Jesus did many wonderful miracles, but we are not saved by the miracles of Jesus. He taught many beautiful lessons, but we are not saved by following the ethical teachings of Jesus. He healed many people from their sickness but the healing of the body does not guarantee the healing of the soul. The fact is that we are not saved through all those marvelous things that Jesus did in His life. The life of Jesus shows that He was the Son of God, but more is necessary for my salvation . . .

Jesus Christ must die on the cross for my sins. Oh, the wonder of it all!! Jesus died for me and for you. The cross of Christ is the bridge from death to eternal life.

Christ not only died to pay for my sins, he arose from the grave that I might be made righteous (Rom.4:25) and might live forever as a child of God. "This is the Good news, the historic gospel, **that Christ died for our sins according to the Scriptures; that He was buried, and that He rose again the third day according to the Scriptures** (I Cor.15:3,4).

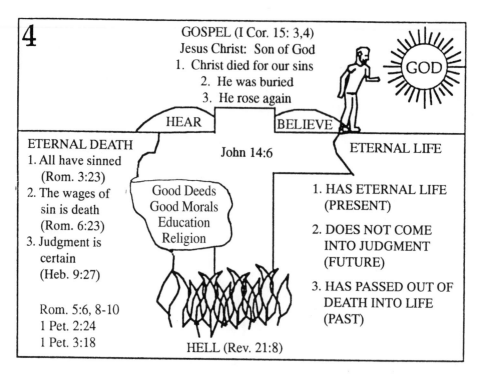

Jesus died to save all men, yet all men are not saved. Why? Because God will not force you to believe. You have a choice, and that choice will determine your eternal destiny. How can you be saved?

Jesus says, **"whoever hears my word and believes him who sent me has eternal life and will not be condemned; he has crossed over from death to life"** (John 5:24). Since you have already heard Jesus' words, you must only believe in order to possess eternal life.

Believe what? Believe that Jesus died on the cross for your sins, was buried and rose again from the dead. Believe He is truly the Son of God, and accept Him as your personal Savior.

Are you willing to believe now? When you do so, you have everlasting life. You will not be judged by God in the future or sent to hell, because all your past, present and future sins have been forgiven by God and covered by the blood of Jesus shed on the cross. You have indeed already passed from death to life.

Jesus says, **"Behold, I stand at the door and knock"** (Rev.3:20). Jesus knocks at the door of your heart. Will you open your heart right now and call upon the Lord in a prayer of faith?

Pray in your own words something like this: **"Dear Father in heaven I acknowledge that I am a guilty sinner and deserve your judgment. But I believe that you loved me and sent Jesus to die on the cross for my sins. I pray that Jesus will come into my heart. Forgive my sins and give me life everlasting. Amen.**

To everyone who calls on the Lord in true faith for salvation, God gives eternal life as He promised (Rom.10:13). All who are willing to believe shall be saved. If you have believed in Jesus, then rest in hope and peace because He will bring every one of His children into heaven.

ENDNOTES:

1. Roy Robertson, *The Timothy Principle* (NavPress, Singapore, 1992), page 58.
2. This can be done on a flip chart, chalk board, an overhead, or any other visual. Robertson, op cit., pages 57-63

# APPENDIX C

## YFC World Congress Statistics in Japan's Provinces

The 1953 Youth for Christ World Congress of Evangelism in Japan produced the largest and widest gospel thrust ever attempted by the YFC movement (see Chapter 16). Every *ken* ("province") in this island nation was targeted for a series of cooperative evangelistic meetings and all but one of the 46 kens and the results for each one are recorded below after the summaries.

Summaries

| | |
|---|---|
| Total Kens That Held Meetings | 45 out of 46 |
| Total Firm Decisions for Christ | 22,042 |
| Total Meetings Held in the 45 Kens | 880 |
| Total Places Where the Meetings Were Held | 434 |
| Average Number of Decisions Per Meeting | 25.05 |

Statistics

| Ken | Number of Decisions | Number of Meetings |
|---|---|---|
| Aichi-ken | 404 | 16 |
| Akita-ken | 200 | 8 |
| Aomori-ken | 35 | 3 |
| Chiba-ken | 409 | 17 |
| Ehime-ken | 1,056 | 40 |
| Fukui-ken | 340 | 26 |
| Fukuoka-ken | 296 | 16 |
| Fukushima-ken | 337 | 17 |
| Gifu-ken | 163 | 6 |
| Gumma-ken | 505 | 18 |
| Hiroshima-ken | 734 | 31 |
| Hokkaido-ken | 925 | 42 |
| Hyogo-ken | 1,392 | 49 |
| Ibaragi-ken | 227 | 12 |
| Iwate-ken | 54 | 7 |
| Kagawa-ken | 136 | 14 |
| Kagoshima-ken | 1,051 | 27 |
| Kanagawa-ken | 760 | 14 |
| Kochi-ken | 106 | 7 |
| Kumamoto-ken (Cancelled-Floods) | 0 | 0 |

| Ken | Number of Decisions | Number of Meetings |
|---|---|---|
| Kyoto-ken | 325 | 23 |
| Mie-ken | 490 | 14 |
| Miyagi-ken | 121 | 1 |
| Miyazaki-ken | 186 | 13 |
| Nagano-ken | 125 | 21 |
| Nagasaki-ken | 256 | 7 |
| Nara-ken | 357 | 21 |
| Niigata-ken | 275 | 16 |
| Okayama-ken | 630 | 27 |
| Oita-ken | 55 | 7 |
| Osaka-ken | 1,032 | 19 |
| Saga-ken | 92 | 7 |
| Saitama-ken | 607 | 18 |
| Shiga-ken | 381 | 17 |
| Shimane-ken | 474 | 17 |
| Shizuoka-ken | 591 | 22 |
| Tochigi-ken | 377 | 15 |
| Tokushima-ken | 1,060 | 17 |
| Tottori-ken | 496 | 22 |
| Toyama-ken | 212 | 15 |
| Wakayama-ken | 422 | 13 |
| Yamagata-ken | 270 | 7 |
| Yamaguchi-ken | 132 | 7 |
| Yamanashi-ken | 467 | 19 |
| Tokyo | 2,681 | 135 |
| Totals | 22,042 | 880 |

Tracts and Literature    556

# Author

Roy Robertson founded The Navigators work in Singapore in 1962. During a 16-mile walk of faith across the island, he claimed God's promises to send people from Singapore to all the earth to multiply laborers.

Before going overseas as the first Navigator missionary in1948, he lived in the home of Dawson Trotman, the founder of The Navigators; and he started the Navigator ministry in his home state of Texas.

As a missionary, Roy personally opened the Navigators work in China, Taiwan, Japan, Singapore and Indonesia. As Asian director he launched and supervised the ministry in the Philippines, Hong Kong, India and Korea; and he was formerly overseas coordinator for The Navigators.

Roy originally met The Navigators in 1941 in Honolulu the day before the Pearl Harbor attack. He served as a Navy pilot until he joined Navigators staff in 1945.

While working as a Navigator missionary Roy founded and directed an autonomous ministry, Training Evangelistic Leadership (TEL), which develops Asian evangelists and gospel teams.

Having retired from the Navigators in 1987, he continues to supervise the TEL ministries in Indonesia, India, Philippines and Hong Kong.

Roy and his wife Phyllis live in Hong Kong. Two of their six children, Janet Lewis and Susan Rice, with their husbands, are Navigator missionaries in Africa. Both their twins Leonard and Lee work with Training Evangelistic Leadership in Asia. Keith studies veterinary medicine in Florida, and Lila is training to be a nurse in Texas.